Who Killed William Shakespeare?

AL	HZ	BE	RE
·8|13	2|14	8|16	2|15

Who Killed William Shakespeare?

The Murderer,
The Motive,
The Means

Simon Andrew Stirling

The
History
Press

An ART & WILL Book

To my parents,
Brenda and Norman,
with love

First published 2013

The History Press
The Mill, Brimscombe Port
Stroud, Gloucestershire, GL5 2QG
www.thehistorypress.co.uk

© Simon Andrew Stirling, 2013

British Library Cataloguing in Publication Data.
A catalogue record for this book is available from the British
Library.

ISBN 978 0 7524 8725 0

Typesetting and origination by The History Press
Printed in Great Britain

Contents

Author's Note

I AM not, and have never been, a Roman Catholic; neither, for that matter, am I an Anglican or a Lutheran. I wish to make this clear from the outset, lest any reader be tempted to accuse me of bias.

Religion in Shakespeare's day was a tortured affair. It is perhaps best to regard it as a sort of spectrum. At one end of this spectrum were the diehard Catholics who remained loyal to the Church of Rome and the form of Christianity which had been practised in England for 1,000 years; many of these 'papists' were in fact converts who, in defiance of the severe penalties for embracing the 'Romish' religion, had adopted the traditional creed.

At the opposite end of the spectrum were those who, for the sake of convenience, we call 'Puritans' (a word which seems to have come into usage in the year of Shakespeare's birth). Following the accession of Queen Elizabeth I in 1558, these extremists sought to purge the Church of England of all remaining vestiges of 'popish superstition' and 'trish-trash'. They frequently called themselves 'the godly' or 'the Elect'.

Between the two extremes were those whom we call Protestants, a word which came from an occasion in 1529 when a minority group of reformers presented a *Protestatio* – or affirmation – of their beliefs at the imperial Diet in Speyer. Initially, the word was applied exclusively to Germans who followed the teachings of Martin Luther and Huldrych Zwingli; only later did it come to be used of all those who defied the orthodoxy of Roman Catholicism.

In reality, these three groups – Catholic, Protestant and Puritan – tended to shade into one another. Even today, the Church of England comprises the 'High' and 'Low' forms of Anglicanism which, respectively, lean towards the Catholic and Calvinist extremes. In Shakespeare's day, there were strict Catholics (best exemplified by those missionaries of the Society of Jesus which had been established by a Spanish ex-soldier, Iñigo López de Loyola: the Jesuits swore absolute obedience to the pope) and hard-line Lutherans; there were also 'soft' Catholics, who attended Protestant church services and celebrated Mass in secret, and easy-going Anglicans who shuddered at the bloody-mindedness of the holier-than-thou Puritans.

Though it has often been argued that one of Elizabeth I's strengths was her commitment to a 'middle way' between the Roman and Germanic extremes, it should be remembered that Protestantism was a relatively new phenomenon, born in the time of Elizabeth's father, and that Puritanism was newer still. From the point of view of the traditionalists – who, in some parts of the country, were the majority – Queen Elizabeth's religious compromises were themselves a form of extremism. The ruthlessness with which the adherents of the old faith were persecuted suggests that Elizabeth's *via media* was no compromise at all. Rather, it was a new form of religion which elevated the power of the State at the expense of the Church.

If religion was a bit of a mess in Shakespeare's day, **currency** was even more of a muddle. Generally, though, England worked on the '£.s.d' system of pounds, shillings and pence. There were 12 pennies in 1 shilling, and 20 shillings in a pound (a 'groat' was 4 pence; a 'guinea' was 21 shillings, or 252 pence). The currency in Britain was not decimalised (£1 = 100p) until 1971.

My own rule of thumb for converting prices in Shakespeare's day into something resembling prices in our own is to multiply by 1,000. Thus, the schoolmaster of Stratford earned £20, which we can multiply by 1,000 to reach a pre-decimal £20,000 – although a more realistic estimate would be to multiply £20 by 240p by 1,000 and then divide by 100 to arrive at £48,000 in modern decimalised currency, which is within the range of a teacher's salary in Britain today – while the dagger that killed Christopher Marlowe cost 12 pence, or approximately £50 in today's money.

Dates are another problem. Catholic Europe adopted the Gregorian calendar, named after Pope Gregory XIII, in 1582. Being resolutely Protestant, the Elizabethan government refused to accept such a 'popish' innovation and England stuck doggedly to the older Julian calendar (named after Julius Caesar) for another 170 years. There was, at the time, a difference of ten days between the two calendars, which led to no end of confusion; as Hamlet observed, 'The time is out of joint'.

According to the Old Style calendar (as the Julian calendar is also known), the year began on 25 March, rather than 1 January. In line with standard practice, I have followed the New Style (Gregorian) dating system, so that what to Will Shakespeare would have been 10 February 1615 is, in our modern calendar, 10 February 1616.

Most of the Shakespeare **quotations** in this book are taken from *The Oxford Shakespeare: The Complete Works*, Second Edition, published in 2005, which is surely the most readable and accessible edition of Shakespeare's works, although I have also consulted other editions, in particular the Arden and New Penguin Shakespeare series. For the *Sonnets*, I have relied on the Quarto edition, published in 1609, preserving much of the original punctuation but updating the spelling as necessary.

For reasons of space, as much as relevance, it has not been possible to refer in this book to everything written by Shakespeare.

Finally, I wish to offer my unconditional and heartfelt **thanks** to: John Cheal, Merima Hadzic, Andrea Nelson, Sally Paley, Tejvan Pettinger, Ralph Richardson, Canon David Rogers, Catherine Simpson, Dr Silvia Uhlemann, the Oxford Preservation Trust and the Worcestershire Archive and Archaeology Service for their help with the images for this book, and special thanks to Richard Peach for allowing me access to his superb photographs of the skull; my teachers and tutors, especially Gary Hedges and Professor Edwin Barrett, and to Vicki Mansfield for the tours of Shakespearean places; those I have had the pleasure of working with and learning from, including those producers (Andrew Brown, Natasha Carlish, Mark Forstater, Tony Garnett, Joy Lale, Chris Parr, Hilary Salmon), directors (Lindsay Anderson, Brian Astbury, Tom Bailey, Sue Colverd, Colin Cook, Richard Digby-Day, Robert Hamlin, Helena Kaut-Howson, Liz Light) and actors (Geoffrey Bayldon, Duncan Campbell-Godley, Stefan Dennis, Richard Griffiths, John Inman, Malcolm McDowell, Ron Moody, Neil Pearson, Alexander Siddig) who particularly inspired me; my editor, Lindsey Smith, and the team at The History Press; and, most of all, to Kim and Kiri, for putting up with me.

Preamble

'The Apotheosis of Shakespeare'

SOMETHING ODD happened in the second half of the eighteenth century. The man known as William Shakespeare was forgotten, his place taken by a national myth. This was the myth of Shakespeare the 'universal' genius.

A by-product of that development was another myth – that Shakespeare the player could not have written the plays which made him famous.

It all started in Shakespeare's garden.

The more tree

WILL SHAKESPEARE bought the 'pretty house of brick and timber' on the corner of Chapel Street in Stratford-upon-Avon in 1597. The 'Great House' had been built about 100 years earlier by Hugh Clopton, a prosperous silk merchant who rose to become Lord Mayor of London. It was the grandest residence in Stratford: three storeys high, with five gables and ten fireplaces, a frontage of more than 60 feet, two barns and two gardens.

By the time Will acquired the property it had become known as New Place and was in need of restoration. He paid for the renovations, selling the leftover stone to the Stratford Corporation, which used it to repair the Clopton Bridge over the River Avon.

In one of the gardens to the rear of New Place, Will planted a mulberry tree. A horticultural tradition in Warwickshire held that a quince tree should be planted on the north side of a property and a mulberry to the south. Whether or not Shakespeare followed this tradition to the letter we do not know – but when he introduced the legend of the mulberry in *A Midsummer Night's Dream*, he did so via the agency of a character named Quince.

As with so much in his life, Will's planting of a mulberry is open to interpretation.

In 1608, King James I issued an edict to the Lords Lieutenant of 'the several shires of England', urging them to 'persuade and require such as are of ability to buy and distribute in that County the number of ten thousand Mulberry plants'. The King was eager to promote a home-grown silk industry, the leaves of the mulberry being the favoured food of the silkworm, and His Majesty led the way by planting 4 acres of mulberries on the site of what are now the gardens of Buckingham Palace.

Many mulberry trees were planted. But they were the wrong kind of mulberry. Had King James really been interested in stimulating a domestic silk-weaving industry (a move fiercely opposed by the silk merchants of London), he should have insisted on the cultivation of the white mulberry, *Morus alba*, rather than the black mulberry, *Morus nigra*, which was enthusiastically but pointlessly planted throughout England.

By ordering the wrong kind of mulberry trees, James I did nothing to encourage silkworms. He might, however, have succeeded in neutralising a potent symbol.

The black mulberry yields a blood-red fruit which stains anything it touches. Also known as the morberry or 'more tree', it was associated with Sir Thomas More, the one-time Lord Chancellor who was beheaded in 1535 for his opposition to the religious policies of King Henry VIII. The Italian name for the mulberry, *il Moro*, had provided Sir Thomas More with his family crest: the impaled head of a North African Moor. Erasmus of Rotterdam referred to his friend as 'the black man' and dedicated his 1509 essay 'In Praise of Folly' to Sir Thomas, the Greek title, *'Morias Enkomion'*, also meaning 'In Praise of More'.

Sir Thomas More had died for his allegiance to the Church of Rome. His bloodstained shirt became a holy relic. Those who honoured him as a Catholic martyr were afflicted with the same 'folly' which had driven More to defy his tyrannical king. They were 'more fools'; 'God's lunatics', in the words of their Puritan enemies.

The very name of More was an anagram of Rome and, through the wordplay of the time, was linked to the idea of Love, *Amor* in Latin, which, as a reflection of *Roma*, came to stand as a metaphor for the Catholic faith.

The planting of a 'more tree' could be an act of defiance. Its dark fruits, 'purple with love's wound', bore witness to More's blood sacrifice. The mulberry became a symbol of the religious 'folly' which led to death (*Mors* in Latin) and of the Catholic resistance to the Protestant policies of King James and his predecessor, Elizabeth I.

In times of sectarian conflict, symbolic acts are imbued with significance. King James ordered the widespread cultivation of black mulberries in order to rob the 'more tree' of its subversive symbolism. This in turn raises questions about Shakespeare's motivation when he planted his mulberry at New Place.

Did the tree represent his Catholic convictions, or was he conniving in a royal scheme to undermine the sacrificial symbolism of the morberry?

'I John Shakespeare'

IT IS a measure of the grandeur of Will's Stratford home that Queen Henrietta Maria spent three days there in 1643 as a guest of Shakespeare's daughter.

After the death of Shakespeare's granddaughter, New Place was sold to Sir Edward Walker, formerly the Secretary at War to King Charles I. The house soon returned to its original owners, the Clopton family, and was remodelled early in the eighteenth century. By 1756, it had come into the possession of the Reverend Francis Gastrell, who chopped down Shakespeare's mulberry.

The townsfolk of Stratford responded to this outrage by smashing the windows of New Place and threatening Gastrell's family with violence.

The remains of the tree were bought by an enterprising watchmaker named Thomas Sharpe, who carved a variety of keepsakes – 'snuff-boxes, goblets, punch-ladles, toothpicks and tobacco-pipes' – from its wood. The mulberry furnished so many souvenirs that Sharpe was suspected of sharp practice. The American author Washington Irving would write of his visit to Stratford in 1815, 'There was an ample supply also of Shakespeare's mulberry-tree, which seems to have had as extraordinary powers of self-multiplication as the wood of the true Cross.' Thomas Sharpe was so stung by these slurs that he:

> called in the Mayor and one of the standing Justices of the Peace of the borough, and ordered a friend to draw up an affidavit, wishing to convince the world to the contrary of such insinuations and enable him to set a proper value upon the relics of the celebrated tree.

He swore 'upon the four Evangelists, in the presence of almighty God' that all his curios were carved 'from the very Mulberry-tree which was planted by the immortal Bard'.

In the meantime, a startling discovery had been made.

A builder named Joseph Mosely was replacing the roof tiles on the Shakespeare Birthplace property on Henley Street when, on 29 April 1757, he came across a hand-stitched document which had been hidden among the rafters. Though the first page was missing, it was clear that the manuscript was some sort of Catholic last will and testament. Almost every one of its handwritten paragraphs began with the words 'I John Shakespeare'.

Mosely passed the document to Alderman Payton of Stratford. The manuscript was also seen by John Jordan, a local tour guide, who created a new first page for it and sent his transcript to the *Gentleman's Magazine*, the editor of which mentioned the discovery to the Shakespeare scholar Edmond Malone. Malone contacted his friend James Davenport, vicar of Holy Trinity Church, Stratford, and received the original five-page manuscript from Alderman Payton.

Malone declared himself 'perfectly satisfied' that the will was genuine when he published the original pages in his *Plays and Poems of William Shakespeare* in 1790. Within a few years, though, he had changed his mind. 'I have since obtained documents,' he wrote, 'that clearly prove it could not have been the composition of any one of our poet's family, as will be fully shewn in his Life.'

Edmond Malone died before he could write his 'Life' of William Shakespeare. No documents pertaining to the 'Spiritual Testament' were found among his papers. Even the original will had vanished, never to be seen again.

Rage and curses

THE DISAPPEARANCE of the 'Spiritual Testament' from Malone's study allowed scholars to dismiss it as a forgery. It was an age of Shakespearean forgeries: Malone himself had exposed a raft of spurious documents – including Shakespeare's Protestant 'Profession of Faith' – as the work of a young fraudster named William-Henry Ireland. But the discovery of the will hidden beneath the roof tiles of the Shakespeare Birthplace was dynamite. It offered compelling evidence that Shakespeare's father had been a closet Catholic willing to 'endure and suffer all kind of infirmity, sickness, yea and the pain of death' for his beliefs – if, that is, the testament was genuine.

It was not until the 1920s that a Spanish version of the will was found by a Jesuit scholar in the library of the British Museum. Entitled *Testamento O Ultima Voluntad del Alma*, it had been printed in Mexico City in 1661, but its author had been Cardinal Carlo Borromeo, Archbishop of Milan, who died in 1584. Copies of the 'Testament of the

Last Will of the Soul' had been smuggled into England by Jesuit priests who passed through Stratford in the summer of 1580.

An English-language copy of the testament, published in 1638, finally came to light in 1966. Consisting of twenty-four miniature pages, this 'Testament of the Soul' corresponded exactly with the document found in the roof space of the Shakespeare Birthplace in 1757. John Shakespeare's 'Spiritual Testament' had not been a forgery after all.

Only the year before John Shakespeare's incriminating testament was discovered, Rev. Francis Gastrell had chopped down Will Shakespeare's mulberry tree, possibly because of its 'papist' associations. Now a document had appeared which identified Shakespeare's father as a committed Catholic.

Rev. Francis Gastrell had left Stratford after the mulberry incident, but he was still the owner of New Place and therefore liable for the property tax which paid for the maintenance of the poor. Gastrell quarrelled with the Corporation over the assessment of his monthly levy, and eventually, in 1759, he razed New Place to the ground.

The preacher must have arrived mob-handed. The Corporation appears to have been powerless to stop him.

Gastrell was marched out of Stratford 'amidst the rage and curses of the inhabitants', and the Corporation passed a by-law forbidding anyone named Gastrell from living in the town.

In the space of four years, Shakespeare's mulberry had been axed, its wood going on to form a host of 'relics'; a Catholic will, signed by Shakespeare's father, had been found among the rafters of the Birthplace; and Will's substantial home had been demolished by the same preacher who had felled his mulberry tree.

Rev. Francis Gastrell's actions require better explanations than his supposed annoyance with the sightseers wishing to view Shakespeare's mulberry and his row with the council over taxes. The mulberry and the 'Spiritual Testament' had revealed Will's family as secret 'papists', and so the physical traces of Shakespeare's existence were attacked and destroyed by a Protestant bigot.

Shakespeare's Jubilee

THERE WAS now a yawning gap on the corner of Chapel Street where Shakespeare's home had stood. The Stratford Corporation started looking for a new way to honour the town's most famous son.

The old Town Hall at the other end of Chapel Street had been blown up during the Civil War, shortly after the Catholic queen, Henrietta

Maria, stayed at New Place. The Town Hall was rebuilt in 1767. The new building of golden stone had an open niche on its north side which was intended to hold a statue of Shakespeare. All that was needed was a benefactor to provide the statue.

The Corporation approached the famous actor and theatre manager David Garrick, offering to elect him an Honorary Burgess of the town and to present him with a testimonial, granting him the Freedom of the Borough, in an ornate box 'made of that very mulberry-tree planted by Shakespeare's own hand'.

Garrick had made his name playing Shakespearean characters. He had even built a temple to Shakespeare in the grounds of his house beside the River Thames. Flattered by the honours and the 'elegant and inestimable box' bestowed on him by the aldermen of Stratford, Garrick saw an opportunity to host a huge festival, during which the new Town Hall would be named Shakespeare's Hall and his effigy of Shakespeare paraded through the streets. He chose to call this festival 'Shakespeare's Jubilee' – even though it took place five years after the bicentenary of Shakespeare's birth, and in the wrong month.

A three-day programme of events was planned. As a letter published in *The Public Advertiser* and the *Gentleman's Magazine* put it, 'The Whole will conclude with the Apotheosis of Shakespeare.'

A large rotunda, known as the Amphitheatre, or the Great Booth, was specially constructed on the riverside in Stratford. The wardrobe of the Drury Lane Theatre was emptied, with 'upwards of 150 large boxes of dresses and scenery' packed up and transported from London, 100 miles away. As the first day of the Jubilee drew near, Stratford was inundated with visitors anxious to take part in the festivities. The numbers vastly exceeded the available accommodation in the town.

'The god of our idolatry'

HALLEY'S COMET passed through the sky on the first night of the Jubilee. To some, this was a sign of impending disaster.

The festival-goers awoke to a 'hateful drizzling rain' on the second day, Thursday 7 September 1769. This soon became a downpour. The Amphitheatre was crowded for the dedication of Shakespeare's statue. David Garrick recited his 'Dedication Ode':

'Tis he! 'tis he! – that demi-god!
Who Avon's flow'ry margin trod,
While sportive *Fancy* round him flew,

Where *Nature* led him by the hand,
Instructed him in all she knew,
And gave him absolute command!
'Tis he! 'Tis he!
'The god of our idolatry!' ...
SHAKESPEARE! SHAKESPEARE! SHAKESPEARE!

Garrick gave way to Mrs Baddeley, who sang the sixth air of the Ode: 'Thou soft-flowing Avon, by thy silver stream, / Of things more than mortal, sweet Shakespeare would dream.' As Sophia Baddeley prepared for her encore, David Garrick threw open the doors of the Amphitheatre. The meadow was flooded. 'Flow on, silver Avon! in song ever flow,' sang Mrs Baddeley, while the river burst its banks.

A masquerade ball was held in the Amphitheatre that evening. Horses waded knee-deep to bring the costumed gentry to the ball. 'Such a flood has not been witnessed there in the memory of a man,' wrote an observer. James Boswell was there, desperately trying to read out his own poem for the occasion and 'dancing with the water over his shoes'. The great fireworks display fell victim to the torrential rain: 'The rockets would not ascend for fear of catching cold, and the surly crackers went out at a single pop.'

The Jubilee horse race went ahead the following noon, but the high point of the festival – a grand procession of 170 persons 'properly dressed, in all the principal characters to be met with in Shakespeare's plays' – was cancelled because of the weather. And so Garrick's Folly, as it came to be thought of, fizzled out. The actor-manager had lost about £2,000 on the event.

The townsfolk of Stratford were blamed for the festival's failings. 'The low People of Stratford upon Avon are without doubt as ignorant as any in the whole Island', wrote one correspondent to the *St James Chronicle*. 'I talked with many, particularly the old People, and not one of them but was frightened at the Preparations for the Jubilee, and did not know what they were about.' The Stratfordians were hardly alone in this – a labourer from Banbury, paid to transport a double-bass viol to the event, apparently believed that he would be witnessing the 'resurrection of Shakespeare'. But the metropolitan elite were especially critical of the people of Shakespeare's hometown: 'It is impossible to describe their Absurdity; and indeed Providence seems by producing Shakespeare and the rest of his Townsmen, to shew the two Extremes of Human Nature.'

The London crowd convinced itself that the residents of Stratford were too comical to be capable of appreciating Shakespeare. Garrick's triumph had been ruined by the local clowns.

Ten days after the Jubilee ended, the *London Chronicle* published an anonymous piece, 'Garrick's *Vagary: or* England *run Mad; with Particulars* of the Stratford Jubilee', in which a character named Nettle fulminated about the people 'running out of Town, pell-mell, after a Brat of *Judaism*, a since foster-child of *Popery*, now, forsooth, revived by an Actor, to the very imminent and most alarming Danger both of Church and State'. It was a satirical portrait, no doubt, but one which reflected the views of some towards Shakespeare (a 'foster-child of *Popery*'). The piece ended in the 'Apollo *Room at the* Shakespeare's *Head*, Covent Garden', with members of the Mulberry Club '*sitting round a Table, on which is a Representation of the* Mulberry *Tree*': 'Let Critics dissent, or let them agree, / We'll sing, and dance round the Mulberry-tree.' Shakespeare's mulberry, the felling of which had sparked outrage in Stratford, had become a metropolitan reminder of a bucolic past that never was.

Avarice and vanity

DAVID GARRICK took his revenge on the people of Stratford. At his Drury Lane Theatre, on 14 October 1769, he presented his stage adaptation of *The Jubilee*. It culminated with the elaborate Pageant of Shakespearean characters which had been rained off in Stratford.

The entertainment opened with an early morning scene in an old woman's house in Stratford. The old woman and her neighbour gossiped fearfully about the Jubilee. They were joined by a country bumpkin who insisted that the pope was responsible for the Jubilee, or maybe the (Catholic) Pretender to the throne, and claimed to have seen men fiddling with gunpowder in a barn, which he assumed was a plot to blow up the town.

The waiters at the White Horse Inn were seen struggling with the demands of hungry guests. Pedlars touting relics from the mulberry tree accused each other of cheating. 'The general Hurry and Spirit of the Whole,' wrote one reviewer, 'give us an agreeable Idea of the Distresses and Bustle of the *Jubilee* at Stratford, and the audience may enjoy both, without having the Inconveniences of partaking either of the one or of the other.'

The Jubilee was performed more than ninety times during the Drury Lane season of 1769–70. Its success made up for the costly and chaotic proceedings in Stratford.

But, as one of Garrick's enemies implied, the whole thing had been more a celebration of David Garrick than of the Bard: 'Avarice and vanity prompted G---k to the deed. He wanted to fleece the people and transmit his name down to posterity, hand in hand, with Shakespeare.'

One of the oddities of the 1769 Jubilee was that not one of Shakespeare's plays was performed during the festival. Not a single sonnet or soliloquy of Shakespeare's was recited. During the whole three-day event only one line from Shakespeare was heard, and that was misquoted. There were plenty of poems and songs *about* Shakespeare, but none of his own. The entire Jubilee was devoted, not so much to Shakespeare, as to the *idea* of Shakespeare.

Garrick's Jubilee drove a wedge between the 'low People' of Will's hometown and the metropolitan sophisticates. Only the educated elite were refined enough to understand Shakespeare (even if they couldn't be bothered to quote him accurately). The Stratfordians were too stupid, too superstitious, to be taken seriously. The flipside, of course, was that the townsfolk were probably horrified by the tasteless spectacle and fearful that their Shakespeare was being taken from them.

As far as Garrick's crowd was concerned, Shakespeare – 'Our SHAKESPEARE' – had become the 'god of our idolatry'. Verily, the Jubilee had seen the Apotheosis of Shakespeare. Except that it was not Will Shakespeare. It was a pseudo-Shakespeare, cut off from his roots and planted on a painted pedestal. Not a flesh-and-blood Shakespeare, but a political construct: a myth.

All that is known

GEORGE STEEVENS was no fan of David Garrick. He had in fact been instrumental in getting Garrick involved in the plan for the Shakespeare statue at Stratford's Town Hall, correctly presuming that Garrick could easily be flattered into overreaching himself.

Steevens had edited and published twenty of Shakespeare's plays in 1766. With the help of Dr Johnson, Steevens then put together a ten-volume *Works of Shakespeare*. Setting the bar for Shakespeare biographers, Steevens set it very low indeed: 'All that is known with any degree of certainty concerning Shakespeare, is – that he was born at Stratford-upon-Avon, – married and had children there, – went to London, where he commenced actor, and wrote poems and plays, returned to Stratford, made his will, died, and was buried.'

Surprisingly little has changed since Edmond Malone quoted Steevens' summary of Shakespeare facts in 1780. Those who stray from the narrow path sketched out by Steevens are deemed guilty of wandering into the fairy dells of speculation. The awful truth is that we know so little about

Shakespeare. 'What we would not give for a single personal letter,' cried Samuel Schoenbaum, 'one page of a diary!'

And yet, this too is a myth. It sprang from the deification of Shakespeare which Garrick achieved with his Jubilee. To preserve the lofty image of 'Our SHAKESPEARE' it was necessary to assert that the Bard was an unknown quantity.

Just as the felling of Will's mulberry gave rise to Garrick's asinine ballad of *Shakespeare's Mulberry-Tree* ('As a relick I kiss it, and bow at the shrine'), with no mention at all of the clergyman who chopped it down or the anger of the townsfolk at its desecration, so the local memory of Shakespeare was ridiculed and ignored in order to allow the 'immortal Bard' to become the focus of patriotic projections. The 'Apotheosis of Shakespeare' created a national poet who was brilliant *because* he was invisible, a 'demi-god' who was never really mortal in the first place.

Little wonder, then, that when the Reverend James Wilmot left London to become the rector of Barton-on-the-Heath, near Stratford, he began to have his doubts about the authorship of Shakespeare's works. How, Wilmot wondered, could the humbly born Shakespeare have been 'received as a friend and equal' by men of culture and breeding? Thus, another myth was born in 1785, when Rev. James Wilmot first suggested that somebody else must have written the plays.

On the one hand, the theory that Shakespeare the player could not have been the playwright was born of sheer snobbery. But, like the axe which was taken to his mulberry, the hatchet used to attack Will's reputation was wielded by extremists: Delia Bacon, who championed Francis Bacon as the 'real' Shakespeare, came from a family of New England Puritans; Thomas Looney, who argued that the Earl of Oxford was the author of the plays, belonged to a proto-fascist sect called the Church of Humanity. The refusal to see Shakespeare as he was owes more to fanaticism than fact.

The three interrelated myths – that of Shakespeare the 'demi-god'; the myth that nothing is known about Shakespeare; and the Alternative Authorship nonsense – all came into being against a backdrop of rising religious tensions.

After the death of the 'Old Pretender', James Francis Edward Stuart, in 1766, the Papacy in Rome formally recognised the Protestant Hanoverian dynasty as the lawful rulers of England. This paved the way for the removal of the penal laws against Catholics, beginning with the first Catholic Relief Act of 1778. This modest Act provoked violent anti-Catholic riots in London. Another fifty years would pass before England's Catholics finally achieved emancipation.

With feelings running so high in the late 1700s it was only to be expected that any hint of Catholicism in Shakespeare's background would be judiciously erased – it would hardly have squared with Garrick's Apotheosis of Shakespeare as the national poet of Protestant England. And so the 'Spiritual Testament' signed by Will's father was conveniently lost and a Protestant 'Profession of Faith' was forged. The real Shakespeare had to be buried for the 'god of our idolatry' to arise.

We have paid a price for this. By denying Shakespeare's Catholic roots, scholars have rendered his life and works unintelligible. His plays and poems are urgent despatches from the front line of a vicious conflict, a brutal power struggle between the old communal world and the new commercial one. There were many victims of this strife, and Will Shakespeare was one of them – but you wouldn't think it from what the academics are prepared to admit.

Means, motive, opportunity

I WITNESSED this censorship when I attended a talk at the Shakespeare Centre in Stratford about the publication of a 'lost' play which forms a crucial piece of evidence in the matter of Will's death.

At one point, the issue of John Shakespeare's incriminating 'Testament' was raised. The country's leading authority on Shakespeare quickly stifled that line of inquiry. Remarking that another academic had dismissed the Catholic document as a 'boilerplate job' – 'there were hundreds of those things around at the time' – the professor swiftly steered the discussion away from the contentious topic.

It is true that thousands of those testaments were smuggled illegally into England. But to pretend that no inference can be drawn from the fact that Will's father signed his name to such a document is facetious. Merely by possessing his copy, Shakespeare's father was guilty of treason.

To downplay the significance of John Shakespeare's testament is to engage in a cover-up – an ongoing, 400-year-old cover-up that extends into all aspects of Shakespeare's life and times.

The popular view of the criminal law in the United States is that a jury must be convinced of three things before judgement can be passed. The jurors must believe that the accused had the ability or *means* to commit the offence, the reason or *motive* to carry it out, and the chance or *opportunity* to do so.

In the first part of this book, we shall examine how Shakespeare met his death (the 'means'). In the second part, we review his life and career (the 'motive'), and in the final section we will consider the circumstances leading up to his murder (the 'opportunity').

During the course of our investigation, a picture of Will Shakespeare will emerge which differs from the familiar, squeaky-clean image of the Bard.

There will be no sweeping of vital evidence under the carpet. We owe him that.

Those who are touched in their property and person,
torn by cruel rage and wounded by the government,
cry aloud to heaven that they are abandoned.

And so all about us are groans,
and complaints,
and tears of blood.

They live in a perpetual dread
of losing their property today,
their liberty tomorrow,
their life the day after,

as has happened to many.

Nicolò Molin
Venetian Ambassador to England
1605

1 George Vertue's 1737 sketch of Shakespeare's funerary monument, Holy Trinity Church, Stratford.

Part One

Means

There thou mayst brain him,
Having first seized his books

William Shakespeare
The Tempest

Being Merry at a Tavern

IT IS by far the most visited parish church in England.

Eight hundred years old, the Collegiate Church of the Holy and Undivided Trinity stands on the west bank of the river in the Old Town of Stratford-upon-Avon. Approaching along a paved avenue lined with lime trees, the visitor steps through the vaulted fifteenth-century porch and, passing the font in which William Shakespeare was baptised, enters an echoing space illuminated by brightly coloured windows.

The best windows light the east-facing chancel, with its medieval choir stalls, its ornate tomb of Thomas Balsall (who built the chancel in 1480) and its recumbent effigy of Shakespeare's friend, John Combe. The high altar is a rare example of a pre-Reformation altar still in use in England; buried for many years under the chancel floor, it escaped the rage of the Puritan reformers.

The grave of William Shakespeare lies in front of the altar. On one side is the grave of his widow, Anne; on the other, the graves of Thomas Nash (who married Will's granddaughter), Dr John Hall (who married Will's daughter, Susanna) and Susanna herself. It is the grave of Will Shakespeare which lures so many visitors to Holy Trinity Church. The gravestone is smaller than those on either side and is inscribed with a four-line doggerel verse, laying a curse upon anyone who 'moves my bones'.

The register of Holy Trinity Church records the burial on 25 April 1616 of 'Will Shakspere gent'. Overlooking the grave from the north wall of the chancel, a funerary monument, installed within a few years of Shakespeare's death, reveals that the poet died on 23 April, aged 53. He was buried two days later under a gravestone which does not bear his name.

An Oxford University student toured Holy Trinity Church in 1694. In a letter to a friend he wrote of Shakespeare's grave that 'they have laid him full seventeen-foot deep, deep enough to secure him'. Combined with the curious injunction on his gravestone not to 'dig the dust enclosed here', the extraordinary depth of the grave ensured that Will's remains were unlikely ever to be disturbed.

A NEW vicar arrived in Stratford in 1662. The Rev. John Ward was eager to find out all that he could about the famous poet who lay buried in his church and gave himself a reminder to look in on Shakespeare's daughter, Judith. Whether or not John Ward spoke with Judith – she died that same year – the parson did glean some information from his parishioners.

'I have heard that Mr Shakespeare was a natural wit,' he wrote, '… he frequented the plays all his younger time, but in his elder years lived at Stratford, and supplied the stage with two plays every year, and for that had an allowance so large that he spent at the rate of a thousand a year, as I have heard.' Those were spectacular outgoings; £1,000 was a great deal of money. Rev. John Ward continued his memorandum: 'Shakespeare, Drayton and Ben Jonson had a merry meeting, and, it seems, drank too hard, for Shakespeare died of a fever there contracted.' This is the only known reference to the circumstances surrounding Shakespeare's death.

Ward's interest in the Bard was far from idle. He concluded his note, 'Remember to peruse Shakespeare's plays and be versed in them, that I may not be ignorant in the matter.' But his memorandum sadly lacks detail; the vicar made no mention of where or when the 'merry meeting' took place. We can, however, hazard some educated guesses.

Traditionally, Shakespeare is said to have been born, as he died, on 23 April. As we shall see, the coincidence of him having died on his birthday, and in the town where he was born, is not without significance. As for a possible venue for the 'merry meeting', we need look no further than a few yards from Shakespeare's home.

New Place stood to the north of Holy Trinity Church, on the corner of Chapel Street. A short distance away, heading along Chapel Street and the High Street, was a half-timbered house known as Atwood's. For five years, a wine merchant named Thomas Quiney had owned the lease on Atwood's for the purpose of running a tavern.

The Shakespeares and the Quineys had been close for years. Adrian Quiney had served with Will's father, John Shakespeare, on the Stratford Corporation. Adrian's son, Richard Quiney, addressed a letter to his 'Loving good Friend and countryman' Will Shakespeare in 1598. It was Richard's son, Thomas, who now ran the tavern on Stratford High Street. On 10 February 1616, a few weeks before Shakespeare died, Thomas Quiney married Will's daughter, Judith, who was still alive forty-five years later when Rev. John Ward came to town.

The tavern run by Will's newly acquired son-in-law was a three-minute stroll from New Place, and so it was perhaps at Atwood's that Shakespeare had his fateful 'merry meeting' with Drayton and Jonson.

OF THE three poets present, only one had a reputation for heavy drinking. This was Ben Jonson, the youngest of the trio.

William Drummond, a Scottish poet who had the pleasure of Jonson's company during the winter of 1618–19, left a character sketch in which he remarked of the 46-year-old Ben: 'He is a great lover and praiser of himself, a contemner and scorner of others, given rather to lose a friend than a jest, jealous of every word and action of those about him (especially after drink, which is one of the elements in which he liveth).' Drummond added that Jonson was 'a dissembler of ill parts which reign in him' and 'a bragger of some good' that he lacked.

Ben's fondness for the bottle, particularly the sweet wine known as Canary, had probably contributed to his burgeoning girth. He weighed in at some 278lb (126kg) and boasted a 'mountain belly' to match his 'rocky face'. That face had once been lean and hollow-cheeked but was now fleshy and pockmarked. His beard and moustache were wispy, a shade or two lighter than his thick dark hair. The portrait of Jonson painted in about 1617, and now in the National Portrait Gallery in London, gives him a broad nose with a pronounced ridge at the top where his eyebrows meet. The playwright Thomas Dekker described him as a 'staring Leviathan' with a 'terrible mouth'.

Michael Drayton had no such reputation for drinking. The eldest of the three poets at the 'merry meeting', he was admired for his probity. The churchman Francis Meres, whose *Palladis Tamia* of 1598 compared his contemporary poets with the poets of the classical world, held him in the highest regard:

As *Aulus Persius Flaccus* is reported among all writers to be of an honest life and upright conversation: so *Michael Drayton* ... among scholars, soldiers, Poets, and all sorts of people, is held for a man of virtuous disposition, honest conversation, and well governed carriage, which is almost miraculous among good wits in these declining and corrupt times ...

His portrait in the National Portrait Gallery, painted in 1599 when he was about 36 years old, presents a thin and scholarly looking man of clean skin and neat appearance, the oval of his face accentuated by a trim gingery beard, his brown hair crowned with a wreath of laurels. A later portrait from 1628 shows that Drayton's jowls had begun to sag and his beard had shrunk to a tuft of greying hairs. His face had lost none of its pallor, while the clear eyes of 1599 had become careworn and distrustful.

Warwickshire folklore recalls the adolescent Shakespeare as an enthusiastic and accomplished drinker. This reputation did not follow him down to London. His theatre company endeavoured to prove that they were 'Men of grave and sober Behaviour'.

Writing later in the seventeenth century, John Aubrey – who noted that Ben Jonson tended to fall into bed drunk – remarked that Will Shakespeare was a 'handsome, well-shap't man, very good company', who was 'the more to be admired *quia* he was not a company keeper' and 'wouldn't be debauched'. When invited to make merry, he would excuse himself, saying 'he was in pain'.

At home, he might have let his guard down. An anecdote preserved in the second volume of Aubrey's *Brief Lives* finds Will in a Warwickshire saloon:

> One time as he was at the tavern in Stratford on Avon, one Combe, an old rich usurer, was to be buried, [Shakespeare] makes this extempore epitaph:
>
> > Ten in the hundred the Devil allows,
> > But Combe will have twelve, he swears and vows:
> > If anyone asks who lies in this tomb,
> > 'Hoh!' quoth the Devil, ''Tis my John o'Combe.'

John Combe of Old Stratford died in 1614, a couple of years before Shakespeare; his effigy lies close to Will's funerary monument in the chancel of Holy Trinity Church. John Combe left Shakespeare £5 in his will. Will in turn bequeathed his sword to John's nephew and heir, Thomas Combe, a Catholic.

A somewhat kindlier version of Will's 'extempore epitaph' for John Combe was recorded by Nicholas Burgh, a Poor Knight of Windsor, in a document dating from 1650. Burgh's manuscript also recalled an occasion when Shakespeare and Jonson had been drinking together:

> Mr. Ben Jonson and Mr. William Shakespeare being merry at a tavern, Master Jonson having begun this for an epitaph: 'Here lies Ben Jonson, / That was once one', he gives it to Master Shakespeare to make up, who presently writes: 'Who while he lived was a slow thing, / And now, being dead, is a nothing'.

A similar anecdote was discovered among the papers of Thomas Plume, Archdeacon of Rochester and vicar of Greenwich, who died in 1704. In Plume's account, Will 'took the pen' from Jonson and wrote:

Here lies Benjamin –
With short hair upon his chin –
Who while he lived was a slow thing,
And now he's dead is no thing.

The playful epitaphs for John Combe (who was dead) and Ben Jonson (who wasn't) were not up to Will's usual standard. They can be compared with a jingle that Shakespeare reputedly wrote to accompany a pair of gloves. The gloves were made by Will's father for the Stratford schoolmaster, Alexander Aspinall, who gave them to his bride, Ann Shaw, who lived near the Henley Street home of the Shakespeare family. The wedding present came with a note: 'The gift is small, / The will is all: / Alexander Aspinall.'

The word 'will' was a slang term – as 'willy' is today – for the penis. Elsewhere, Shakespeare made use of the term 'glove' as a familiar metaphor for the female genitals, and so the wedding gift became, as the ditty suggested, a token of something more meaningful: the easing of the groom's enlarged 'will' into his bride's little 'glove' when the marriage was consummated.

Something of the same bawdy nature can be glimpsed in Will's jokey epitaph for Ben Jonson. Nicholas Burgh and Thomas Plume recorded slightly different versions of this epitaph, but the tenor of both was the same – Ben, while he lived, was a 'slow thing' and, once dead, would be 'nothing'.

Then, as now, a 'thing' could be a penis. Shakespeare is known to have used 'thing' and 'no thing' to designate the male member and its female counterpart. This sheds an unsavoury light on his off-the-cuff epitaph for Jonson. Ben himself had started it off with 'Here lies Ben Jonson, / That was once one'. Shakespeare then took the pen and wrote that Ben was a 'slow thing' – a dullard, a flaccid penis – who died and became 'no thing', a rotting pudendum.

Before long, Jonson was recounting his own version of the impromptu epitaph. He told the Scottish poet William Drummond (who noted how quick Ben was to take offence, especially when he had been drinking) that his 'Epitaph, by a companion written, is:

Here lies Benjamin Jonson dead,
And hath no more wit than a goose in his head,

That as he was wont, so doth he still
Live by his wit, and evermore will.'

('Ane other', wrote Drummond in 1619: 'Here lyes honest Ben / That had not a beard on his chen.')

Jonson's account of his epitaph 'by a companion written' was clearly a sanitised version of the ones later recorded by Burgh and Plume. Gone are the dubious references to slow things and no things. Instead, Ben contrives to live eternally by his wit, even though he has less wit in his head than a 'goose'.

Coming within three years of Will Shakespeare's death, Ben's own account of his epitaph suggests that other versions were already doing the rounds. These alternative versions, later written down by Nicholas Burgh and Thomas Plume, made it clear that Shakespeare was the companion who had made up the original.

We are left with the impression that some sort of epitaph game was played by Shakespeare and Jonson while they were 'being merry at a tavern'. Shakespeare was said to have composed an extempore epitaph for his friend, John Combe, in a Stratford tavern in 1614. The occasion of the Jonson epitaph was quite possibly the 'merry meeting' of 1616, at which the poets 'drank too hard' and Will caught the 'fever' that killed him. Ben was soon promoting his own, more self-flattering version of the epitaph, thereby implying that the alternative account was already in circulation. This would suggest that a third party was there to witness the moment when Shakespeare insulted Jonson with his 'no thing' jibe.

That person was probably Michael Drayton, the third poet at the 'merry meeting'.

LIKE SHAKESPEARE, Drayton was a native of the Woodland, the spiritual and geographical heart of England. Born in the village of Harthill, on the north-eastern boundary of the Forest of Arden, he was about a year older than Shakespeare.

In his childhood Michael Drayton entered into service with the Goodere family of Polesworth. His first patron was Sir Henry Goodere. An important local figure, Goodere served as High Sheriff of Warwickshire in 1570, but was committed to the Tower of London the following year over his dealings with Mary, Queen of Scots. He recovered his fortunes, however, and was later knighted, becoming a trusted Gentleman of the Privy Chamber.

Drayton remained in service with the Gooderes of Polesworth Hall until the death of Sir Henry in 1595, when he was 'bequeathed' to the dazzling Lucy Harington, whose parents were based at Coombe Abbey, near Coventry. Lucy married Edward Russell, Third Earl of Bedford, at about the same time as she inherited the poet Drayton. As Lucy, Countess of Bedford, she became the 'universal patroness of poets', but her relations with Drayton soon soured. He complained in a bitter verse that she had abandoned him in favour of 'deceitful *Cerberon*', a 'beastly clown too vile of to be spoken'. It is probable that this beastly 'Cerberon' was Ben Jonson, who dedicated his satirical play *Cynthia's Revels* to the Countess of Bedford in 1600.

By 1602, Drayton had a new patron, Sir Walter Aston, whose mother was the daughter of Sir Thomas Lucy, the lord of the manor of Charlecote, near Stratford. Sir Thomas Lucy was a magistrate, a Member of Parliament and a fanatical persecutor of Catholics: among those who suffered at his hands was a glove maker of Stratford called John Shakespeare and his eldest son, William.

Unlike Will Shakespeare and Ben Jonson, Drayton never married. The love of his life was Anne Goodere, the daughter of his first patron. She became his 'Idea' – his Muse – and he dedicated his pastorals and a collection of sonnets to her in the early 1590s. Around the time of her father's death in 1595, Anne married Sir Henry Rainsford of Clifford Chambers, a manor just 2 miles south of Stratford-upon-Avon. The lovelorn Drayton took to spending his summers at the half-timbered Manor House, with its clear view of the wooden spire of Holy Trinity Church. He would remain the devoted poet-shepherd, 'Rowland of the Rock', forever inseparable from his 'Idea' and her marital home of 'dear Clifford'.

It was during one of his extended stays at Clifford that Drayton was cured of a recurring fever by Dr John Hall of Stratford. Hall's notes reveal that Drayton was given an emetic with syrup of violets, which 'worked very well both upwards and downwards'. In 1607, Dr John Hall married Shakespeare's daughter, Susanna. He also treated Drayton's beloved 'Idea', Lady Anne Rainsford.

Drayton was also a close friend of Will Shakespeare's 'cousin', Thomas Greene, a trained lawyer and a minor poet in his own right – Greene composed a sonnet 'To Master Michael Drayton', which was prefixed to Drayton's long poem 'The Barons' Wars' of 1603. That same year, Greene was appointed Steward of Stratford-upon-Avon, and between 1603 and 1611 he and his family lived at New Place as guests of the Shakespeares, who probably stood as godparents to Greene's children, William and Anne.

When Shakespeare retired from the public stage in 1611, Thomas Greene and his family moved out of New Place and into a large house in Stratford's Old Town. Five years later, after the death of Will

Shakespeare, Greene promptly resigned his position as town clerk, sold his house and relocated to Bristol, more than 60 miles away. Writing to his old associates in 1617, he referred to his years with the Stratford Corporation as his 'golden days'.

MICHAEL DRAYTON merely dabbled in writing for the theatre. He collaborated with other playwrights – Anthony Munday, Henry Chettle and Thomas Dekker – and was a good friend to Francis Beaumont, but he is best remembered for his poetry.

Ben Jonson also expected to be chiefly remembered for his poetic achievements. Among Ben's published *Epigrams* are two he addressed to Lucy, Countess of Bedford, who had once favoured Drayton. Perhaps Jonson had Drayton in mind when he wrote that the 'bright and amiable' Lucy had:

>   a better verser got,
> (Or *Poet*, in the court account) than I,
> And who doth me (though I not him) envy.

In a later poem, entitled 'The Vision of Ben Jonson, on the Muses of his Friend, M. Drayton', Jonson openly displayed the ambivalence of his feelings towards the Warwickshire poet: 'It hath been questioned, MICHAEL, if I be / A Friend at all; or, if at all, to thee.' As Professor Sara Van Den Berg observed in the *Cambridge Companion to Ben Jonson*, 'It is impossible to decide the poet's answer to [this] initial premise.'

What makes Jonson's equivocation so remarkable is that his 'Vision' was written as a preface to Drayton's 1627 collection of his best poems. After showering Drayton's poetry with overblown praise, Ben concluded his dedicatory verse:

> I gratulate it to thee, and thy Ends,
> To all thy virtuous, and well chosen Friends,
> Only my loss is, that I am not there:
> And, till I worthy am to wish I were,
> I call the world, that envies me, to see
> If I can be a Friend, and Friend to thee.

Eleven years on from the fabled 'merry meeting', Ben Jonson was quibbling – was he, or was he not, a friend to Michael Drayton? It is a strange sort of dedication. Jonson indicated that he was 'not there' among Drayton's 'virtuous and well chosen' friends, and he challenged the reader to determine whether he was, or even could be, Drayton's friend. The praises he heaped on Drayton's work sound disingenuous and tongue-in-cheek. If the reader still doubted Jonson's friendship, the fault lay entirely with Ben.

One of the poems published by Drayton in his 1627 miscellany was 'The Shepherds' Sirena'. In this, he depicted his idyllic rural retreat as threatened by 'Roguish swineherds, that repine / At our flocks like beastly clowns'. He had previously referred to 'deceitful *Cerberon*' as a 'beastly clown', but he now gave another name to his nemesis, the ringleader of the 'Roguish swineherds':

Angry OLCON sets them on,
And against us part doth take,
Ever since he was out-gone
Off'ring Rhymes with us to make.

The mention of 'Angry OLCON' might mean little were it not for an earlier poem, Drayton's Eighth Eclogue of 1606, in which he had shown his resentment towards 'Sirena' – Lucy, Countess of Bedford – for having transferred her patronage to 'deceitful *Cerberon*'. Rewritten in 1619, the Eighth Eclogue went on to denounce 'great OLCON, which a PHOEBUS seemed:

Whom all good Shepherds gladly flocked about,
And as a God of ROWLAND was esteemed,
Which to his praise drew all the rural Rout:
        For, after ROWLAND, as it hath been PAN,
        Only to OLCON every Shepherd ran.

As the poetic 'Rowland', Drayton had seemingly been in awe of 'great OLCON', as had the other poets or 'Shepherds' who flocked to greet him. But great Olcon had since deserted Drayton, and 'to the stern Wolf and deceitful Fox, / Leaves the poor Shepherd and his harmless Sheep.' Great Olcon had offered to make rhymes with Drayton and his companions, but he had been 'out-gone' – surpassed, bested, outdone. Olcon then departed angrily, abandoning poor 'Rowland' to the 'stern Wolf and deceitful Fox' and inciting his 'Roguish swineherds' to menace Drayton in his rural paradise.

This was how things stood in 1619, three years after the 'merry meeting' in Stratford. Only the year before, Drayton had struck up a long-running correspondence with William Drummond of Hawthornden. Drummond was in his early thirties at the time. He was the laird of Hawthornden Castle, 7 miles south of Edinburgh, and he was well connected: his father had been a gentleman-usher to King James I of England, while his mother's brother was secretary to James' queen, Anne of Denmark.

Soon after Drayton and Drummond began writing to each other, Ben Jonson set out on foot from London to Edinburgh. The 300-mile journey took him seventy-one days – no mean undertaking for an overweight, middle-aged alcoholic.

Jonson spent a fortnight or more with Drummond at Hawthornden Castle over Christmas 1618. Drummond's notes of their conversations included Ben's version of his 'Epitaph, by a companion written'. They also discussed Michael Drayton. Jonson told Drummond that 'Drayton feared him, and he [Ben] esteemed not of him.' He declared that Drayton's 'long verses pleased him not' – so the praises he lavished on Drayton's poems in 1627 were hardly sincere – and he complained that Sir William Alexander, the poet, playwright, First Earl of Stirling and close friend of Drummond's, had been 'not half kind to him, and neglected him, because [Sir William was] a friend to Drayton'.

Drummond's notes also refer to a lost play of Jonson's:

> He hath a pastoral entitled The May Lord. His own name is Alkin, Ethra the Countess of Bedford's, Mogibell Overbury, the old Countess of Suffolk an enchantress ... In his first story, Alkin cometh in mending his broken pipe. Contrary to all other pastorals he bringeth the clowns making mirth and foolish sports.

It is not known when *The May Lord* was written. Jonson's most recent biographer, Ian Donaldson, suggests that he wrote it 'for private study' in 1618. William Drummond perhaps sent details of it in a letter to Drayton after Jonson's visit, giving Drayton time to add the stanzas referring to 'great OLCON' to his Eighth Eclogue, published in 1619.

By his own admission to Drummond, Jonson had characterised himself as 'Alkin', a name borrowed from classical mythology. The Roman poet Gaius Valerius Flaccus portrayed Alcon as a skilled archer whose arrows never missed their mark. Jonson no doubt flattered himself into thinking that his satirical barbs invariably struck home.

The 'great OLCON' and 'Angry OLCON' of Drayton's poems was surely the Alcon or 'Alkin' with whom Jonson wished to be identified. In the first scene of *The May Lord*, as Jonson told Drummond, 'Alkin cometh in mending his broken pipe'. Drayton would soon write of 'Olcon' that he 'forsakes the Herd-groom and his Flocks, / Nor of his

Bag-pipes takes at all no keep'. Those who knew of *The May Lord*, including such noble patrons as Lucy, Countess of Bedford, and William Herbert, Third Earl of Pembroke, would have recognised Drayton's allusion to 'OLCON', the angry poet-satirist, and his 'beastly clowns'.

Evidently, by the winter of 1618–19, the relationship between Drayton and Jonson had broken down. There had been bad blood between them before, when Jonson stole Lucy, the 'universal patroness of poets', from Drayton, but Drayton's Eighth Eclogue of 1619 suggests that they had then buried their differences. 'Olcon' had been considered a 'God of Rowland', second only to Drayton in the admiration he received from other poets. But then, after some sort of rhyming contest, instigated by 'Olcon', Jonson abandoned Drayton to the tender mercies of the 'stern Wolf and deceitful Fox'.

Jonson, meanwhile, was telling William Drummond that 'Drayton feared him'. Drayton would later claim that 'Angry OLCON' had unleashed his roguish followers against him. They threatened to destroy his treasured peace and quiet at Clifford Chambers by attacking him with 'holly whips' and 'hazel goads'. This was published in the volume of 1627, which Jonson commended with his 'Vision ... on the Muses of his Friend, M. Drayton', even though he 'esteemed not' of Drayton, whose 'long verses pleased him not'.

SOMETIME BEFORE Christmas 1618, Ben had offered to make 'Rhymes' with Drayton and another poet. We know from William Drummond's sketch that Jonson was 'given rather to lose a friend than a jest', and on this occasion he was 'out-gone'. The occasion might well have been the 'merry meeting' of 1616, when Shakespeare, Drayton and Jonson were gathered together, 'being merry at a tavern'.

Jonson had commenced his own rhyming epitaph before passing it to Shakespeare, who completed it with a pungent pun: 'Who while he lived was a slow thing, / And now he's dead is a no-thing.'

Shakespeare then died 'of a fever there contracted', according to Rev. John Ward's informants in Stratford. Ever since, Drayton had lived in fear of Jonson and his 'swineherds'.

The manor of Clifford Chambers, though now part of Warwickshire, in Shakespeare's day lay in the neighbouring county of Gloucestershire. The sixth volume of *The History of the County of Gloucestershire*, published in 1965, remarks of the moat-encircled Manor House that one of its rooms was 'called after Drayton', who stayed there so often, 2 miles from Stratford-upon-Avon.

Another room was named after Ben Jonson, who was also said to have visited 'dear Clifford – place of health and sport'.

2

A Sculptor's Workshop

THROUGH MUCH of the eighteenth century it was widely accepted that Ben Jonson had been a persistent opponent of Shakespeare's. A Scotsman, Robert Sheills, wrote in 1753 that Jonson was 'in his personal character the very reverse of Shakespear, as surly, ill-natured, proud, and disagreeable, as Shakespear with ten times his merit was gentle, good-natured, easy, and amiable.' The Shakespearean actor Charles Macklin made a similar claim five years earlier, remarking that Jonson was 'by nature *splenetic* and *sour*':

> This made him many enemies, who towards the close of his life endeavoured to dethrone *this tyrant* ... And what greatly contributed to their design, was the *slights* and *malignances* which the *rigid* Ben too frequently threw out against the *lowly* Shakespeare, whose fame since his death ... was too great for Ben's *envy* either to *bear* with or *wound*.

Jonson was eventually rehabilitated, though, and today he is generally thought of as a loving friend to Will Shakespeare. The evidence for this supposed fondness rests almost entirely on an uncritical reading of the poem 'To the memory of my beloved', which Jonson wrote for the First Folio of Shakespeare's plays in 1623, and a couple of anecdotes – Rev. John Ward's reference to the 'merry meeting' of Shakespeare, Drayton and Jonson, and an account of the 'wit combats' which arose whenever Shakespeare and Jonson were together in London's Mermaid Tavern.

In his *History of the Worthies of England*, Thomas Fuller imagined Jonson and Shakespeare as being like:

> [a] Spanish great galleon and an English man-of-war. Master Jonson, like the former, was built far higher in learning; solid, but slow in his

performances. Shake-speare, with the English man-of-war, lesser in bulk but lighter in sailing, could turn with all tides, tack about, and take advantage of all winds, by the quickness of his wit and invention.

Every meeting of Shakespeare and Jonson at the Mermaid was thus an intellectual rerun of the Spanish Armada: Ben was bigger, but Will was quicker. Unfortunately, Thomas Fuller was born just three years before Shakespeare quit the public stage; he is unlikely to have witnessed any of these apocryphal 'wit combats' at first hand.

Contemporaries certainly saw the two poets as being in competition with one another. Early in the seventeenth century, students at Cambridge University performed a satirical play, in which the actor William Kempe dismissed university-educated playwrights:

> Few of the university men pen plays well, they smell too much of that writer *Ovid*, and that writer *Metamorphoses* ... Why, here's our fellow *Shakespeare* puts them all down, I and *Ben Jonson* too. And that *Ben Jonson* is a pestilent fellow, he brought up *Horace* giving the Poets a pill, but our fellow *Shakespeare* hath given him a purge that made him bewray his credit.

To 'bewray' was to defile or befoul. Shakespeare's 'purge' had caused Jonson to soil his own reputation, to shit himself.

It was this ongoing rivalry that prompted the identification of Will and Ben as the subjects in *The Chess Players*, a painting of about 1603. Attributed to the Dutch artist Karel van Mander (died 1606), the painting shows two men hunched over a chessboard. The figure on the right is moving one of the pieces; his hair, under a wide-brimmed hat, is dark and lank, his lips pursed in concentration. Opposite him sits a fleshier man with brown hair and a furrowed brow. His right hand is raised, as if in alarm: he is about to be checkmated.

If Karel van Mander's painting really did depict *Ben Jonson and William Shakespeare Playing at Chess*, as the work is sometimes described, then it would be the only portrait of Shakespeare known to have been executed during his lifetime. But the identification of the players is speculative. The financier J.P. Morgan would have been willing to pay up to US $1 million for the painting had there been proof that it was Jonson and Shakespeare.

That proof was not forthcoming.

THERE IS no hard evidence that any of the surviving portraits said to be of Shakespeare were painted while he was alive.

The most famous Shakespeare portrait graced the title page of his *Comedies, Histories, & Tragedies*, better known as the First Folio, which was published seven years after his death. The image was engraved by Martin Droeshout the Younger – 22 years old at the time – and commended 'To the Reader' by Ben Jonson:

> This Figure, that thou here seest put,
>> It was for gentle Shakespeare cut;
> Wherein the Graver had a strife
>> with Nature, to out-do the life:
> O, could he but have drawn his wit
>> As well in brass, as he hath hit
> His face; the Print would then surpass
>> All, that was ever writ in brass.
> But, since he cannot, Reader, look,
>> Not on his Picture, but his Book.

Jonson implied that the engraving was about as realistic as anyone could have hoped, short of capturing Will's remarkable intelligence. And yet there are problems with the image. The head is too big for the body. A clear line runs down the side of the face, especially below the formless earlobe. The moustache is a clumsy stippling of stubble. The odd lighting produces a bright highlight on the bulbous forehead and white crescents under the eyes. The whole head seems to float on a stiffly starched collar.

Strikingly similar to the Droeshout engraving is the so-called 'Flower Portrait', donated by Mrs Charles Flower to the Royal Shakespeare Company in the nineteenth century. Painted over an image of the Virgin Mary with the Christ child and St John the Baptist, the Flower Portrait bears the inscription, 'Willm Shakespeare 1609'. For many years it was presumed to have been the original from which Martin Droeshout made his more famous engraving, but it was discovered in 2005 that the pigment used for the gold braid on Shakespeare's doublet was not available before the early 1800s. The Flower Portrait, it would seem, is a clever forgery.

The Droeshout engraving for the First Folio also bears comparison with the bust of Will Shakespeare which forms part of his funerary monument in Stratford. The bust was carved from a block of limestone by Gheerart Janssen, a London-based sculptor who had previously crafted the effigy of Will's friend John Combe, which is also in the chancel of Holy Trinity Church.

Various repairs have been carried out on the Shakespeare bust over the centuries. As early as 1649, the bust had to be 're-beautified', probably because it had been damaged by Puritan extremists during the Civil War. The bust was restored in 1748–49 and underwent further repairs in the nineteenth century. In 1911, it was noted that the head of the bust was loose, resting precariously on the shoulders, and in 1973 the sculpture was prised from its plinth by intruders who were apparently looking for something inside it.

Even allowing for the vicissitudes of vandalism and re-beautification, the funerary bust is uninspiring, aptly described by J. Dover Wilson as resembling a 'self-satisfied pork butcher'. The face seems flabby. There is no neck to speak of, and if the enlarged forehead of the Droeshout engraving hints at intellect, the bald pate of the Janssen bust suggests only portly middle age. With his left hand resting on a writing cushion and a goose quill poised in his right, Shakespeare does not look like the finest writer in the English language – more like a retired clerk taking names at a local meeting.

The cartoonish Droeshout engraving and the stolid funerary bust seem so unrealistic because they were both made after Shakespeare's death. The Droeshout image gives the game away. The bold line running down the side of the face creates the impression that what we are actually looking at is a mask: specifically, a death mask.

DR LUDWIG Becker was buried in Queensland, on a flat, arid plain with the mountains of the Grey Range faintly visible in the distance. He had succumbed to malnutrition on 29 April 1861 while taking part in the doomed Burke-Wills expedition which had set out nine months earlier to explore the Australian mainland from south to north.

Becker was a talented artist and naturalist from Darmstadt in Germany. In his thirties, he had held a post at the ducal palace in Darmstadt before moving to Mainz where, in 1847, he came across a small oil-on-parchment painting in a shop owned by an antiquarian named Jourdan. The painting had previously belonged to Count Franz Ludwig von Kesselstatt, Canon of Mainz Cathedral, whose collection was sold after his death in 1841. Dr Becker found it intriguing.

It was described as 'A deceased man crowned with a laurel wreath 1637'. The vendor was happy to provide Becker with a letter stating that he had bought the 'small picture with the date 1637, *showing Shakespeare on his deathbed*' at the auction of the Count von Kesselstatt's effects in 1842.

Professor Nikolaus Müller, supervisor of the Mainz Gallery, also confirmed in a letter to Becker, dated 28 February 1847, that the deathbed portrait had enjoyed a 'prominent place' in the Kesselstatt collection, where it had borne the inscription 'Shakespeare, according to Tradition'. Müller claimed that 'among the numerous scholars, antiquaries and outstanding artists' who had seen the collection, 'not the slightest doubt obtained about the authenticity of the picture of Shakespeare'. Indeed, the late Count von Kesselstatt had 'turned down many very large offers from those who wanted to buy it'.

Becker assumed that the portrait of the bed-bound corpse had been copied from a death mask. He discovered that a 'plaster head' had also formed part of the Kesselstatt collection. After two years of searching he found this 'male image in plaster' in a second-hand shop, surrounded by rags and junk. On the back edge of the death mask, inscribed while the plaster was still soft, was a small cross followed by 'A° D$_m$ 1616'.

The following year, Dr Becker's brother became secretary to Prince Albert in England. Becker himself left Germany, travelling first to Edinburgh and then on to London, where he left the deathbed portrait and the death mask in the care of the British Museum. The mask was exhibited as 'Shakespeare's Death Mask' and was displayed in Stratford-upon-Avon for the 300th anniversary of Shakespeare's birth.

In 1856, Professor Richard Owen – the anatomist who coined the term 'dinosaur' – was appointed superintendent of the natural history department of the British Museum. After careful study, Professor Owen concluded that the bust of Will Shakespeare in Holy Trinity Church, Stratford, had probably been sculpted using the death mask as a model.

MAKING A death mask was a fairly straightforward process. The face of the corpse would be washed and lathered with soap. A band of cloth was then wrapped around the hairline and ears. Soft wax was spread over the face to create a 'flying mould'. This wax mould was then lightly oiled and liquid plaster of Paris poured into it.

John Parker Norris, a Philadelphia-based attorney, examined the death mask of Shakespeare in 1884. He noted that 'Some hairs adhere to the moustache and beard on the mask, and also on the eyebrows and eyelashes.' These human hairs were 'reddish brown or auburn' and, Norris felt, matched the hair colour of the Shakespeare effigy in Holy Trinity Church.

The face of the death mask is naturally in a state of repose, the eyes closed and the cheeks sunken slightly. The forehead is high and broad, the nose long and pointed, aquiline, with a prominent rhinion at the end of the nasal bone. The moustache is full and slopes downwards to obscure the corners of the mouth, leaving the philtrum exposed, and there is a neat goatee between the bottom lip and the point of the chin. J. Parker Norris observed in 1884 that the nose had been 'touched up' with a knife, and additional lines had been cut into the beard and moustache for emphasis.

The moustache and beard of the death mask do not match the Droeshout engraving or the funerary bust – the latter shows a thin, rather effete moustache which curls upwards at the ends. There is, however, a sketch made of the Shakespeare bust by Sir William Dugdale in 1636. Reproduced as an engraving in his *Antiquities of Warwickshire* in 1656, Dugdale's pre-Civil War sketch looks much more like the death mask: the nose is the same length, the cheeks are hollow, and the moustache slopes downwards, leaving the philtrum clear. The differences between the Dugdale sketch and the bust in its present form suggest that the bust was not just 're-beautified' in 1649; it was substantially altered.

The death mask discovered by Becker had perfectly preserved the tiny wrinkles and pores of the skin, the crow's feet and creases, and even the crystalline tears which had seeped out from the conjunctiva to gum the eyelashes together. This is a natural part of the decomposition process. Normally, those tears would have been cleaned away when the face was prepared for the flying mould. Their presence indicates that the mask was made a day or two after the subject's death.

Will Shakespeare died on 23 April 1616. The death mask would appear to have been made in some haste shortly before he was buried two days later.

In *The Death Mask of Shakespeare*, J. Parker Norris revealed another detail of the mask. 'Over the right eyebrow,' he wrote, 'there is an indentation or scar on the forehead of the Mask extending towards the right side.'

There is no sign of any such indentation on the forehead of the Shakespeare bust in Holy Trinity Church. But the sketch of the bust made by Dugdale in 1636, before it was 're-beautified', shows a distinct black mark above the right eyebrow.

PROFESSOR RICHARD Owen's suggestion that the Shakespeare bust might have been modelled on the death mask was immediately taken up by Henry Wallis, an artist associated with the Pre-Raphaelite Brotherhood.

Wallis had launched his career in 1853 with an exhibition of paintings which depicted, in meticulous detail, various interiors relevant to the life of Shakespeare, including *The Room in Which Shakespeare Was Born* and the staircase leading up to that room (*Shakespeare's House, Stratford-upon-Avon*, with additions by Sir Edwin Landseer). His best known work

is *The Death of Chatterton* (1856), for which he persuaded the writer
George Meredith to pose as Thomas Chatterton and set up his easel in
the very Gray's Inn garret where the young poet had poisoned himself.

In 1857, Wallis exhibited his latest work. Entitled *A Sculptor's
Workshop, Stratford-upon-Avon, 1617*, it was surely inspired by Richard
Owen's recent comments about the death mask. The painting is now in
the Royal Shakespeare Company's collection.

A Sculptor's Workshop presents an imaginary scene. In vibrant,
summery colours it shows Gheerart Janssen at work on the bust for
Shakespeare's funerary monument. The sculptor kneels before his
finished effigy, a mallet in one hand and a chisel in the other. Ben Jonson
stands over him, cradling a plaster of Paris death mask in his left hand.
The forefinger of Ben's right hand points to the precise spot, above the
right eyebrow of the mask, where J. Parker Norris would detect an
'indentation or scar on the forehead'.

A second death mask hangs neglected in a small, high, murky window.

The main shopfront window, which is open, frames the golden-grey
spire of Holy Trinity Church (an anachronism: the stone spire was not
built until 1763). A perspective line is formed by the River Avon, which
flows away from the workshop, past the willows of the churchyard. On
the window sill stands a bronze statuette.

Two young children are playing with figurines on the workshop floor.
A third child, older than the other two, stands in the open doorway with
her finger raised to her lips. She is gazing up at Ben Jonson, her expression
ruminative and wary.

Henry Wallis was drawing attention to Jonson's supposed supervision
of the Shakespeare effigy and the possibility that the bust was modelled
on the death mask. Ben's finger jabs at the 'indentation or scar' on the
mask, as if instructing the sculptor to make a final alteration to the
limestone bust.

This brings us back to the statuette on the window sill. It appears to
represent Hercules overpowering Achelous. The story, as told by Ovid,
one of Shakespeare's favourite classical authors, cast Achelous as the
god of a river prone to flooding. Wallis positioned the statuette so as to
make Achelous the spirit or *genius loci* of the flood-prone River Avon.
When Achelous taunted his rival Hercules with his low birth, Hercules
flew into a rage. 'I am better with my hands than with my tongue,' said
Hercules, 'provided I can defeat you in the fight, you can have your
verbal victory!'

The Greek myth recalls the 'merry meeting' of Shakespeare and Jonson
and their strained epitaph game – the 'Rhymes' which, according to

Michael Drayton, who was there, Ben offered to make with Shakespeare, only to become angry when he was 'out-gone'. Hercules had been similarly incapable of controlling his rage 'as a hero should'. He attacked the river god. Achelous turned himself into a snake and then a bull. Hercules wrestled the bull to the ground and tore off one of its horns, mutilating the river god's brow.

In *A Sculptor's Workshop*, Henry Wallis showed Ben Jonson pointing directly at the mutilated brow of Shakespeare's death mask while, behind him, Hercules and Achelous (who is plainly associated with Shakespeare's River Avon) are frozen in perpetual struggle.

It is perhaps no accident that the attitudes of the two young children playing with figurines on the workshop floor almost exactly mirror those of the figures in Karel van Mander's supposed portrait of *Ben Jonson and William Shakespeare Playing at Chess*. Henry Wallis seems to have used his depiction of *A Sculptor's Workshop* to drop heavy hints about the long-running rivalry between Shakespeare and Jonson, the taunts which led to a physical assault, the mutilation of a brow, the 'indentation or scar' on the forehead of the death mask and Ben Jonson's role in approving the image of Shakespeare sculpted for his funerary monument in the Church of the Holy Trinity.

FOUR YEARS after Wallis exhibited *A Sculptor's Workshop*, Dr Ludwig Becker starved to death at the Koorliatto Waterhole in northern Australia. Eight months later, his brother Ernst returned to Darmstadt in Germany, taking the death mask with him. Professor Richard Owen had been keen to purchase the death mask for the British Museum, but only if evidence could be produced to explain how it had come into the possession of Count von Kesselstatt. That evidence did not come to light until 1995, when it was discovered that the count had travelled to London in 1775 at the age of 22.

The American artist William Page, president of the National Academy of Design in New York, spent seven days studying the death mask in Germany in 1874 and then travelled to Stratford, where he compared his measurements of the mask with the funerary bust of Shakespeare. His findings, published in *A Study of Shakespeare's Portraits* (1879), were quoted by J. Parker Norris in his *Death Mask of Shakespeare*. 'Of these twenty-six measures,' Page had written, 'at least ten or twelve fit exactly corresponding points in the Shakespeare bust.'

A similar experiment was carried out in 1911 by the German historian Paul Wislicenus and the sculptor Robert Cauer. Their painstaking comparison of the death mask and the bust revealed an extraordinary degree of correspondence: the 'face on the [bust] is exactly the same size as the mask', wrote Wislicenus: 'the eyebrows are the same, the eyes are identically placed, as are the bridge of the nose, the mouth, the temples, cheeks, jawbone and chin.'

In short, 'it is the same head.'

Shortly thereafter, Europe was plunged into the first of two world wars. British interest in the death mask did not survive the conflict, presumably because the mask was in enemy hands. The plaster of Paris mask was put up for auction in 1960. It was bought by the director of the Hessen State and University Library and has since been kept in the library of Darmstadt Castle.

IT IS almost certain that the bust of Shakespeare which overlooks his grave was modelled on his death mask, as was the Droeshout engraving for the First Folio of 1623. Ben Jonson considered the latter a reasonable likeness, and given that Martin Droeshout had been just 15 years old when Shakespeare died, it is probable that he based his engraving on a pre-existing image.

The theory that both images – engraving and effigy – were modelled on the death mask was put to the test in the 1990s by Hildegard Hammerschmidt-Hummel, Professor of English Literature and Culture at the universities of Marburg and Mainz. With the help of forensics experts at the BKA, Germany's federal criminal investigation agency, Professor Hammerschmidt-Hummel compared several Shakespearean images, using such electronic methods as photogrammetry, computer tomography, laser scanning and a 'Trick Image Differentiation Technique' developed by the BKA specialists. Photomontages of the funerary bust and the death mask offered 'very special and convincing proof' that the images were of the same person. Similarly positive results were obtained for the death mask and the Droeshout engraving.

Two more images of Shakespeare were also subjected to these tests.

The 'Chandos Portrait' was the first item acquired for the National Portrait Gallery when it was founded in 1856. It presents a down-to-earth image of the Bard. A swarthy countryman gazes at us with watchful brown eyes. The receding hairline exposes a high forehead. The nose – like those of the death mask and the Droeshout engraving – is distinctively long. The shape of the face is oval, with a halo of dark brown curls and a soft brown beard. The light-brown moustache parts above the middle of the lips, inclining gently towards the edges of the mouth. A simple gold ring hangs in the lobe of the left ear.

The painting is named after one of its owners, James Brydges, Duke of Chandos, who died in 1789. A note made in 1784 by the Shakespeare scholar Edmond Malone on a copy of the Chandos Portrait states that the original had 'formerly belonged to Sir William Davenant'. Davenant was Shakespeare's godson and – as we shall see – quite possibly his natural son. His alleged ownership of the Chandos Portrait would suggest that the painting is an authentic image of the Bard. The examinations carried out by the BKA experts showed that it compares with the Shakespeare engraving and the bust: the dimensions are the same; the images match.

The Garrick Club in London possesses the most impressive and dashing portrait of Will Shakespeare. This is the so-called 'Davenant Bust'. It was found by William Clift, the first curator of the Hunterian Museum in the Royal College of Surgeons and father-in-law to Sir Richard Owen, the anatomist who studied the death mask of Shakespeare. From Owen, the bust passed to the Duke of Devonshire, who disclosed that it had been rescued when the Duke's Playhouse in Lincoln's Inn Fields was pulled down in 1848. The Duke's Playhouse was opened by Sir William Davenant in 1661, and according to the Duke of Devonshire the terracotta bust had been 'placed over one of the Stage Doors, the bust of Ben Jonson (accidentally destroyed by the workmen) occupying a corresponding place over the other door'.

The face of the Davenant Bust is fiercely intelligent and, one could say, aristocratic. The nose is long, thin, pointed, the forehead high. The delicate moustache parts over the philtrum and descends to the sides of the small, beautifully shaped lips. The beard is short and follows the line of the chin, leaving the cheeks clean. The cheeks themselves are slightly hollow. The hair billows in luxuriant curls. The eyes, in particular, are irresistible: they are piercing, challenging, all-observing.

Once again, the forensics experts of the BKA who examined the Davenant Bust in the 1990s became convinced of its authenticity. Comparing it with the death mask of Shakespeare, a BKA specialist concluded that 'what we are seeing here is one and the same person'.

Minute scrutiny of the Davenant Bust, the Chandos Portrait, the Droeshout engraving, the funerary bust and the death mask revealed certain common features which appear to have been pathological in nature.

There is a swelling on the upper left eyelid of the Droeshout engraving and the Chandos Portrait, and evidence that a similar swelling was removed from the Davenant Bust in the course of restoration. The caruncle in the left-hand corner of the left eye is enlarged. The distorted left eye of the death mask protrudes markedly in comparison with the right, as if it had been forced forwards. There is also a distinctive depression, roughly oval in shape, in the forehead of the death mask, which matches similar depressions visible on the Davenant Bust, the Chandos Portrait and the engraving by Droeshout.

The 'indentation or scar' above the right eyebrow of the death mask can also be seen on the Davenant Bust and the portraits of Shakespeare.

Concentrating on the unusual swellings around the left eye, Professor Hammerschmidt-Hummel consulted medical experts, including Professor Walter Lerche, then medical director of the Ophthalmic Clinic at the Wiesbaden Land-Capital Hospital, who diagnosed Mikulicz syndrome, a chronic condition affecting the tear-producing and salivary glands. It usually affects both sides of the face and generally occurs in conjunction with other diseases, such as leukaemia or sarcoidosis. Professor Hammerschmidt-Hummel was moved to put forward the theory that Shakespeare died of a degenerative disorder of the immune system.

There is, however, another explanation – one hinted at by Henry Wallis in his painting of *A Sculptor's Workshop, Stratford-upon-Avon, 1617*.

It involves the mutilation of Shakespeare's brow resulting from a blow to the face: a blow, or blows, which also caused the swellings around the left eye and the 'fever' from which Shakespeare died.

3

Marred by a Jagged Hole

FOR MORE than 100 years, the death mask dated 1616 and the deathbed portrait, dated 1637, had been kept together. Both items were seemingly acquired as a job lot by the Count von Kesselstatt in London and both were believed to be of Shakespeare.

It was Hermann Schaaffhausen, Professor of Anatomy at the University of Bonn, who noticed that the face of the corpse in the deathbed portrait resembled the portrait of Ben Jonson which hung in the picture gallery of Dulwich College, London.

Ben Jonson died on 6 August 1637. This matches the date given in gold on the deathbed miniature. The head in the portrait wears a crown of laurels; Jonson was, to all intents and purposes, England's first Poet Laureate.

Like his contemporary, Professor Richard Owen of the British Museum, Hermann Schaaffhausen was an anatomist and palaeontologist with an interest in evolutionary theory. He saw Dr Ludwig Becker's discovery of the Shakespeare death mask as little more than an excuse to exhume the skull of William Shakespeare.

Professor Schaaffhausen published an article, 'On Shakespeare's Death Mask', in the 1875 annual of the German Shakespeare Society, arguing that the mask bore similarities to other Shakespearean portraits. 'Should we be afraid to rely on this evidence,' he wrote, 'there is an easy way of settling the question. We can dig up Shakespeare's skull and compare the two.'

There was an obvious drawback to this proposal. The inscription on Shakespeare's gravestone blessed 'the man that spares these stones' and cursed anyone who 'moves my bones'. But Schaaffhausen was undaunted. He declared that 'there is no desecration in entrusting the noble remains of the poet to the enquiring eye of science.'

Schaaffhausen's article sparked an international debate. One man who entered the fray was Clement Mansfield Ingleby, the Warwickshire-born Vice President of the Royal Society of Literature and an honorary member of the German Shakespeare Society. In 1861, Ingleby had become one of the first trustees of the Shakespeare Birthplace Museum. In 1883, he published an essay with the unwieldy title, 'Shakespeare's Bones: The Proposal to Disinter Them, Considered in Relation to Their Possible Bearing on his Portraiture: Illustrated by Instances of Visits of the Living to the Dead'.

Drawing on the documented exhumations of such luminaries as Oliver Cromwell, John Milton, Robert Burns, Francis Bacon and Ben Jonson, C.M. Ingleby outlined his case for opening the grave in Holy Trinity Church and extracting Shakespeare's skull in order to compare it with the various portraits of the Bard. Still, the curse of Shakespeare's gravestone exerted its baleful influence, and the science-versus-superstition furore rumbled on.

Soon after he published his proposal to disinter Shakespeare's bones, C.M. Ingleby received a letter written from the vicarage at Beoley, a small village a few miles from Stratford. Requesting a copy of 'Shakespeare's Bones' from its author, the letter disclosed that 'further revelations are in progress which will set at rest this much agitated question'.

The 'much agitated question' was whether or not to exhume the skull of Will Shakespeare from his Stratford grave. The 'further revelations' were about to be published by the Reverend C.J. Langston, who had an astonishing story to tell.

THE ANCIENT Roman road of Icknield Street passes 6 miles to the west of Stratford-upon-Avon. Heading north, it runs through the Warwickshire towns of Alcester and Studley. The road to Birmingham then separates from the old Roman road before beginning its ascent of Gorcott Hill. Partway up the hill stands a fine Elizabethan house known as Gorcott Hall. Throughout the eighteenth century it was home to a family named Chambers. For the most part, they were upstanding members of society: they provided vicars for several surrounding parishes and were the lords of the manor of Studley from about 1785. But every family has its black sheep, and in the Chambers family his name was Frank.

In the 1780s, Frank Chambers was employed by a medical practice in Alcester – most likely Jones and Sons, surgeons, of Henley Street. Some youthful indiscretion then caused Frank to leave the country. He was in France to witness the early stages of the Revolution, but returned to Alcester in about 1791 and resumed his duties as a doctor's assistant.

Among his local acquaintances was William Seymour-Conway, the younger brother of Francis Seymour-Conway, Earl of Yarmouth. On the death of his father in June 1794, Lord Francis became the Second Marquess of Hertford and inherited the grand Palladian mansion of Ragley Hall, which stands on a hill outside the town of Alcester.

Sometime in the autumn of 1794, the newly elevated marquess hosted a dinner at Ragley. The conversation turned to David Garrick's 'Jubilee', held several years earlier, and then to the topic of Shakespeare's funerary bust. Captain Fortescue wondered whether the bust really did look like the Bard.* The captain's question elicited a lisping reply from the gruff Dr Parr: 'You had best dig him up, John Fortescue; may I be there to see it.'**

A local squire then recalled that Horace Walpole – Gothic novelist, antiquarian and fourth son of the 'prime minister' Sir Robert Walpole – had offered 300 guineas to anyone who could present him with the skull of William Shakespeare.

Frank Chambers had been at the dinner. He resolved to dig up Shakespeare's skull. Summoning three local ne'er-do-wells to his room above the surgery on the corner of Malt Mill Lane in Alcester, he explained that he wanted their help in procuring the skull of 'a chap who has been dead nearly two hundred years'. Chambers told the men that he would pay them £3 for their services, with plenty of drink as an added incentive.

The three recruits were Thomas Dyer, Harry Cull and one Hawtin.*** Chambers arranged to meet the three young men one dark night at Holy Trinity Church, Stratford-upon-Avon.

On the appointed night, Chambers was delayed. He stumbled through the churchyard to find his confederates already digging up a tomb on the south side of the church.

---

* The Fortescues were associated with the village of Weethley, adjacent to Ragley; Captain John Fortescue of the Royal Navy died, aged 86, on 9 May 1808 and was buried in the nearby chapel at Cookhill.

** Born in 1747, Dr Samuel Parr was a schoolmaster and preacher residing, at the time of the Ragley dinner, in the vicarage at Hatton, near Warwick, where he was the assistant curate.

*** The *Topography & Dictionary of Warwickshire*, published in 1830, lists one 'Thos. Dyer' as a carpenter and joiner living in Bleachfields, Alcester; the census of 1841 indicates that the 65-year-old carpenter was then based in the High Street – he would have been about 18 when Frank Chambers hired him. Harry Cull was perhaps the father of George Cull, an agricultural labourer of the nearby village of Sambourn, aged 25 at the time of the 1841 census. A John Hawtin, possibly the son of Chambers' collaborator, was listed in the 1841 census as a 45-year-old labourer of Alcester.

Hawtin had been seeing a young woman who was in service with the Rev. James Davenport, vicar of Holy Trinity. Quizzed about Shakespeare's grave, the maid had remembered that there was a tomb just outside the church which bore that name. Chambers arrived to discover Dyer, Hawtin and Cull breaking into the grave of William Shakespeare Payton, son of Alderman Payton, who had died as recently as 1789.

Chambers cleared up the confusion, explaining that the grave they sought was *inside* the church. Tom Dyer, who had some experience as a blacksmith, forced the lock on a side door. Hawtin acted as lookout while the others quietly entered the church. Groping their way into the chancel, they found the correct grave, identifiable by its four-line 'curse'.

Dyer and Cull scraped away the mortar around the stone slab. The grave was prised open. Inside, the gang found a layer of brown mould scattered with fragments of fire-damaged glass. Delving into the earth, they turned up a few odd bones and teeth, a metal disc bearing the name 'Ashwin' and a worn bronze ring with a faded inscription.*

The robbers rummaged up to their armpits in the grave mould. Finally, Harry Cull removed a large stone and Tom Dyer pulled out an old skull and jawbone.

Chambers later recalled that the skull 'was smaller than I expected, and in formation not much like what I remembered of the effigy above our heads.' Only the year before, Edmond Malone had prevailed upon Rev. Davenport to cover the Shakespeare bust with a layer of whitewash (it was repainted in its original colours by Collins of London in 1851). The funerary bust of Shakespeare would have loomed out of the chancel wall over the heads of the grave robbers like a ghost in the moonlight.

The gravestone was replaced and dust from the church floor swept over the cracks. The gang made its way back to Alcester, 7 miles away across the Alne hills. At Oversley Bridge, Chambers gave the men their money, and a little later he treated them to 9 quarts of ale – roughly 6 pints each – at an Alcester inn known, appropriately, as The Globe.

At home, Chambers made a more detailed study of the skull, lending his findings to a Dr Booker, but the notes were then lost.**

Chambers next wrote in confidence to Horace Walpole, telling him that Shakespeare's skull was available in return for the promised reward. Walpole was then nearing the age of 80 and staying with his

---

* A Thomas Ashwin, resident in Chapel Street, was listed in 1830 as the Chief Magistrate of Stratford and agent to the County Fire Office.
** Perhaps Matthew Booker, curate of Alcester from 1785 to 1808, or more likely the Rev. Dr Luke Booker of Dudley, of whom more anon.

cousin, Field Marshal Henry Seymour Conway, in Berkshire.* Walpole had no intention of handing over the 300 guineas. He sent his agent – Thomas Kirgate, Walpole's printer and occasional secretary – who tried to negotiate an unconditional loan of the skull or, failing that, a tooth which he could show to Horace Walpole. Chambers stood his ground, and Walpole's man left Alcester empty-handed.

A few days later, Frank Chambers paid a visit to Samuel Parr at the vicarage of Hatton, north of Stratford. The church bells were ringing in the Christmas season. Chambers discovered that his friend John Bartlam was staying with Dr Parr.** During the evening, Chambers delicately raised the matter of the skull.

Samuel Parr immediately assumed that the skull had been stolen by the actor David Garrick during the disastrous Shakespeare Jubilee of 1769. Chambers began to stammer that the skull had remained in its grave throughout the Jubilee.

The bullish Dr Parr cut him short: 'Well then, sir, there let it be' – and he reminded Chambers of the gravestone's inscription, 'And cursed be he that moves my bones.'

The wretched Chambers quickly changed the subject. The following morning, John Bartlam walked with him part of the way back to Alcester. Suddenly, Bartlam exclaimed, 'Chambers, you have that skull!'

On hearing Chambers' confession, Bartlam made him promise to return the skull to its proper resting place.

Chambers met up again with Thomas Dyer. They hatched a plan to replace the skull, but Chambers was unavoidably detained. Dyer insisted that he could return the skull to its grave all by himself.

Visiting Holy Trinity Church the next Sunday, Chambers noticed that an 'ominous crack' had appeared in the gravestone. He tracked Dyer down to the Four Alls Inn at Wexford-on-Avon, where the carpenter was drinking. He admitted that he had found the gravestone too heavy to manhandle.

'You rascal!' cried Chambers. 'Then you never buried that skull!'

Dyer assured him that 'the old chap was there beneath, as safe as a door-nail'. But Chambers was unconvinced, and when a relative later asked him if the skull had really been restored to its Stratford grave, he replied in the words of the skull's original owner: '"Twere to consider too curiously, to consider so.'

Such was the burden of an article published more than eighty years later under the heading, 'How Shakespeare's Skull Was Stolen', in the

---

* Conway was uncle to the second Lord Hertford, at whose Ragley dinner table the adventure had begun.
** Rev. John Bartlam was born in Alcester in 1770.

October 1879 edition of *Argosy* magazine. Its author identified himself
as 'A Warwickshire Man'. He was in fact the Rev. Charles Jones, rector
of Sevington in Kent. Just before his article was published he had,
according to *The Times* newspaper of 26 September 1879, changed his
surname to Langston.

The census of 1881 shows that Charles Langston, then 43 years
old, was still living in the rectory at Sevington. By the beginning of
1884, though, he had moved into the vicarage at Beoley, close to his
birthplace of Alcester. He wrote to C.M. Ingleby from Beoley Vicarage
on 2 January 1884, requesting a copy of the latter's proposal to disinter
Shakespeare's bones.

Ingleby had mentioned Langston's 1879 article in a footnote.
'The vraisemblance of this narrative is amazing,' wrote Ingleby in
'Shakespeare's Bones'. 'But for the poverty of the concluding portion,
which is totally out of keeping with the foregoing part, one might almost
accept this as a narrative of fact.'

What C.M. Ingleby had picked up on was the wealth of incidental
detail in 'How Shakespeare's Skull Was Stolen'. Langston claimed to
have pieced his narrative together from the diaries of Dr Frank Chambers
and the memories of Frank's nephew, coyly identified as 'the late Mr. M'.
It so happens that these are the only two individuals in the vicar's
account who cannot be positively identified.*

The publication of C.M. Ingleby's 'Shakespeare's Bones' in 1883
revived interest in Langston's story, prompting him to write to Ingleby
with the information that 'further revelations are in progress that will
set at rest this much agitated question'. Following a flood of enquiries,
Langston issued a new pamphlet in 1884. Priced at one shilling, it built
on the account he had previously published in 1879. It was entitled,
'How Shakespeare's Skull was Stolen and Found'.

ONE OF Frank Chambers' 'closest companions' had been a 'Lieutenant
J.L.' or Lieutenant Joseph Langston of the Royal Marines. Lt. Langston
served under Capt. Charles Brisbane on HMS *Goliath* and was grievously
wounded whilst capturing the French corvette *Mignonne* off the coast of
Haiti on 28 June 1803.

The Rev. Charles Jones Langston was a descendant of this naval hero
and had inherited a packet of letters written by Frank Chambers to

---

*   The 'late Mr. M.' might have been Henry Morris, surgeon, of Studley, who
      died on 10 January 1870, aged 60. In 1846, Mr Morris bought the Pound
      House in Alcester from one Charlotte Langston.

'Lieutenant J.L.'. These letters included references to a 'surprising visit', a 'strange account', and something that Chambers could only discuss with his friend in private.

Rev. C.J. Langston had also acquired some papers which had belonged to the lieutenant's brother-in-law, who was the surgeon named Jones under whom Chambers had studied in Alcester. Among these papers, Langston found a small piece of bone. 'Dark on the outside; slightly curved, of irregular outline, measuring two inches by one, and a quarter of an inch in its thickest part,' wrote the vicar. 'I observed that it was formed of numberless tiny cells, and there was a coating of brown mould on the inside.'

The manuscript which had been folded around this fragment contained an account of a 'startling adventure'. Frank Chambers had written up this account for the benefit of his friend, unaware that Lieutenant Joseph Langston had died of his wounds onboard the *Goliath*.

Five years had passed since the grave-robbing expedition to Stratford when, on a bitingly cold night in December 1799, Dr Chambers was called out to an 'outlandish parish'. He was met there by Tom Dyer. Sworn to secrecy, Chambers was led through the churchyard and smuggled into the church by way of an 'irregular opening in the masonry'.

He found himself inside a vault filled with coffins and ornamental urns. A ragged, prematurely aged woman lay moaning on a bench.

Chambers surmised that Thomas Dyer and two accomplices had been stealing lead from the coffins and melting it down to produce counterfeit coins. The woman had been badly burned when a boiling kettle tipped over.

The doctor attended to the woman's burns and then persuaded Dyer to return with him to Alcester to fetch a palliative. They set off down the frosty lane, passing Gorcott Hall, the home of the Chambers family, at which point Dyer began to talk.

'One good turn deserves another, doctor, and I don't mind a-telling you as how I was drove away in a fright from Stratford Church before I could bury that old skull.'

Dyer now claimed to have hidden the skull inside a vessel in the vault that Chambers had just visited. He added that he had clipped a 'bit out on him to leave a kind of mark', and with that he handed Chambers the fragment of bone so that the doctor could identify the skull when he returned to tend to the injured woman.

Frank Chambers left no account of any return visit to the 'outlandish parish', leading Rev. Charles Jones Langston to conclude that the skull had not been returned to its Stratford grave.

Langston noted that the skull fragment had been wrapped in a torn piece of paper. It was part of a bill, written in Chambers' hand: 'Dr. to Thomas Dyer. / For refixing clapper of new bell ... 4s. 3d. / For seeing to stays and clips ... 3s. 8d.'

Rev. C.J. Langston spent a fruitless week searching the local parishes but found nothing which matched the details given in Chambers' account of his 'startling adventure'. One day, Langston's horse cast a shoe as he was riding past Gorcott Hall on the Alcester to Birmingham road. It occurred to him that Gorcott must have been the hall mentioned in Frank Chambers' letter.

Langston continued his journey up Gorcott Hill and turned off the main road at the Bowling Green Inn. After a while he came to an old sandstone church perched on a hillside. Everything was exactly as Chambers had described it. Examining the building, Langston noticed that an old ventilation grating had been filled in. This, it would seem, was the 'irregular opening in the masonry' through which Chambers had slithered into the church vault.

Looking through the churchwarden's account book, Langston came across an entry for 1799: 'Paid to Thomas Dyer of Alcester, for repairing new bell, as per bill, 17s. 3d.' Chambers had revealed in his letter that the white house adjacent to the churchyard had been vacant when he visited the 'outlandish parish'. Langston discovered that the vicarage adjoining the churchyard was indeed unoccupied for several months after the death of the Rev. William Brittain in December 1799. The next incumbent had been John Bartlam, that favourite pupil of Dr Samuel Parr's, who had known as early as Christmas 1794 that his friend Frank Chambers had stolen Shakespeare's skull.

Langston next explored the inside of the church, finding a 'remarkable mortuary chapel, surrounded by magnificent tombs under canopies'. The floor to this chapel turned out to be hollow. Locating the entrance to the vault, Langston squeezed through and descended into the crypt.

By the light of a lantern he surveyed the 'numerous open coffins'. Some had been ransacked and one 'delicate form, still bearing the sweet odours of foreign embalming, being probably that of Mary Sheldon, nun at Louvain, had been wantonly mutilated'.[*] Probing further, Langston noticed a narrow opening into a separate chamber beneath the effigies of William and Elizabeth Sheldon.[**] This underground space contained a 'heap of gigantic bones'. In the corner, Langston found a 'plain

---

[*] Mary Sheldon died in 1676.

[**] William Sheldon (1589–1659) married Elizabeth Petre (died 1657), daughter of William, Second Baron Petre, in 1611.

earthenware vessel' which had held the viscera of the 'Right Worshipful' Ralph Sheldon.

Langston lugged this heavy jar out into the larger vault. The vessel was filled with 'a sediment of dark mud ... mingled with clippings and rude pellets of lead'. He peered inside, and later wrote, '"Oh rapture!" resting on these was an undersized skull, with a prominent forehead marred by a jagged hole. Over that hole I placed the fragment I had brought with me: it fitted exactly. THE VERITABLE SKULL OF WILLIAM SHAKESPEARE WAS THERE.'

IN HIS account of 'How Shakespeare's Skull was Stolen and Found', Rev. C.J. Langston avoided admitting that the church in which he discovered the missing skull was his own, the Church of St Leonard in Beoley. Today, it is a thriving place of worship, tucked away from the road, its well-tended graveyard affording pleasant views across the River Arrow towards Bromsgrove.

The village of Beoley lies on the northern outskirts of Redditch. It falls within Worcestershire, although the eastern part of the village adjoins Shakespeare's county of Warwickshire. The manor of Beoley was sold in 1549 to William Sheldon, whose son Ralph built the Sheldon Chapel on the side of St Leonard's Church. The black marble slab which serves as the chapel's altar was reputedly presented to Ralph Sheldon in 1580 by Pope Gregory XIII.

One of the most prominent Catholics in the English Midlands, Ralph Sheldon died in 1613. His life intersected with Will Shakespeare's in a number of ways.

Rev. Charles Jones Langston was living in the vicarage beside the churchyard of St Leonard's when he published his expanded story in 1884. He oversaw the restoration of Beoley Church in 1885, but then retired to the City of Bath. Describing himself as 'formerly Vicar of Beoley', he retained his fascination with Shakespeare – he was planning a new article entitled 'Shakespeare in his cups' – and he died in Bath on 12 December 1912 at the age of 74.

For all its extraordinary detail, his account of 'How Shakespeare's Skull was Stolen and Found' doesn't quite stand up. It strains credulity that Thomas Dyer should have hidden the skull in the Beoley crypt the very night before he summoned Dr Chambers to the 'outlandish parish'. Remarkably, though, there is a rogue skull in the vault beneath the Sheldon Chapel at St Leonard's Church.

It was photographed by Richard Peach for *The Village* magazine in October 2009. Inspecting the lone skull, Peach found that there was a 'jagged hole left by a missing fragment of bone'. But the hole was at the base of the skull. The forehead was intact. Like Henry Wallis in his painting of *A Sculptor's Workshop*, Rev. Charles Jones Langston had deliberately drawn attention to Shakespeare's brow.

Langston described the skull as 'undersized'. The skull in the Beoley crypt does seem small, partly because the lower jaw is missing, as are the zygomatic (cheek) bones and parts of the maxilla (upper jaw), which appear to have been snapped off. The break at the corner of the orbital region on the left side of the skull is particularly ragged, leaving sharp burrs of bone. If this fracture had occurred before death it could have created a swelling on the upper left eyelid comparable with the visible swellings on the Droeshout engraving and the Chandos Portrait of Shakespeare.

Above the right eyebrow of the skull is a darkly discoloured region commensurate with the 'indentation or scar' observed by J. Parker Norris on Shakespeare's death mask. This discoloured patch occupies the same position on the skull as that indicated by Ben Jonson's finger in *A Sculptor's Workshop* and appears as a groove above the right eyebrow on the Davenant Bust. The star-shaped mark seems to be related to a small fracture in the supraorbital process immediately above the right eye. This fracture extends through to the underside of the supraorbital ridge and appears to have been replicated on the Davenant Bust. Another fracture can be seen along the fissure of the temporal and parietal bones.

Two parallel scratches ascend across the forehead of the skull from the discoloured region above the right eyebrow. These same scratches are suggested in the Droeshout engraving for the First Folio of 1623. They are seemingly apparent in Sir William Dugdale's pre-Civil War sketch of the funerary bust in Stratford and are hinted at on the Davenant Bust and the Chandos Portrait. They are also present on the death mask discovered in Germany by Dr Ludwig Becker: a three-dimensional computer image of Shakespeare's face, based on the death mask and produced in 2010 by a team led by Dr Caroline Wilkinson, Professor of Craniofacial Identification at the University of Dundee, replicates these parallel scratches as furrows in the brow.

The skull shows signs of an uneven forehead – including a roughly oval depression, mid-brow, probably indicating a sunken fontanelle caused by dehydration in early childhood – which are also clearly discernible on the Davenant Bust because somebody in the past has attempted to scratch them smooth.

Beneath the left eyebrow of the skull there is a fracture in the orbital cavity: a sliver of bone is missing from the upper right side of the medial wall. The death mask reveals that the skin had relaxed into this aperture, and the effect is reproduced in the Chandos Portrait and the Droeshout engraving. The inner eye socket fracture in the skull is surely related to the dark grey slit which can be seen on the inner corner of the left eyelid of the death mask – a thin lateral scar running from the eyeball to the bridge of the nose, which has seldom been noticed, but which might hold the key to Shakespeare's death.

The relaxation of the skin tissue would also explain the presence of faint lines on the Chandos Portrait, the Davenant Bust and the death mask. These lines follow the outline of the skull's broken maxilla bone. The damage to the left eye socket of the skull can also be traced in the Shakespeare portraiture.

The broken fissure between the temporal and parietal bones on the right side of the skull suggests a rupture to the middle meningeal artery, leading to an epidural haematoma. The resulting increase in intracranial pressure could have caused a midline shift in the brain, which in turn forced the left eyeball forwards as the brain pressed against the aperture in the fractured eye socket. This would account for the protruding left eye of the death mask and possibly the swollen caruncle visible in the posthumous portraits of Shakespeare, caused by the displacement of the lachrymal bone (the smallest, most delicate bone in the face) in the lower front part of the eye socket.

These symptoms, taken in conjunction with the broken maxilla and the swollen eyelid caused by the damage to the frontal and zygomatic bones, are indicative of traumatic craniofacial injury. The nature of this injury will be considered in the following chapters.

It is possible that Rev. C.J. Langston was right, in that the 'VERITABLE SKULL OF WILLIAM SHAKESPEARE' is indeed hidden away beneath a private family chapel at Beoley, 12 miles from Stratford. How it came to be in the vault of the region's most staunchly Catholic family is a matter for the latter part of this book.

For now, we shall note only that there is a ring of eight bells in the tower of St Leonard's Church. Two of them are recent additions. Another was the 'new bell' which Thomas Dyer fixed in 1799. Two of the early eighteenth-century bells are inscribed with the name of John Whateley.

The name Whateley will prove to have an important bearing on the life of Will Shakespeare.

A Depression in forehead (non-fatal)

B Scratch in forehead in line with wounds to left eye socket

C Fracture in upper medial wall of left eye socket

D Sharp burrs where temporal bone and eye socket are broken

E Fissure in right eyebrow (sinus region)

F Partial separation of temporal and parietal bones

G Discoloured region above right eyebrow

H Parallel scratches in forehead above right eye

2 The Beoley skull.

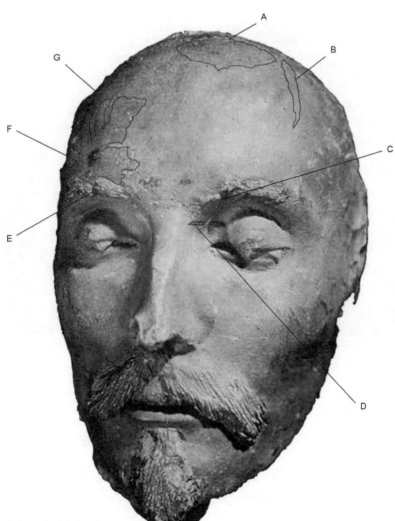

A Depression in forehead
B Scratch in forehead in line with wounds to left eye socket
C Visible outline of damage to left eyebrow
D Thin grey slit or scar between bridge of nose and left eyeball
E Fissure in right eyebrow
F Depressed region above right eyebrow
G Parallel scratches in forehead above right eye

3 The Darmstadt death mask.

A Depression in forehead
B Scratch in forehead in line with wounds to left eye socket
C Visible outlines of damage to left eyebrow
D Visible outlines of damage to temporal bone and left eye socket
E Fissure in right eyebrow
F Depressed region above right eyebrow
G Parallel scratches in forehead above right eye

4 The Davenant bust.

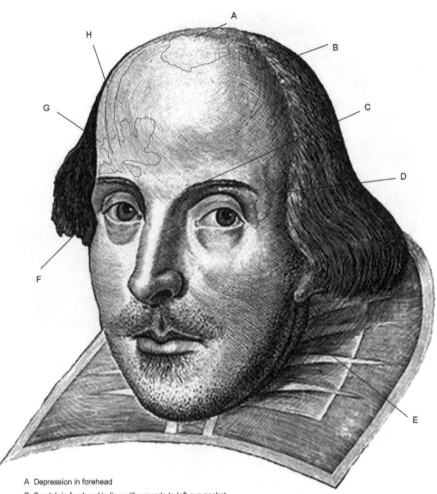

A Depression in forehead
B Scratch in forehead in line with wounds to left eye socket
C Visible outlines of damage to left eyebrow and eye socket
D Visible outlines of damage to temporal bone and left eye socket
E Outline of death mask
F Fissure in right eyebrow
G Depressed/discoloured region above right eyebrow
H Parallel scratches in forehead above right eye

5 The Droeshout engraving, 1623.

A Depression in forehead
B Scratch in forehead in line with wounds to left eye socket
C Visible outlines of damage to left eyebrow and eye socket
D Visible outlines of damage to temporal bone and left eye socket
E Visible outline of broken maxilla
F Fissure in right eyebrow
G Depressed/discoloured region above right eyebrow
H Parallel scratches in forehead above right eye

6 The Chandos Portrait.

As He Hath Hit His Face

SHAKESPEARE WAS familiar with the work of the French writer Michel de Montaigne. In an essay of 1580, Montaigne recalled that his brother, Captain Saint-Martin, had been just 23 years old when he was 'struck by a ball a little above the right ear' while playing tennis. There being no sign of a contusion, his brother 'did not sit down or rest, but five or six hours later he died of an apoplexy that this wound gave him'.

Captain Saint-Martin was unlucky enough to have been struck very close to the pterion. Situated between the top of the ear and the end of the eyebrow, the pterion is where four bones meet. It is the weakest part of the skull. Some physicians refer to it as 'God's little joke'. The middle meningeal artery runs beneath the pterion, and any damage to this part of the skull can result in an epidural bleed which reaches its peak six hours or so after the injury.

The build-up of blood increases the pressure inside the skull, squeezing the delicate tissues of the brain and leading to hydrocephalus ('water on the brain') and a restriction in blood flow. The body responds by raising the blood pressure and dilating the cerebral blood vessels, further increasing the intracranial pressure, until a deadly herniation occurs. The victim experiences headaches, nausea, vomiting, delirium and convulsions. Speech is slurred, co-ordination is impaired. Limbs become weak or numb. A lucid interval is followed by a sudden deterioration. The victim loses consciousness and slips into a coma.

According to the recollections of the people of Stratford, as recorded by Rev. John Ward in 1662, Shakespeare 'died of a fever' contracted as a result of his 'merry meeting' with Drayton and Jonson.

A separate tradition had Shakespeare completing an epitaph started by Jonson when they were 'being merry at a tavern'.

Michael Drayton would acknowledge that he had been an admirer of 'great Olcon' – Ben Jonson – but after Ben was bested or 'out-gone' when he offered to make 'Rhymes' with the Warwickshire poets, he had turned angry. William Drummond, who observed in 1619 that Jonson was 'jealous of every word and action of those about him (especially after drink ...)', also noted Ben's remark that 'Drayton feared him'.

Drayton let at least ten years go by before he honoured Will Shakespeare's 'comic vein' and 'clear ... rage' in verse; perhaps Drayton was too scared of Ben Jonson's beastly followers, those 'Roguish swineherds', to make a more fulsome public statement.

Jonson did not comment on Will's death until seven years after the 'merry meeting', when he commended Martin Droeshout's engraving of Shakespeare 'To the Reader' of the First Folio. Ben remarked that 'the Graver had a strife / with Nature to out-do the life' of his subject, and exclaimed: 'O, could be but have drawn his wit / As well in brass, as he hath hit / His face ...'

The Droeshout engraving was almost certainly modelled on a death mask of Shakespeare. A death mask would also have formed the template for the funerary bust of Shakespeare in Holy Trinity Church and two images associated with Shakespeare's godson: the Chandos Portrait and the Davenant Bust. These images all reveal certain pathological features – a swelling on the upper left eyelid, a protruding left eye, scratches on the forehead and an 'indentation or scar' above the right eyebrow.

These features match those of the 'stolen' skull discovered by Rev. C.J. Langston in the vault beneath the Sheldon Chapel in Beoley Church.

In his 1857 painting, *A Sculptor's Workshop*, Henry Wallis depicted Ben Jonson overseeing the completion of Shakespeare's funerary bust. Ben is seen cradling a death mask and indicating the region immediately above the right eyebrow with his finger. Two details included by Henry Wallis in his painting are worthy of comment.

The statuette of Hercules and Achelous which overlooks the River Avon represents the mythic struggle between the hot-headed hero and the shape-shifting river god. Hercules attacked Achelous, mutilating his brow, after the god of the river mocked his lowly origins.

In the top right-hand corner of Wallis' painting hangs another, discarded death mask. Wallis seemingly intuited that there had been *two* death masks of Shakespeare. One was made shortly after his death, when the facial oedema caused by his injuries would have given him a puffy, 'pumpkin-face' appearance. A second mask was hurriedly cast when the tissues had relaxed. The differences between the two masks would account for the variations in the posthumous images of Shakespeare: the swollen eyelid, the flabby cheeks, the vague or upward-curving moustache.

The presence of alcohol in Shakespeare's bloodstream would have exacerbated his symptoms. He probably had no recollection of the assault (post-traumatic amnesia), and within a few hours he had succumbed to what looked like a raging fever.

It was not the first time Ben Jonson had killed a man.

JONSON'S ANCESTRAL roots lay in the troubled Borders country between England and Scotland. His tutor, William Camden, had this to say about the region: 'In this territory, the Jonstons are men of greatest name: a kindred ever bred to war; between whom and the Maxwells there hath been professed an open enmity over long, even to deadly feud and bloodshed.' They were a quarrelsome lot of thieves and raiders but, as Camden observed in his *Britannia*, able to sweet-talk their way out of trouble: 'But say they be taken: so fair spoken they are and eloquent, so many sugared words they have at will sweetly to plead for them, that they are able to move the judges and adversaries both.' These qualities of his ancestors – the tendency towards 'open enmity' and the 'many sugared words they have at will' – were evident in Ben Jonson.

He was born in 1572, or thereabouts. In one poem he gave his birthday as 11 June. His father, a minister of the Church, died a month before Ben was born. His mother soon remarried and the family moved into a narrow, stinking lane between Charing Cross and the River Thames in Westminster.

An unknown benefactor paid for Ben to be schooled at the Royal College of St Peter. There, he came under the influence of the deputy master at Westminster, the historian and antiquarian William Camden, from whom Ben acquired his extensive knowledge of the classics and his prodigious memory. Jonson would tell Drummond in 1618 that he could 'repeat whole books' that he had read. He remained a voracious reader for the rest of his life.

It is unclear whether or not Ben completed his schooling at Westminster. William Drummond later noted that Jonson had been 'put to school by a friend' but then 'taken from it, and put to ane other craft (I think it was to be a Wright or Bricklayer)'. John Taylor the Water Poet, writing at the time of Ben's death in 1637, claimed that it was Jonson's stepfather who had dragged him away from his studies:

Then was he forced to leave the academ',
And lay by learning (that unvalued gem);
Behold a metamorphosis most strange:
His books were turned to bricks, a sudden change ...

The stigma of having followed his stepfather into the bricklaying business would never leave him. Students at Cambridge University joked about it in 1601 – Jonson was the 'wittiest fellow of a bricklayer in England' ('He were better to betake himself to his old trade of bricklaying,' came the reply).

Almost the exact same words were used seventeen years later, when Jonson's *Pleasure Reconciled to Virtue* failed to impress the Court. 'The poet is grown so dull,' wrote Sir Nicholas Brent, 'divers think fit he should return to his old trade of bricklaying again.' As late as 1633, after another of his plays had bombed, Ben was advised that a 'brickhill's fitter for thee than a stage'.

According to the notes made by William Drummond, Jonson 'could not endure' his new occupation and so 'went he to the Low Countries'.

War had been simmering in the Spanish Netherlands for thirty years, ever since the Protestants of the Low Countries – roughly, modern Holland, Belgium and Luxembourg – had rebelled against their Spanish overlords. Queen Elizabeth I had been cajoled by some of her Protestant advisers to intervene on the side of the Dutch Protestants. She despatched her favourite, Robert Dudley, Earl of Leicester, with a modest army to the Low Countries in 1585. The campaign was a disaster. Leicester's nephew, the brilliant poet Sir Philip Sidney, died horribly at Zutphen. The earl returned in disgrace to England in 1587 and died 'of a continual fever' the following year. Ben Jonson would later tell William Drummond that the former royal favourite had been poisoned.

Jonson was probably recruited in 1591, when English forces were sent to reinforce the army of the States-General under Maurice of Nassau. His principal memory of his military adventures was recorded by Drummond in 1619: 'In his service in the Low Countries, he had, in the face of both the Camps, killed ane enemy and taken opima spolia from him.'

Ben had, by his own account, killed an enemy soldier in single combat. By the sound of it, Jonson was the champion chosen to represent his army in this ritualistic duel. He won, and took all the spoils – '*opima spolia*' – from his victim.

BACK IN London, a few years later, Jonson killed again. As William Drummond put it, 'and since his coming to England, being appealed to in the fields, he had killed his adversary, which had hurt him in the arm, and whose sword was 10 inches longer than his; for the which he was imprisoned, and almost at the gallows.'

Ben had returned to his studies and, in the words of John Aubrey, 'acted and wrote, but both ill, at the Green Curtain, a kind of nursery or obscure playhouse somewhere in the suburbs'. In November 1594 he married Anne Lewis, whom he described to Drummond as 'a shrew yet honest'.

By 1597, he had broken into writing for the theatre. *The Isle of Dogs*, a notorious satire penned by Jonson and Thomas Nashe, was performed that year and soon brought to the attention of the queen's chief interrogator, Richard Topcliffe, who was ordered to investigate 'that seditious play'. Sensing danger, Thomas Nashe fled to Great Yarmouth. Jonson stayed put and, in the summer of 1597, was arrested along with two actors from the Earl of Pembroke's company.

Ben Jonson, Robert Shaw and Gabriel Spenser were accused of 'lewd and mutinous behaviour' by performing a play which contained 'very seditious and scandalous matter'. Jonson was charged as 'not only an actor, but a maker of part of the said play'. In the hope of discovering 'what is become of the rest of their fellows that either had their parts in the devising of that seditious matter, or that were actors or players in the same', Richard Topcliffe committed Jonson, Shaw and Spenser to the Marshalsea prison. Two spies were placed in Jonson's cell in an attempt to wheedle information out of him.

The Privy Council, meanwhile, decreed that 'no plays shall be used within London or about the City, or in any public place during this time of summer' and that 'those playhouses that are erected and built only for such purposes shall be plucked down'. As the impresario Philip Henslowe noted in his diary that August, 'restraint is by the means of playing *The Isle of Dogs*'.

Fortunately, the Privy Council's instructions were ignored. Jonson, Robert Shaw and Gabriel Spenser were released from the Marshalsea in October 1597, having come close to shutting down the London theatres altogether.

Less than a year later, on 22 September 1598, Ben Jonson fought with Gabriel Spenser in the 'fields' just north of London. The cause of their dispute is not known.

Philip Henslowe, the meticulous manager of the Lord Admiral's Company, which Spenser had joined after he was freed from prison, wrote to his son-in-law, the actor Edward Alleyn, a few days after Spenser was buried in Shoreditch: 'Since you were with me I have lost one of my company which hurteth me greatly, that is Gabriel, for he is slain in Hoxton Fields by the hands of Benjamin Jonson, bricklayer.'

Ben was formally arraigned in October 1598. The jury heard that he had 'feloniously and wilfully struck and beat the said Gabriel' with a 'certain sword of iron and steel called a Rapier, of the price of three shillings, which he then and there had in his right hand and held drawn'. Jonson had given Spenser, 'in and upon the same Gabriel's right side, a mortal wound, to the depth of six inches and the breadth of one inch, of which mortal wound the same Gabriel Spenser then and there died instantly'.

The jurors found him guilty.

Jonson then displayed the knack of his Annandale ancestors for wriggling off the hook. The record states that he 'confesses the indictment, asks for the book, reads like a clerk, is marked with the letter T, and is delivered according to the form of the statute'.

He avoided the death penalty by pleading benefit of clergy, an arcane procedure dating from a time when ordained priests could claim to be outside the jurisdiction of the secular courts. As he later remarked, he was 'saved by the book'. His ability to read out the 'neck-verse' from Psalm 51 got his sentence commuted. He was branded with a hot iron on the base of his right thumb with a letter T, for Tyburn, the site of the 'gallow's tree'. It was a reminder that he had escaped hanging once. There would be no such leniency for a second offence.

It seems incredible that a man with a history of violence should have got off so lightly. But then, Jonson's victim on this occasion had been no angel.

Just two years earlier, Gabriel Spenser had killed James Feake at the Shoreditch home of a barber named Richard Easte. The inquest heard that, on the evening of 3 December 1596, 'divers insulting and reproachful words were said and spoken between the aforesaid James Feake and Gabriel Spenser'. Feake had picked up a candlestick, ready to throw it at Spenser. Whereupon Spenser, 'having a sword called a rapier, of iron and steel, of the price of five shillings, being in the scabbard', attacked Feake, striking and beating him and:

> giving then and there to the same James, with the sword being in the aforesaid scabbard, a certain mortal wound, six-inches deep and two-inches wide, on the face – that is to say, between the pupil of the right eye, called the ball of the eye, and the eyebrows – penetrating to the brain.

Feake had 'languished and lived in languor' for three days before dying of 'the aforesaid mortal wound'.

It could be said that Gabriel Spenser got his comeuppance when Jonson stabbed him to death in Hoxton. At the same time, we can be sure that the manner in which Spenser had killed James Feake – a blow to the face, in the form of a sword, still in its scabbard, thrust into the eye socket, between the eyeball and the eyebrow – was not lost on Ben Jonson.

ONE OF the two 'damned villains' who had been placed with Ben Jonson in his cell in the Marshalsea prison was probably the spy called Robert Poley. Jonson would intimate as much in his poem, 'Inviting a Friend to Supper':

And we shall have no *Pooly*, or *Parrot* by;
Nor shall our cups make any guilty men:
But, at our parting, we will be, as when
We innocently met.

The risk of being overheard, and one's words twisted into something incriminating, was an ever-present one, for that was how the government kept its eyes on the people.

Robert Poley (or Pooley) had spent time in the Marshalsea before. Queen Elizabeth's spymaster, Sir Francis Walsingham, had locked him up in 1583, when Poley was eager to 'do Her Majesty and the State some special service'. By the summer of 1585, Poley was in Paris, liaising with Thomas Morgan, the chief agent acting for Mary, Queen of Scots. Robert Poley was instrumental in setting up a 'secret' channel of communication between Mary, then under house arrest in England, and her supporters in France.

Poley's next move was to befriend an impressionable young Catholic named Anthony Babington, who was encouraged to write to Mary, using the communication channel which Poley had helped to establish, giving details of a harebrained scheme to assassinate Queen Elizabeth and place Mary on the throne. Mary's reply was intercepted, deciphered and probably altered by Walsingham's code-breaker, Thomas Phelippes. This gave Sir Francis Walsingham what he had been angling for: hard evidence that Mary, Queen of Scots, was complicit in a conspiracy against her cousin, Elizabeth.

Too late, Anthony Babington began to suspect that he had been framed. He wrote a last desperate letter to his false friend, Poley: 'Farewell, sweet Robyn, if as I take thee, true to me. If not, adieu, *ominium bipedum nequissimus* [most wicked of all two-legged creatures].'

Babington was brutally executed, along with six others, on 20 September 1586. Few Catholics were in any doubt as to who had been the 'chief actor' of the plot and the 'chief instrument to contrive and prosecute the matter' – it was Robert Poley. Even Ben Jonson's tutor, William Camden, held Poley to be a 'most cunning counterfeiter and dissembler'.

Thanks to Poley's efforts, the charming Mary, Queen of Scots, was charged with high treason and beheaded on 8 February 1587. Her execution deprived the beleaguered English Catholics of a much-loved figurehead.

Robert Poley was already a figure of some notoriety, then, when he met with three men on 30 May 1593 at the house of a widow named Eleanor Bull on Deptford Strand, near the royal palace of Greenwich. The others who joined Poley that Wednesday morning were Nicholas Skeres, a criminal and government spy who had also played a part in the Babington Plot; Ingram Frizer, a fraudster who occasionally worked with Skeres; and one Christopher Marlowe, Cambridge graduate, government agent and groundbreaking playwright.

MARLOWE WAS 29 years old. Born a couple of months before Will Shakespeare, his background was similar to that of the Warwickshire poet: Shakespeare's father was a glove maker; Marlowe's was a shoemaker.

Hailing from Canterbury in Kent, Marlowe went up to Corpus Christi College, Cambridge, in the winter of 1580. He graduated Bachelor of Arts on Palm Sunday 1584 and remained at the university to take his Masters degree.

In June 1587, the Privy Council in London wrote to the Cambridge University authorities. The burden of the letter was preserved in the Council's minutes:

> Whereas it was reported that Christopher Morley [sic] was determined to have gone beyond the seas to Reames and there to remain, Their lordships thought good to certify that he had no such intent, but that in all his actions he had behaved himself orderly and discretely whereby he had done her Majesty good service & deserved to be rewarded for his faithful dealing.

The university authorities had suspected that Marlowe was planning to defect to the English college for Catholics at Rheims in northern France. The Privy Council was keen to stress that Marlowe had in fact been acting for 'the benefit of his Country' and should not be 'defamed by those that are ignorant in th'offices he went about'. Almost certainly, Marlowe had been employed as a spy or 'projector'.

For Marlowe, 1587 was a watershed. On 16 November, the Lord Admiral's Company of players accidentally shot dead three members of the audience at London's Rose Theatre. This happened during a performance of *The Second Part of the Bloody Conquests of Mighty Tamburlaine*, the sequel to Marlowe's successful *Tamburlaine the Great*. Marlowe's spectacular career had begun – literally – with a bang.

Over six years, from 1587 to 1593, Kit Marlowe penned a stream of challenging, electrifying plays – *Dido, Queen of Carthage* (co-written, perhaps, with Thomas Nashe and first published in 1594); *The Jew of Malta* (first performed in 1592); *Edward the Second*; *The Massacre at Paris* and *The Tragical History of the Horrible Life and Death of Doctor Faustus*. At the same time he was engaged in covert activity for the government. In January 1592, he was arrested in the Dutch town of Vlissingen and charged with making counterfeit coins. Deported back to England, he was interviewed by Lord Burghley, the queen's most trusted adviser. No action was taken against Marlowe over what was then a capital offence. The likelihood is that Marlowe had been working for Lord Burghley in the Low Countries, where the shadowy Robert Poley was also active in the early 1590s.

The beginning of the end for Kit Marlowe came on 21 March 1593. On that day, the English Parliament voted to extend the privileges available to Protestant immigrants who had fled to London from the Continent. The government welcomed these refugees, not least of all because their enterprise was helping to prop up the ailing economy, but ordinary Londoners felt threatened by these 'strangers' who, it was thought, were better treated than the native citizens. During the parliamentary debate on the matter, Sir Walter Raleigh had been almost alone in decrying the special treatment offered to the émigrés. 'In the whole cause I see no matter of honour,' he said, 'no matter of charity, no profit in relieving them.'

Within days, placards had appeared all over London warning of violent reprisals against the immigrants. The most inflammatory of these was posted on the wall of the Dutch Churchyard on 5 May. It was signed 'Tamburlane' and made several sly references to the plays of Christopher Marlowe.

The Privy Council ordered that all necessary steps be taken to apprehend those responsible for the 'lewd and malicious libels'. One of the first to be caught in the net was Thomas Kyd, a playwright who had previously shared a room with Marlowe. Among the papers found in Kyd's chamber was a short document containing 'Vile heretical conceits denying the deity of Jesus Christ our Saviour'. Kyd was interrogated, suffering 'pains and undeserved tortures'. Under duress, he claimed that the 'heretical' manuscript had belonged to Marlowe.

On 18 May, one of the Queen's Messengers was sent to fetch Marlowe from the 'house of Mr Tho: Walsingham in Kent'. The playwright was staying at the country home of his patron, who was also the young cousin of the late spymaster, Sir Francis Walsingham. Marlowe returned to London and, on 20 May, undertook to appear daily before the Privy Council until all matters were resolved.

Richard Baines was the government agent who had informed against Marlowe in Vlissingen. He now prepared a 'note containing the opinion of one Christopher Marley'. Baines alleged that Marlowe openly advocated atheism and held all Protestants to be 'hypocritical asses'. He concluded his note: 'I think all men of Christianity ought to endeavour that the mouth of so dangerous a member should be stopped.'

More damning evidence was supplied by another agent, Richard Cholmeley, who reportedly stated that 'Marlowe is able to show more sound reasons for atheism than any divine in England is able to give to prove divinity, & that Marlowe told him he hath read the atheist lecture to Sir Walter Raleigh & others.'

This was the key. Raleigh's speech in Parliament in March had captured the popular mood of discontent with the Protestant refugees. Lord Burghley and his industrious son, Robert Cecil, now had evidence of a sort linking Raleigh and Marlowe to atheism.

Ten days after Marlowe was brought back to London, four men met at the house of the widow, Eleanor Bull. They talked from ten till twelve, took lunch, and then talked in the garden all afternoon. At about six o'clock they went indoors for supper.

An argument broke out over the 'reckoning' – the bill for their refreshments. Marlowe was lying on the bed. The others were sitting at a table, Ingram Frizer in the middle, with Robert Poley and Nicholas Skeres on either side of him. Marlowe allegedly leapt up from the bed and grabbed Frizer's dagger, striking him twice across the head and causing two flesh wounds. Though Frizer was trapped between Poley and Skeres he somehow wrested the dagger from Marlowe's hand.

At the inquest, held on Friday 1 June 1593, it was heard that Ingram Frizer, 'in defence of his life, with the dagger aforesaid of the value of twelve pence, gave the said Christopher a mortal wound above his right eye, of the depth of two inches and the width of one inch'. Marlowe 'then & there instantly died'.

The killing had taken place 'within the verge' – that is, within a 12-mile radius of the queen's person – and so the inquest was conducted by the coroner to the royal household. The widow in whose house Marlowe died was a 'cousin' to Blanche Parry, formerly the Chief Gentlewoman of the queen's most honourable Privy Chamber and Keeper of Her Majesty's Jewels. Another 'cousin' of Eleanor Bull was the powerful Lord High Treasurer, Lord Burghley.

Ingram Frizer was, like Marlowe, working for Thomas Walsingham. Robert Poley, as a note signed by Sir Thomas Heneage, vice-chamberlain of the royal household, indicates, was employed 'in Her Majesty's

Service' at the time. Nicholas Skeres was then a servant to Robert Devereux, Second Earl of Essex and sworn enemy to Sir Walter Raleigh.

On 28 June 1593, the queen issued a formal pardon to Ingram Frizer.

There can be little doubt that the murder of Christopher Marlowe was covered up by the Elizabethan authorities. The story told by Frizer, Poley and Skeres is scarcely believable. More likely, the murder was bungled. Frizer and his accomplices had perhaps sought to bludgeon Marlowe with the pommel of a dagger as he lay on the bed. But Marlowe had struggled, wounding Frizer, and in the heat of the moment Frizer forced his dagger into Marlowe's eye socket, between the eyeball and the eyebrow.

Four years later, Ben Jonson was sharing a prison cell with Robert Poley. A year after that, Jonson was back in prison, having killed Gabriel Spenser in a duel.

By the strangest of coincidences, both Poley and Spenser had recently been involved in struggles which resulted in deaths caused by near-identical injuries to the socket of the right eye.

5

We Wondered, Shakespeare

THE MYTH that Kit Marlowe died in a tavern brawl was put about by Puritans gloating over the unseemly death of a playwright. His fellow poets were kinder. George Peele honoured him as 'the Muses' darling' while Thomas Nashe remarked that Marlowe's pen 'was sharp-pointed', like the 'poignard' that killed him. 'His tongue & his invention were foreborn: what they thought they would confidently utter,' wrote Nashe. 'His life he contemned in comparison of the liberty of speech.' Michael Drayton also expressed his admiration for Marlowe, and even Will Shakespeare would pay tribute to his trailblazing contemporary.

When Shakespeare died, twenty-three years later, there were no instantaneous responses. Not a single note or letter survives in which his death was mentioned. Even his fellow Warwickshire poet, Sir Fulke Greville – who, as Recorder of Stratford, was effectively the town's registrar and coroner – refrained from comment. In contrast to the death of Marlowe, Will's demise was greeted with a lingering silence.

FIVE YEARS after Will's death, work began on the first edition of *Mr. William Shakespeares Comedies, Histories, & Tragedies*. Two of Will's longest-standing colleagues, Henry Condell and John Heminges, had gathered together the 'True Originall Copies' of thirty-six of his plays, fully half of which had not previously been published.

After months of preparation, about 1,000 copies of the First Folio went on sale in December 1623. Will's memory was assured – and not a moment too soon. Only the year before, the poet Henry Peachum had issued his *Compleat Gentleman*, in which he discussed those writers and artists who should be studied by a cultured individual; Shakespeare was not included among them.

All the effort which went into the First Folio would have been wasted if the Puritan faction had resolved on seizing and burning the books. To avert such a calamity, Condell and Heminges sought the protection of two patrons who were themselves entwined with the Puritan clique at the heart of the government. The First Folio was duly dedicated to that 'MOST NOBLE AND INCOMPARABLE PAIR OF BRETHREN', William Herbert, Third Earl of Pembroke, and his younger brother, Philip, First Earl of Montgomery.

As Lord Chamberlain, Pembroke exercised supreme control over plays and their publication; his brother Montgomery would succeed him in that post in 1625. The patronage of the Herbert brothers might have protected the First Folio, but there was a catch. Ben Jonson received £20 each year from his patron, the Earl of Pembroke, to spend on books. The price of securing the Lord Chamberlain's protection was the involvement of Ben Jonson in the publication of Shakespeare's *Comedies, Histories, & Tragedies*.

Ben got the first word in, commending 'To the Reader' the Martin Droeshout engraving of Shakespeare on the title page. Jonson also provided the first, and by far the longest, prefatory poem in the First Folio, and seems to have determined who else would get a look in.

One who lost out was William Basse, a minor poet from Oxfordshire. In a short tribute, entitled 'On the death of William Shakespeare', Basse called on the ghosts of three celebrated poets to make space for Will's remains in Westminster Abbey:

Renownèd Spenser, lie a thought more nigh
To learnèd Chaucer; and rare Beaumont, lie
A little nearer Spenser, to make room
For Shakespeare in your threefold, fourfold tomb.

But there would be no Poets' Corner tomb for Shakespeare. William Basse acknowledged that, since Chaucer, Spenser and Beaumont had got there first, there simply wasn't room for Shakespeare in their 'sacred sepulchre'. So Basse advised the 'rare tragedian' to 'sleep alone' under the 'carvèd marble' of his Stratford monument, the 'lord, not tenant' of his 'unshared' grave.

William Basse's affectionate eulogy was omitted from the First Folio. It would not appear in print until a new edition of Shakespeare's *Poems* was published three years after Ben Jonson's death. Even so, Jonson took a sideswipe at Basse in his own poem for the First Folio, which he entitled 'To the memory of my beloved, The AUTHOR MASTER WILLIAM SHAKESPEARE, AND what he hath left us'.

After boasting that he harboured no feelings of envy towards Shakespeare, Jonson rambled for some fourteen lines before getting on with the job:

> I therefore will begin. Soul of the age!
> The applause, delight, the wonder of our stage!
> My Shakespeare, rise. I will not lodge thee by
> Chaucer or Spenser, or bid Beaumont lie
> A little further to make thee a room.

This was plainly a sneer at William Basse. Ben preferred to lump Shakespeare with three different poets:

> For if I thought my judgement were of years
> I should commit thee surely with thy peers,
> And tell how far thou didst our Lyly outshine,
> Or sporting Kyd, or Marlowe's mighty line.

Marlowe had been stabbed to death, his name subsequently blackened by the Puritans. Kyd had been tortured into smearing Marlowe and died a broken man. John Lyly had been denied a promised position at the Court; his efforts to procure royal patronage were repeatedly blocked by Lord Burghley, and he died in penniless obscurity.

None of these three had been honoured with a Westminster Abbey grave. It was a pretty tarnished trio with whom Jonson wished to 'commit' his Shakespeare.

THE ASSUMPTION that Jonson was a fond friend of Shakespeare's rests almost entirely on the prefatory poem he wrote for the First Folio. A comparison of his poem 'To the memory of my beloved' with his 'Vision … on the Muses of his Friend, M. Drayton', which appeared just four years later, raises doubts about Jonson's sincerity.

Ben's poem to Drayton opened and closed with a question: was he, could he even be, a friend to Drayton? Between those two questions, Ben sought to camouflage his ambivalence with a verbal fireworks display:

> It was no dream! I was awake, and saw!
> Lend me thy voice, O Fame, that I may draw
> Wonder to truth! and have my vision hurled,
> Hot from thy trumpet, round about the world.

The conclusion – 'I call the world, that envies me, to see / If I can be a friend, and friend to thee' – expresses the hope that the overblown praises might have settled the matter. And yet there are reasons to suspect that Ben was being disingenuous. He had told William Drummond that 'Drayton feared him, and he esteemed not of him', and that Drayton's 'long verses pleased him not'. Drayton, meanwhile, complained that his life had become miserable since 'great Olcon' turned 'angry' after he was 'out-gone' in some sort of rhyming contest. Ben's hyperbole, his extravagant compliments, appears to have been a smokescreen. He was no friend at all to Michael Drayton.

Similarly, in his poem 'To the memory of my beloved', Ben laid it on with a trowel for Shakespeare: 'But stay, I see thee in the hemisphere / Advanced, and made a constellation there! / Shine forth, thou star of poets ...'

There is a curious passage in which Ben apparently pays tribute to Will's artistry:

> Look how the father's face
> Lives in his issue, even so the race
> Of Shakespeare's mind and manners brightly shines
> In his well-tunèd and true-filèd lines,
> In each of which he seems to shake a lance
> As brandished at the eyes of ignorance.

If 'shake a lance' sounds like a pun on Shakespeare's name, the passage as a whole contains something nastier – the references to 'the father's face' and a weapon 'brandished at the eyes' are taunting reminders of something, like the 'as he hath hit / His face' remark in Ben's commendation of the Droeshout engraving. It is as if Jonson couldn't help himself: even in the midst of a praise poem for Shakespeare he had to hark back to the outcome of the 'merry meeting'.

We are left with a conundrum. If Ben's poetic eulogy for Shakespeare was a genuine outpouring of affection, what are we to make of his equally extravagant poem to Drayton? And if, in the latter, Jonson was playing with Drayton, like a cat with a mouse in its paws, why should we imagine that he was being any more upfront and guileless when showering Shakespeare with compliments?

Maybe the poet John Dryden was right when he called Ben's Shakespeare eulogy 'an insolent, sparing, invidious panegyric'.

Jonson in fact anticipated that some would doubt his sincerity, writing, 'Or crafty malice might pretend this praise, / And think to ruin where it seemed to raise.' He might have fooled modern critics, but Ben failed to convince the poets of his own time that his praises of Shakespeare were genuine.

ELSEWHERE, HE was more disparaging of Shakespeare. He considered *Pericles* a 'mouldy tale', 'nasty' and 'stale', which might explain why it was left out of the First Folio. In his *Timber: or, Discoveries Made Upon Men and Matter*, Ben also found fault with Will's *Julius Caesar*: 'Many times he fell into those things, could not escape laughter: As when he said in the person of *Caesar*, one speaking to him; *Caesar thou dost me wrong*. He replied: *Caesar never did wrong, but with just cause*: and such like; which were ridiculous.' Those same *Discoveries* – Ben's reflections on his writing career, published after his death – contain what is perhaps his most considered response to Shakespeare's work:

> I remember, the Players have often mentioned it as an honour to Shakespeare, that in his writing, (whatsoever he penned) he never blotted out a line. My answer hath been, would that he had blotted out a thousand. Which they thought a malevolent speech. I had not told posterity this, but for their ignorance, who chose that circumstance to commend their friend by, wherein he most faulted. And to justify my candour, (for I loved the man, and do honour his memory (on this side Idolatry) as much as any.) He was (indeed) honest, and of an open and free nature: had an excellent Phantsie; brave notions, and gentle expressions: wherein he flowed with that facility, that sometime it was necessary he should be stopped ...

It is true that the players had remarked of Shakespeare that 'he never blotted out a line'. Henry Condell and John Heminges said as much in their dedicatory epistle to the First Folio: 'His mind and hand went together, and what he thought he uttered with that easiness that we have scarce received from him a blot in his papers.'

Their observation is akin to what Thomas Nashe had to say about Christopher Marlowe: 'His tongue & his invention were foreborn: what they thought they would confidently utter.'

Chillingly, Ben's response echoed the note made by Richard Baines about Marlowe's opinions: 'I think all men in Christianity ought to endeavour that the mouth of so dangerous a member may be stopped.'

Ben's judgement on Shakespeare – 'sometime it was necessary he should be stopped' – meant much the same thing. Shakespeare's mouth needed to be corked.

To ram the point home, Jonson added '*Sufflaminandus erat*; as *Augustus* said of *Haterius*'. *Sufflaminandus erat* – 'the brake had to be applied'. Shakespeare wrote not wisely, but too well. 'The wit was in his own power,' mused Jonson; 'would the rule of it had been so too.'

Ben's disagreement with the players over Shakespeare's refusal to censor himself seems to have taken place when the First Folio was going to press. He had perused their dedication, 'To the Great Variety of Readers', and took issue with what they were saying. Shakespeare never knew when to shut up. Sooner or later, the brake had to be applied.

Like Marlowe before him, 'it was necessary he should be stopped'.

BEN'S LENGTHY praise poem was followed in the First Folio of 1623 by an execrable sonnet, 'Upon the Lines and Life of the Famous Scenic Poet, Master William Shakespeare'. It was written by Hugh Holland:

> Those hands which you so clapped go now and wring,
> You Britons brave, for done are Shakespeare's days.
> His days are done that made the dainty plays
> Which made the globe of heav'n and earth to ring.

And so on, until the limp finale: 'For though his line of life went soon about, / The life yet of his lines shall never out.'

Hugh Holland was Jonson's friend. They had both studied under William Camden at Westminster School. We can infer that the Welshman's lacklustre sonnet was only included in the First Folio because Ben wanted it so.

Though Condell and Heminges had done most of the work on the First Folio of Shakespeare's *Comedies, Histories, & Tragedies*, the publication bore the hallmarks of a Ben Jonson production. The first words in the volume were his – his commendation 'To the Reader' of the Droeshout engraving. The Condell and Heminges dedication to those 'singular good LORDS', the Earls of Pembroke and Montgomery, was followed by their epistle 'To the Great Variety of Readers'. Then came Jonson's long prefatory poem, 'To the memory of my beloved', and the inferior sonnet by Hugh Holland. And that, had Ben had his way, would have been that. The First Folio might have burst the bubble of silence surrounding Shakespeare's death, but it did so under Jonson's strict supervision.

Then, a month before the First Folio was released, fire tore through Jonson's lodgings. His books and papers were incinerated.

Ben seemingly tried to make light of the catastrophe in his mock-serious poem, 'An Execration Upon Vulcan', but the fire left him stunned, embittered – and distracted.

At the eleventh hour, two more poems found their way into the First Folio.

PAGES FIVE and six of the First Folio were taken up with the poems of Jonson and Holland. A Table of Contents followed on page seven. Then came a separate sheet, on which were printed two additional poems and a list of 'The Names of the Principal Actors in all these plays'. This folded sheet – pages eight and nine – appears to have been inserted at a late stage in the printing process.

The first of the last minute additions was signed 'L. Digges' and entitled 'TO THE MEMORY of the deceased Author Master W. Shakespeare'. It began, '*Shake-speare*, at length thy pious fellows give / The world thy Works: thy Works, by which, out-live / Thy Tomb, thy name must'. As if to rub salt into Jonson's wounds, the poet toyed with the word 'fire':

> Nor Fire, nor cank'ring Age, as *Naso* said,
> Of his, thy wit-fraught Book shall once invade ...
> Till these, till any of thy Volume's rest
> Shall with more fire, more feeling be expressed ...

The twenty-two-line poem also referred in passing to Will's *Julius Caesar* – 'Or till I hear a Scene more nobly take / Than when thy half-Sword parleying *Romans* spake'. The poet, Leonard Digges, would expand on this in a longer eulogy:

> So have I seen, when Caesar would appear,
> And on the Stage at half-drawn parley were,
> Brutus and Cassius: O how the Audience
> Were ravish'd, with what wonder they went thence ...

Digges would contrast the mesmerising effect of Shakespeare's tragedy with Ben Jonson's tiresome efforts:

> ... When some new day they would not brook a line
> Of tedious (though well-laboured) *Catiline*;
> *Sejanus* too was irksome: they priz'd more
> Honest Iago, or the jealous Moor.

The longer of Digges' two eulogies appeared five years after his death – and three years after Jonson's – alongside the previously unpublished 'On the death of William Shakespeare' by William Basse. They prefaced a new edition of *POEMS: WRITTEN BY WIL. SHAKESPEARE. Gent.*, which was published by John Benson, a London bookseller, in 1640.

Benson furnished his volume with a new engraving of Shakespeare. This was in fact a mirror image of an engraving of Ben Jonson, made by Robert Vaughan in about 1627. Vaughan's engraving of Jonson showed him crowned with a laurel wreath, a cloak draped over his left shoulder and a pair of gloves in his left hand. William Marshall's new engraving of Shakespeare showed Will with a cloak over his right shoulder and a sprig of laurels clutched in his tiny gloved hand – as if he had snatched the wreath from Jonson's head. Printed beneath this engraving were lines which parodied Jonson's contributions to the First Folio: 'This Shadow is renowned Shakespear's? Soul of th'age / The applause? Delight? The wonder of the Stage ...' In addition to the William Basse tribute, omitted from the First Folio, and the longer Leonard Digges eulogy, Benson's 1640 edition of Shakespeare's *Poems* included an anonymous 'Elegy on the death of that famous Writer and Actor, Master William Shakespeare'. Jonson's earlier comments on Shakespeare were derided:

> Nor is it fit each humble muse should have
> Thy worth his subject, now thou'rt laid in grave.
> No, it is a flight beyond the pitch of those
> Whose worthless pamphlets are not sense in prose.

Jonson had habitually composed his dramas in prose before converting them into verse, 'for so his master Camden had learned him'. But if Ben was only alluded to in the lines cited above, the next line named him outright: 'Let learnèd Jonson sing a dirge for thee, / And fill our orb with mournful harmony; / But we need no remembrancer.' In a further dig at Ben Jonson – who was then in no position to fight back – the anonymous versifier of 1640 declared that Shakespeare had been the 'chiefest tutor' of his age, the 'only favourite' of the 'widowed stage'.

A final encomium by John Warren appeared in the 1640 edition of the *Poems*, under the title, 'Of Master William Shakespeare'. It is worth quoting in full:

> What, lofty Shakespeare, art again revived,
> And Virbius-like now show'st thyself twice lived?
> 'Tis Benson's love that thus to thee is shown,
> The labour's his, the glory still thine own.
> These learnèd poems amongst thine after-birth,
> That makes thy name immortal on the earth,

Will make the learnèd still admire to see
The muses' gifts so fully infused on thee.
Let carping Momus bark and bite his fill,
And ignorant Davus slight thy learnèd skill,
Yet those who know the worth of thy desert,
And with true judgement can discern thy art,
Will be admirers of thy high-tuned strain,
Amongst whose number let me still remain.

The repetition of 'learnèd' recalled the inscription surrounding Robert Vaughan's engraving of Ben Jonson: *doctissimi poetarum anglorum* – 'most learned of English poets'.

Momus – 'carping Momus' – was the Greek god of ridicule and mean-spirited criticism. In one of Aesop's fables he was moved by envy to deride the craftsmanship of his fellow gods. Most famously, Momus mocked Hephaestus, the Greek god of fire, just as Jonson had mocked the Roman equivalent in his 'Execration Upon Vulcan'.

In Roman mythology, Virbius ('twice a man') was brought back to life after he had been killed by his own horses. Ben Jonson's admirers, after his death in 1637, published a collection of his poems under the title *Jonsonus Virbius: or, The Memory of Ben Jonson revived*. John Warren noted in 1640 that 'lofty Shakespeare' had been similarly revived, 'Virbius-like', in Benson's edition of his poems.

The 'ignorant Davus' of Warren's poem was another Roman figure, a loathsome upstart of a slave who criticised his master, the poet Horace, as a 'slave many times over'.

John Warren's poem of 1640 began with a shot across the bows of the Sons of Ben – those *Jonsonistas* who had imagined their mentor revived, like Virbius, in his published poems. He then invoked Jonson as the monstrous slave-critic, 'ignorant Davus', and that depraved genius of mockery and savage criticism, 'carping Momus'. Ranged against the Tribe of Ben were the genuine admirers of Shakespeare's 'high-tuned strain'.

The 1640 publication of Shakespeare's *Poems* was an unmistakably anti-Jonsonian production, hinting strongly that Jonson's false praise of Shakespeare in the First Folio had been motivated purely by envy.

HAD IT not been for Ben Jonson's preoccupation with the fire which had ravaged his study, he would have prevented the inclusion of Leonard Digges' poem in the First Folio of 1623 on the grounds that Digges was firmly in the pro-Shakespeare camp.

The younger son of the mathematician Thomas Digges, Leonard was an Oxford-educated translator who had travelled in Spain; on the flyleaf of a 1613 edition of Lope de Vega's poems he compared the Spanish poet with 'our Will Shakespeare'.

In 1603, Digges' widowed mother married Thomas Russell, whose manor of Alderminster lay 4 miles from Stratford-upon-Avon. Russell was related by marriage to the more doggedly defiant Catholics of the region – the Sheldons of Beoley, the Throckmortons of Coughton and the Arden family of Shakespeare's mother. He became one of Will's most trusted associates: Shakespeare named Thomas Russell as one of just two overseers of his will. Leonard Digges was, therefore, the stepson of a man who probably knew more than most about the death of Will Shakespeare.

The second poem inserted, late in the day, in the First Folio was written by Digges' friend and colleague James Mabbe, a Fellow of Magdalene College, Oxford. Mabbe's brief eight-line poem opened with a startling admission: 'We wondered, Shakespeare, that thou went'st so soon / From the world's stage to the grave's tiring-room.' After such a prolonged period of silence, Mabbe's tribute 'To the memory of Master William Shakespeare' came like a lightning bolt. Though they had kept their thoughts to themselves, there were some in Shakespeare's circle who had 'wondered' at his sudden exit from the theatre of the world.

SHAKESPEARE'S FUNERARY monument was in place near his grave in Holy Trinity Church by the time the First Folio came out. Leonard Digges referred to it in his poem of 1623:

> *Shake-speare*, at length thy pious fellows give
> The world thy Works: thy Works, by which, out-live
> Thy Tomb, thy name must when that stone is rent,
> And Time dissolves thy *Stratford* Monument,
> Here we alive shall view thee still. This Book,
> When Brass and Marble fade, shall make thee look
> Fresh to all Ages ...

The inspiration for Digges' comments came partly from the Roman poet Horace, who wrote in his third Ode that he had created in his poetry 'a monument more lasting than bronze'.

According to the inscription on Shakespeare's Stratford monument, he died on 23 April 1616. Will met his end on his fifty-second birthday.

A similar fate had befallen one of his dramatic characters.

The *Tragedy of Julius Caesar* was the first play performed at the Globe Theatre in London when it opened its doors in the summer of 1599. The play presented the assassination of 'immortal Caesar' by a group of conspirators led by Brutus and Cassius.

In Mark Antony's famous 'Friends, Romans, countrymen' speech, he skilfully turns the Roman mob against Caesar's assassins. The conspirators flee, pursued by Mark Antony and Octavius Caesar. Finally, the opposing armies meet at Philippi in Macedonia.

The quarrel between Cassius and Brutus on the eve of the climactic battle was recalled by Leonard Digges in his poem of 1623: 'Or till I hear a Scene more nobly take / Than when thy half-Sword parleying *Romans* spake'.

Cassius was born at Philippi. The battle takes place on his birthday, 'as this very day / Was Cassius born'. He begins to suspect that his moment has come: 'This day I breathèd first. Time is come round, / And where I did begin, there shall I end. / My life is run his compass.' When he mistakenly believes that his friend has been captured by the enemy, Cassius turns to his slave Pindarus:

> Come hither, sirrah. In Parthia did I take thee prisoner,
> And then I swore thee, saving of thy life,
> That whatsoever I did bid thee do
> Thou shouldst attempt it. Come now, keep thine oath.
> Now be a freeman, and, with this good sword
> That ran through Caesar's bowels, search this bosom.
> Stand not to answer. Here, take thou the hilts,
> And when my face is covered, as 'tis now,
> Guide thou the sword.

Cassius covers his face. Pindarus runs him through: 'So, I am free, yet would not so have been / Durst I have done my will.'

Like Cassius, Shakespeare died on his birthday, and in the town where he was born.

The poet Horace had also been at the Battle of Philippi – he survived by dropping his shield and running away.

This was the same Horace who was indirectly invoked by John Warren in his poem of 1640. Warren implied that Shakespeare, like Horace, had been rudely criticised by a slavish underdog.

Ben Jonson's translation of Horace's *Art of Poetry* was published in 1640. Ben was previously known for his Pindaric ode, 'To the immortal memory, and friendship of that noble pair, Sir Lucius Cary and Sir

H. Morison'. Of the two forms of ode to emerge from classical antiquity, that of the Roman Horace tended to be personal in nature, while those of the Greek poet Pindar focused more on public celebrations of great individuals and major events.

It was Shakespeare who wrote in the Horatian mode. Ben Jonson followed in the tradition of Pindar, whose Latin name was Pindarus.

Jonson resented the success of *Julius Caesar*, dismissing parts of it as 'ridiculous'. His attempts to match Will's Roman tragedies – *Sejanus His Fall* (1603) and *Catiline His Conspiracy* (1611) – paled in comparison. They were, as Leonard Digges remarked, 'tedious' and 'irksome'.

The score was settled when Jonson – a Pindar in his own right – killed Shakespeare on his birthday, and in the town of his birth, just as Pindarus had slain his master Cassius at Philippi.

THREE POETS had a 'merry meeting'. They drank too hard. There was a poetic competition, a game of epitaphs, as Jonson offered to make 'Rhymes' with Shakespeare and Drayton.

Shakespeare took up the challenge, and Jonson was 'out-gone'.

As they made their way from the tavern, a scuffle broke out. Perhaps Jonson threw a cloak over Shakespeare's head – the cloak with which Cassius had covered his face; the same cloak which appeared in the 1627 engraving of Jonson and the 1640 engraving of Shakespeare – and then struck him a blow in the region of his left eye.

The weapon was possibly the 'dagger with a white haft' which Jonson routinely carried, and which he later presented to a like-minded preacher named Zouche Townley. The point of the dagger entered Will's eye socket, to the side of his nose, and pierced the thin wall of the orbital cavity, between the eyeball and the eyebrow.

Shakespeare jerked backwards. Jonson repeatedly stabbed at Will's forehead, the blade slashing through his eyebrows and scratching his skull. A crunching blow left its impression above Will's right eye. The delicate bones of Shakespeare's skull shattered.

He regained consciousness moments later, but within hours he was comatose. His symptoms – vomiting, delirium, convulsions – were misdiagnosed as a 'fever', from which he died.

The world fell silent, afraid to speak of the matter. But there were those who had their doubts. These emerged, after many months, when a fortuitous fire at Jonson's house allowed James Mabbe's poem to be published in the First Folio: 'We wondered, Shakespeare, that thou went'st so soon / From the world's stage to the grave's tiring-room.'

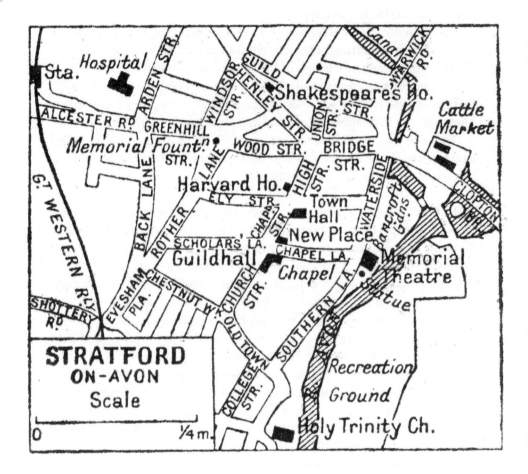

7 Map of Stratford-upon-Avon, 1922, showing the Shakespeare Birthplace ('Shakespeare's House'), New Place, the (Guild) Chapel and Holy Trinity Church. *The Probert Encyclopaedia*

Part Two

Motive

There is an old adage in police circles:
if you want to know how a man died,
look at how he lived.

M.J. Trow
Who Killed Kit Marlowe?

6

Now am I in Arden

ONE OF the best-known passages from Shakespeare is John of Gaunt's paean to England from *The Tragedy of King Richard the Second*:

> This royal throne of kings, this sceptred isle,
> This earth of majesty, this seat of Mars,
> This other Eden, demi-paradise …
> This blessèd plot, this earth, this realm, this England.

Most anthologies end the passage there, on a patriotic high note. But the speech continues:

> … This land of such dear souls, this dear dear land,
> Dear for her reputation through the world,
> Is now leased out – I die pronouncing it –
> Like to a tenement or pelting farm.

The England of the oft-quoted part of the John of Gaunt speech no longer existed. It was 'now bound in with shame, / With inky blots and rotten parchment bonds.' The land had been betrayed, parcelled up and sold by its self-serving leaders and their lawyers: 'That England that was wont to conquer others / Hath made a shameful conquest of itself.' This 'shameful conquest' had begun when Shakespeare's father was a boy.

BOUNDED BY the River Tame to the north and the River Avon to the south, the Forest of Arden was a sprawl of scrub and copses, stippled with isolated farmsteads and secluded manor houses defended by moats.

In about 1200, one William of Arden granted the manor of Knowle to his wife. It is in the register of the medieval guild house at Knowle that we first come across the Shakespeare name. Thomas Shakespeare of Balsall, a descendant of the fourteenth-century Adam of Oldeditch, joined the Knowle Guild in 1486.

By 1526, the Shakespeares were rubbing shoulders with the local gentry; in that year, the names of Richard, John and William Shakespeare and their wives were entered in the book of the Guild of St Anne, alongside those of George Throckmorton of Coughton, Edward Ferrers of Baddesley Clinton, William Clopton of Stratford and Robert Catesby of Lapworth. Eighty years later, these same families would all be embroiled in the infamous 'powder treason' or Gunpowder Plot.

The Richard Shakespeare named in the guild book of Knowle was probably the grandfather of the poet. He was the bailiff of the Benedictine priory at Wroxall, where 'Domina Jane' Shakespeare was the sub-prioress. Richard Shakespeare was also the tenant of a hillside farm in Snitterfield, 3 miles north of Stratford, which he rented from Robert Arden of Wilmcote. The son of Richard Shakespeare would marry the daughter of Robert Arden in 1557; their firstborn son would arrive seven years later. He would be baptised *Gulielmus filius Johannes Shakspere* – 'William son of John Shakespeare' – in the Collegiate Church of the Holy and Undivided Trinity, Stratford-upon-Avon, on 26 April 1564.

Born in about 1530, Will's father, John Shakespeare, was in his childhood when a hurricane of reform was unleashed on the country. King Henry VIII had married his brother's widow, Katherine of Aragon, but her failure to produce a male heir led Henry to seek an annulment of the marriage. This was opposed by Katherine's nephew, the Holy Roman Emperor Charles V, who held sway over the pope. As the diplomatic negotiations dragged on, Henry's patience wore thin. He was infatuated with one of Katherine's maids of honour, the dark-eyed Anne Boleyn, and when the pope refused to grant Henry an annulment of his marriage he responded by declaring himself the 'only supreme head in earth of the Church of England'.

King Henry's expensive foreign policies, combined with the costs of maintaining dozens of royal palaces, required an urgent injection of cash. Thomas Cromwell, appointed vicar-general in 1535, commissioned a nationwide census of Church property. He quickly followed this with a 'visitation' designed to find evidence of 'unthrifty, carnal, and abominable living' in the monasteries.

In 1536, the 'little and small abbeys, priories and other religious houses' were suppressed. Three years later, the larger 'monasteries, abbacies, priories, nunneries, colleges, hospitals, houses of friars, and other religious and ecclesiastical houses and places' were forcibly dissolved.

In all, about one-fifth of the landed wealth in England changed hands, seized from the Church and granted or sold to King Henry's supporters.

Charitable institutions, like Knowle's medieval Guild of St Anne, were abolished. Domina Jane Shakespeare and her fellow nuns were cast out of their priory at Wroxall. Part of the priory was pulled down and a private mansion built on the site.

Will Shakespeare's codeword for the wanton destruction of religious buildings and 'superstitious' images was 'Time'. In his sonnets especially, Time is 'sluttish', 'never-resting', a 'bloody tyrant'; its 'millioned accidents / Creep in 'twixt vows, and change decrees of Kings':

When I have seen by time's fell [cruel] hand defaced
The rich proud cost of outworn buried age,
When sometime lofty towers I see down razed,
And brass eternal slave to mortal rage ...

Time, here, is an active force – a brutal agent of change. Shakespeare would have known that 'time' was the first-person imperative of the Latin verb *timeo*, meaning to 'fear'. 'Time' therefore had the shadow meaning, 'Dread!' Leonard Digges, in his poem for the First Folio of 1623, used 'time' in its Shakespearean sense as a violent despoiler of images: 'when that stone is rent, / And Time dissolves thy *Stratford Monument*'. Like those reformers who dissolved the monasteries and helped themselves to the wealth of the Church, 'time' tended to destroy far more than it created.

The first coins minted during the reign of Mary, the elder daughter of King Henry VIII, bore the motto *Veritas temporis filia* – 'Truth, daughter of time'. Mary Tudor was a devout Catholic who tried to undo some of the damage wreaked in her father's name. If she was 'Truth', then Henry VIII was 'time': the same 'time', which, as Shakespeare would lament, had razed the lofty towers of the old religious houses, leaving only 'Bare ruin'd choirs, where late the sweet birds sang.'

King Henry's determination to abandon Queen Katherine and wed Anne Boleyn had set in motion a seemingly unstoppable process of ruin and redistribution. The Shakespeares were directly affected – Richard Shakespeare lost his post of bailiff to the Wroxall priory – as were most families in the land.

Anne Boleyn would not live to see the results of King Henry's obsession with her. Married in secret in 1533, the couple had a child – the future Queen Elizabeth I – but Henry soon grew tired of his demanding wife and claimed that she had bewitched him. Anne was charged with adultery, incest and treason, and was beheaded on 19 May 1536. Within days, King Henry had married Jane Seymour, who would finally present him with the son and heir he so wanted.

THE DEATH of King Henry VIII in 1547 roughly coincided with the start of John Shakespeare's apprenticeship. He left the rented farm in the village of Snitterfield to train in the nearby town of Stratford as a glover and 'whittawer' specialising in fine leather goods.

Fewer than 2,000 souls inhabited Stratford, where there were almost as many elm trees as there were people. The glove-making trade was popular: between 1570 and 1630 at least twenty-three glovers were based in the town. Which of them took the teenage John Shakespeare under his wing is unknown. It might have been William Badger. By 1552, John Shakespeare was living next door to Badger's brother on Henley Street. George Badger, John's neighbour for many years, was a woollen draper and 'obstinate' Catholic who sired sixteen children and died at the age of 83, having played a minor role in the Gunpowder Plot of 1605.

John's period of apprenticeship lasted a little longer than the six-year reign of King Henry's priggish successor, Edward VI. Aged 9 at the time of his father's death, King Edward had been raised by Protestant tutors and insisted that the pace of religious reform should increase. More church lands were confiscated, more shrines vandalised. Those who were willing to plunder the Church made fortunes. Pilgrimages were banned. Plain tables replaced altars, and the parish priest became little more than a State-appointed mouthpiece.

King Edward died of consumption on 6 July 1553, aged just 15. Though an attempt was made to place Lady Jane Grey on the throne as a puppet-queen, Mary Tudor, the half-sister of Edward VI, swept into London on a wave of popular approval. The juggernaut of reform was halted. Under Queen Mary, England would return to the Catholic fold.

One of King Edward's last acts had been to grant Stratford a charter of incorporation. Local government had all but collapsed with the suppression of its medieval guild. The royal charter of 1553, allowing the town to establish a council of aldermen, came at an opportune moment for John Shakespeare, just as he was setting himself up in business.

He took his first step on the ladder of civic responsibility in 1556, when he was appointed one of two ale-tasters for the borough. Stratford stood on a vital trading route and relied on its brewing industry. As Will's friend Richard Quiney (whose godfather, Thomas Badger, was the father of John Shakespeare's neighbour) would later observe, the town was 'ancient in this trade of malting & have ever served to Birmingham from whence, Wales, Salop [Shropshire], Cheshire & Lancashire are also served'. In his mid-twenties, John Shakespeare was deemed 'able and discreet' enough to ensure that measures were accurate and standards were met.

In that same year, 1556, John bought his combined house and workshop on Henley Street, in what was one of the more affluent parts of the town. The following year, he married the youngest daughter of his father's landlord. Mary Arden was in her late teens and had grown up in a bustling single-storey farmhouse in Wilmcote, a couple of miles away to the north.

Via his mother, Mary, Will Shakespeare would be related to most of the leading Catholic dynasties in the Midlands: the Sheldons of Barcheston and Beoley, the Throckmortons of Coughton, the Catesbys of Lapworth and, most important of all, the Ardens of Park Hall, a manor which lay to the east of Birmingham. Though the precise relationship between Mary Arden and Edward Arden, the head of the family, is unclear, the family name gave Will Shakespeare an emotional claim to the 'wild wood' of Arden.

It was a region he would celebrate in *As You Like It* as a woodland retreat more 'free from peril than the envious court'. Like his spirited Rosalind, Will was 'forest-born'. This would prove to be a dangerous heritage.

THE REIGN of Queen Mary was cut short by a tumour. Had she lived longer, she might have reconciled her country to the Holy Mother Church. Many reformers fled to the Protestant centres of Europe when she became queen. Of those who stayed, some refused to temper their criticism of her Catholic faith. After an abortive rebellion, the more extreme Protestants were tried for heresy. The punishment was burning. Between February 1555 and the end of Mary's reign, some 280 zealots were put to death in this hideous manner, several of them within a 40-mile radius of Stratford-upon-Avon.

At the funeral for Queen Mary in November 1558, John White, Bishop of Winchester, warned that 'the Wolves be coming out of Geneva, and other places of *Germany*'. The Protestants were returning, their attitudes hardened, eager to avenge the deaths of their martyrs and hopeful that Elizabeth, the red-haired daughter of King Henry and Anne Boleyn, would resume the process of reforming the Church and the State.

John Shakespeare became one of four unwaged constables for Stratford in 1558. Armed with a club, he would have dealt with any unrest in the town as the nation lurched again from Roman Catholicism to Protestantism.

That same tumultuous year saw the birth of John and Mary's first child, a daughter named Joan. Baptised by a Catholic priest, little Joan was buried a year or two later by a Protestant vicar. Mary Shakespeare gave birth to another daughter in 1562, but Margaret Shakespeare lived for less than a year.

No sooner had Elizabeth I ascended the throne than she signalled her intention to press ahead with the reforms initiated by her father. The Act of Supremacy required anyone taking public office to swear an oath of allegiance to the queen as supreme governor of the Church of England. The Act of Uniformity established the form that would be taken by the Church and made it a legal obligation for everyone to attend services on Sundays. All vestiges of 'popery' were to be removed from every church in the land.

John Shakespeare became chamberlain to the Stratford Corporation in 1561, making him treasurer to the town and manager of its civic properties. In January 1564, he authorised the payment of two shillings to workmen for 'defaysing ymages in the chapell'.

The chapel of the Guild of the Holy Cross stood on the corner of Church Street, opposite the Great House which John's eldest son would eventually buy. The interior of the chapel had been a riot of colour, the walls painted with murals depicting St George and the dragon, the martyrdom of Thomas Becket, the Exultation of the Cross, the Dance of Death and the Last Judgement.

Under John's supervision, these images were 'defaced' – covered over with whitewash. Further payments were issued in 1565 and 1566 for the breaking of the rood screen and the removal of a large painted cross. The Corporation had left it as long as it dared, waiting until the town's leading Catholic citizen, William Clopton, had gone into exile, before complying with the royal command. Even then, the steps taken to despoil the chapel's imagery were half-hearted: some of the medieval murals can still be seen today.

John Shakespeare supplemented his income from glove making with a little 'brogging' or trading in wool without a licence. Stratford had links with the sheep-farming communities of the Cotswolds and, further afield, with Wales. In 1564, a Welshman named Lewes ap Williams was elected to serve as bailiff or mayor to the Corporation.

John's illicit sideline might have occasioned a journey or two into Wales, and it was on just such a journey that he possibly visited the shrine of St Winefride at Holywell in Flintshire. Tradition held that St Winefride, a chaste noblewoman, was decapitated by a jealous lover; a spring had burst forth where her head hit the ground. The well-water turned pebbles red, and the shrine of St Winefride – the 'Lourdes of Wales' – came to be associated with matters gynaecological. The last Catholic monarch of Britain, James II, visited the well in 1687 to pray for a healthy son and was rewarded with the birth of James Francis Edward Stuart, the 'Old Pretender', the following June.

After six years of marriage, John and Mary Shakespeare were childless, two daughters having died in infancy. There is, as we shall see, some evidence that John did make a pilgrimage to St Winefride's Well to pray for a male child, regardless of the fact that the law forbade such traditional Catholic practices as 'well-wishing'.

With or without St Winefride's influence, a boy was born to John and Mary on the feast day of St George, Sunday 23 April 1564.

It is not known who stood as godfather to William Shakespeare. The possibilities include the glove-maker William Badger and a whittawer, William Wilson, another of John's Henley Street neighbours. There was also a certain 'Allen' who was paid by John Shakespeare in 1564 for 'teaching the children'. Charlotte Carmichael Stopes, writing in 1907, gave his full name as William Allen.

One William Allen who was in the area was an Oxford-educated Lancastrian who had left England in 1561 because he refused to swear an oath of allegiance to the Protestant queen. Dr William Allen returned to work secretly as a Catholic missionary in 1562, first in his native Lancashire and then in the Oxfordshire region, before finally quitting his homeland forever in 1565. He was ordained as a priest and, on Michaelmas Day 1568, he founded the first English College for Catholics at Douai in northern France.

The possibility exists that Will Shakespeare was named in honour of Dr – later Cardinal – William Allen. Perhaps John Shakespeare felt that he owed it to his supernatural patron, St Winefride, to baptise his firstborn son with the name of a leading Catholic dissident who had been 'teaching the children' of Stratford when Will was born. He would soon have reason to be thankful that he did. An entry in the register of Holy Trinity Church, Stratford, records that, on 11 July 1564, 'Here began the plague'.

The dreaded contagion lingered in the town for six months, claiming more than 200 lives. Roger Greene, who lived a couple of doors up from the Shakespeares on Henley Street, lost four children to the outbreak of 1564. But the infant Will Shakespeare survived.

THE FAMILY grew: Gilbert Shakespeare was born in 1566, then Joan in 1569; Ann Shakespeare followed in 1571 (she died at the age of 8), Richard in 1574 and, lastly, Edmund Shakespeare in 1580.

John Shakespeare became an alderman of Stratford in 1565. Three years later, he was elected bailiff, the town's equivalent of mayor. The combination of civic success, material prosperity and marriage into the local gentry inspired him to apply for a coat of arms which would reflect his social status. But for reasons which have never been properly explained, John's application was left to gather dust on a shelf at the College of Arms for three decades.

The first hints that all was not well came in 1570, when John became Chief Alderman of Stratford. He was informed against twice in that year for demanding excessive interest on business loans. Known as 'usury', this practice had been outlawed in 1552 as a 'vice most odious and detestable'. Though John rode out that particular storm, he was accused in 1572 of illegally trading in large quantities of wool. The same man – James Langrake of Whittlebury in Northamptonshire – informed against him on both occasions. Langrake had been accused of raping a servant in 1570; he appears to have been one of the many criminals who were encouraged by the Elizabethan regime to betray others for personal gain.

The beginnings of John's troubles coincided with a nationwide crackdown on Catholics. The religious policies of Queen Elizabeth and her Protestant ministers had provoked a violent uprising in the northern counties in 1569. Rather too late for the northern rebels, Pope Pius V issued a papal bull, *Regnans in excelsis*, in February 1570. The bull denounced Elizabeth as 'the pretended Queen of England and the servant of crime' and released her Catholic subjects from their allegiance to her.

The Church had never acknowledged the legitimacy of Elizabeth's birth – even her father, King Henry, had declared her illegitimate – and this raised doubts about her right to rule. There were many who believed that her cousin, Mary, Queen of Scots, held the stronger claim to the English throne. A confirmed Catholic, Mary Stuart had fled from her Protestant persecutors in Scotland, throwing herself on Elizabeth's mercy in 1568. But Elizabeth was jealous of her beautiful cousin and kept her prisoner for the remainder of her days.

The ill-judged papal bull of 1570 inflamed an already tense situation. Mary, Queen of Scots, instantly became a greater threat to the excommunicated Elizabeth and her Protestant supporters. The massacre of thousands of Protestants in France in 1572 only ramped up the hostility of the English Protestants towards their Catholic neighbours. Drastic anti-Catholic legislation was introduced in 1570 and 1572. The fact that John Shakespeare's legal difficulties stemmed from that time, and that his application for a coat of arms was overlooked, is unlikely to have been a mere coincidence.

THINGS CAME to a head in 1575, when Will Shakespeare was 11. Master John Shakespeare made one of his most significant purchases that year, extending his Henley Street premises by buying the western two-thirds of the building. The Shakespeare family now owned one of the largest properties in Stratford, part of which survives to this day as the Shakespeare Birthplace museum.

Also in 1575, an event took place that would make a lasting impression on Will Shakespeare.

There had been much gossip and speculation about the relationship between Queen Elizabeth and her favourite, Robert Dudley, especially after Dudley's first wife died in a mysterious accident. In 1564, Elizabeth had raised Dudley to the earldom of Leicester. By the mid-1570s, however, the earl was losing his youthful glamour, and in the summer of 1575 he gambled a fortune on nineteen days of 'princely pleasures' designed to seduce his fickle monarch.

The venue for the 'princely pleasures' was Leicester's renovated castle at Kenilworth, 12 miles north of Stratford. On 18 July, a water pageant was staged for the queen's amusement. It opened with a prologue spoken by Triton 'upon a swimming mermaid', after which the Lady of the Lake and her nymphs appeared on 'floating Islands' and Arion sang a 'delectable ditty' while seated on a mechanical dolphin, 24 feet in length, with a small orchestra housed in its belly. Unfortunately, Arion's voice was 'hoarse and unpleasant', but he saved the day by tearing off his mask and announcing that 'he was none of Arion, not he, but honest Harry Goldingham, which blunt discovery', a witness wrote, 'pleased the Queen better than if it had gone through the right way'.

A mechanical dolphin would have been a memorable sight. Will referred to it, many years later, in the opening moments of *Twelfth Night* – 'like Arion on the dolphin's back, / I saw him hold acquaintance with the waves / So long as I could see.' The same remarkable scene was recalled by Oberon in *A Midsummer Night's Dream*:

> Thou rememb'rest
> Since once I sat upon a promontory
> And heard a mermaid on a dolphin's back
> Uttering such dulcet and harmonious breath
> That the rude sea grew civil at her song
> And certain stars shot madly from their spheres
> To hear the sea-maid's music.

Impressive as they were, the 'princely pleasures' of 1575 marked the start of a protracted period of disaster for the Shakespeare family. Elizabeth's visit had cost the Earl of Leicester a staggering sum and availed him nothing: the Virgin Queen moved on, 'in maiden meditation, fancy-free', as Will would put it. Leicester's dreams of becoming the de facto King of England were dashed.

Adding insult to injury, the High Sheriff of Warwickshire had refused to wear the earl's livery during the queen's visit and had called Leicester an 'upstart' and an 'adulterer'.

Leicester was a committed Protestant. The High Sheriff of Warwickshire in 1575 was a Catholic. He was none other than Edward Arden, the head of Will's mother's family.

Warwickshire quickly divided along tribal, sectarian lines. The Protestant followers of the Earl of Leicester now had an excuse to terrorise the Catholics who sided with Edward Arden of Park Hall.

One of Leicester's most puritanical supporters was Sir Thomas Lucy of Charlecote, near Stratford. Sir Thomas had been knighted by Leicester in 1565, and the queen had visited his Charlecote Park home in 1572. His mother, Anne Fermer, came from East Neston in Northamptonshire, her family being the lords of the manor which included the village of Whittlebury, home to a certain James Langrake. Sir Thomas Lucy, in a show of loyalty to the queen at the time of her visit to his estate, had made use of James Langrake to accuse John Shakespeare of illegal business transactions.

Sir Thomas Lucy had been eager to make life difficult for Alderman Shakespeare. Now, Leicester's quarrel with Edward Arden presented him with a golden opportunity. Suddenly, after twenty years of steadfast public service, John Shakespeare stopped attending meetings of the Stratford Corporation. He also ceased going to church – for fear, it was claimed, of being prosecuted for debt. In an attempt to protect himself from the seizure of his assets, John began selling or mortgaging his various properties to family members on the understanding that they would revert to him after a set time.

As a child, Will Shakespeare would have seen his father proudly escorted to the guild hall beside the Guild Chapel by mace-bearing sergeants in buff uniforms. But as Will entered his teens, his father became a furtive recluse, disposing of his more obvious wealth and keeping a very low profile indeed.

HE HAD reasons to be fearful. John Shakespeare was a prominent figure in Stratford-upon-Avon. Through his marriage, he was connected to the extended Arden family, and it is possible that his eldest son received part of his education at Park Hall, deep in the Warwickshire Woodland.

One of Will Shakespeare's cousins had been tutored at Park Hall by Edward Arden. Two years older than Will, Edward Throckmorton of the Catholic clan based at Coughton, 8 miles from Stratford, was 'distinguished for his perfection in every kind of virtue requisite for constituting a saintly youth'. In 1580, Edward Throckmorton departed for the English College in Rome, dying there two years later, aged 20. Before he left England, Throckmorton had established a Catholic school of his own, to which 'other youths flocked from all parts of the county for education as well in letters as in virtue'.

Henry Foley, writing his *Records of the English Province of the Society of Jesus* in 1878, would observe that Edward Throckmorton 'attracted all hearts to himself by his charming affability, sweetness, and sedateness of manner', so that many, 'and those not of the lowest class, begged earnestly of the uncle with whom he lived that their children might be admitted into Edward's service, with the intention that they should be instructed by him, and moulded according to his own character'.

The possibility that Will Shakespeare was educated, at least in part, by the uncle – Edward Arden – with whom Edward Throckmorton lived before his departure for Rome is seldom entertained by his biographers. As the eldest son of Alderman Shakespeare, Will would have qualified for a free place at the King's New School in Stratford. But even that institution was riddled with Catholicism. The schoolmaster there during Will's teen years was Simon Hunt, who defected to the English College set up by Dr William Allen in France, as did the brother of Hunt's successor, John Cottam. Robert Debdale of Shottery, hard by Stratford, left the King's New School to train overseas for the priesthood, as did George Cawdrey, who lived across the street from the house in which Will Shakespeare grew up.

The extent to which the Stratford Corporation was complicit in hiring Catholic schoolmasters and facilitating the defections of those who wished to continue their schooling at Dr William Allen's English colleges is unclear. But there is no doubt that friends, neighbours and kinsmen of Will Shakespeare made the journey into exile: they included his cousin Edward Throckmorton, who died in Rome, and one Robert Arden of Warwickshire, who eventually became Canon of Toledo.

Dr William Allen had founded his first English College at Douai, in a part of France that was then under Spanish control. When Protestant forces took control of Douai, Allen reopened his college at Rheims, in the forested region of the Ardennes. For some fifteen years, from 1578 to

1593, there was a direct link between Ardennes and the Forest of Arden, and when Will came to write his *As You Like It* in 1599 he was happy to blur the distinction between his native region and the home of the Catholic exiles.

As with Shakespeare's England, the world of *As You Like It* is one of division. A new order has overthrown the old. Duke Frederick has usurped the place of Duke Senior, banishing his brother to a wandering life in the forest, where the exiles live 'like the old Robin Hood of England'.

Orlando, the youngest son of Sir Rowland de Bois, has also been disinherited by his brother, who treats him like an animal and denies him an education. 'The world esteemed thy father honourable,' says the usurping Duke Frederick to Orlando, 'But I did find him still mine enemy.' Much the same might have been said to Will Shakespeare by the ultra-Protestant Sir Thomas Lucy.

Orlando is warned that his brother is out to get him: 'Your virtues, gentle master, / Are sanctified and holy traitors to you.' In a world driven by greed and envy, honesty and a noble disposition are seen as threatening to the social order, a kind of treason. As Duke Frederick remarks of his 'gentle' niece, Rosalind, 'the people praise her for her virtues / And pity her for her good father's sake'.

Orlando and Rosalind are banished, like their fathers before them, to the Forest of Arden or Ardennes. Disguised as a boy, Rosalind discloses that 'an old religious uncle of mine taught me to speak'. This same uncle is mentioned by Orlando who, unaware that the 'forest-born' boy is in fact his beloved Rosalind, confirms that he:

> ... hath been tutored in the rudiments
> Of many desperate studies by his uncle,
> Whom he reports to be a great magician
> Obscurèd in the circle of this forest.

Will Shakespeare, too, had an 'old religious uncle' who tutored youths in the heart of the forest: Edward Arden, who was now a marked man.

7

Herne the Hunter

DURING HIS travels through the Midlands in the early 1560s, Dr William Allen had concluded that many people only attended Protestant church services because they were forced to by law. They would, he presumed, readily embrace the Catholic faith again – irrespective of the penalties for doing so – if they had priests to minister to their needs. Consequently, Allen set up his colleges in Europe to train young Englishmen for the priesthood.

The Elizabethan government had sworn to detain, interrogate and execute any priest who entered the country. Those who were schooled in Dr Allen's English colleges were under no illusions: to return to their homeland was to face the likelihood of imprisonment, torture and a horrific death.

There were English spies, informers and *agents provocateurs* stationed throughout Europe. By the time the first Jesuit priests were preparing to cross the Channel in the summer of 1580, their descriptions had already been passed on to the Privy Council.

Arriving at Dover, Thomas Cottam was instantly arrested. The younger brother of John Cottam, master of the King's New School in Stratford, Thomas was found to be carrying a letter and Catholic keepsakes from Robert Debdale to his family in Shottery.

Edmund Campion and Robert Persons fared better. Persons, a West Countryman with an impudent swagger, landed at Dover on 17 June and bluffed his way past the officials. Campion, a brilliant Oxford scholar who wrote plays for his fellow Jesuits, arrived a week later, disguised as a jewel merchant. Both men quickly made their way northwards to Warwickshire.

At some point in the summer of 1580, John Shakespeare met with Campion or Persons, perhaps at Bushwood Hall in leafy Lapworth, where Father Campion was a guest of the Catesbys; Father Persons, meanwhile, stayed with Edward Arden at Park Hall and at the Snitterfield home of Edward Grant, a business associate of John Shakespeare's.

It seems likely that John met with Edmund Campion. John's youngest son was born that year and given the name Edmund. The secret meeting was the occasion on which John Shakespeare received his copy of the 'Testament of the Last Will of the Soul', originally composed by Cardinal Carlo Borromeo, Archbishop of Milan, with whom Campion and Persons had spent several days as they travelled from Rome to England. Later found squirreled away among the rafters of the Shakespeare family home on Henley Street, John's 'Testament' was one of many distributed by the Jesuits. The following year, in 1581, Dr William Allen noted that Father Persons needed another 'three or four thousand or more of the *Testaments*, for many persons desire to have them'.

By signing his name to the 'Testament', Will's father promised to 'live and die obedient unto the Catholic, Roman & Apostolic Church' and called upon the 'glorious and ever Virgin Mary' to be his 'chief executrix', along with his personal patron, whom he named in the document as 'saint Winefrid'.

John's copy of the 'Testament' is an embarrassment to those scholars who like to think of Will and his family as conforming Protestants. It branded Will's father as a dissident, potentially a traitor. John Shakespeare identified St Winefride as his particular patron, lending weight to the possibility that he had made an illegal pilgrimage to her Holywell shrine to pray for a son. That son was 16 when his father received his copy of the 'Testament'. John had anticipated the arrival of the Jesuits, naming his lastborn son Edmund in honour, perhaps, of Father Campion, much as the name of his firstborn son might well have been inspired by Dr William Allen.

In that heady summer, when the first Jesuit priests came to succour the beleaguered Catholics, Alderman Shakespeare was ready to confirm his commitment to the faith of his forefathers.

CAMPION'S NEXT destination was the northern county of Lancashire. It is possible that one of the Jesuit's travelling companions was the teenager, Will Shakespeare.

As with Wales, there were links between Stratford and Lancashire, forged by the wool and brewing trades. But there was more to these connections than malt and fleeces. The Stratford Corporation repeatedly hired Lancashire-born masters to teach the schoolchildren. Only one non-Lancastrian taught at the King's New School during Shakespeare's youth, and that was Thomas Jenkins, who had been tutored at Oxford by Edmund Campion.

Lancashire, specifically the area around Preston, and the Midlands, particularly around Stratford, were hotbeds of Catholic resistance. They formed two points of a triangle, the third point being Dr William Allen's English College at Rheims.

The Stratford schoolmaster in 1580 was John Cottam, whose brother Thomas was seized at Dover that summer. The home of the Cottam brothers was Dilworth, near Preston, where the neighbouring estate belonged to Alexander Hoghton. The Cottams knew the Hoghtons well: in his will, Alexander Hoghton left his 'servant' John Cottam a generous reward. In that same will, dated 3 August 1581, Alexander bequeathed his musical instruments and his players' costumes to his half-brother, Thomas Hoghton:

> And if he will not keep and maintain players, then it is my will that Sir Thomas Hesketh, knight, shall have the same Instruments and play clothes. And I most heartily require the said Sir Thomas to be friendly unto Fulk Gillam and William Shakeshafte now dwelling with me, and either to take them into his Service or else to help them to some good master, as my trust is he will.

Alexander Hoghton also made provision for 'William Shakeshafte' to receive an annuity of 40 shillings.

Having stayed with William Catesby at Lapworth, Edmund Campion made his way up to the Hoghton estate in Lancashire. It is now widely accepted that Will Shakespeare made the same journey, and that he was the 'player' identified as William Shakeshafte in Alexander Hoghton's will of 1581.

The Shakeshafte surname was not uncommon in the Preston area. As such, it would have offered some degree of cover for a young poet residing in a Catholic household, far from his proper home.

John Aubrey, the seventeenth-century gatherer of biographical titbits, remarked that Shakespeare 'understood Latin pretty well, for he had been in his younger years a schoolmaster in the country'. Aubrey's source was the son of one of Will's theatrical colleagues, and there were other contemporary references to Will having been a 'schoolmaster'.

An apostate priest would inform on ten Catholic households in Lancashire, including that of the Hoghtons, which kept 'recusants as schoolmasters' ('recusancy' being the refusal to attend Protestant church services). The priest divulged this information in 1592, at the same time as John Shakespeare was listed among the recusants – 'obstinate papists, shelterers of seminaries' – of Stratford.

One of the motives for Will to have removed himself to a remote part of the country was to relieve his family of an additional financial burden. At

16, he was liable to be fined for recusancy. He could avoid this by taking refuge in a large private house and acting as tutor to the children of the family. The fact that 'William Shakeshafte' was associated in Alexander Hoghton's will with 'play clothes' and musical instruments would suggest that Will doubled as an entertainer, a young man of many parts.

He was probably recommended to the Hoghton family by the Stratford schoolmaster, John Cottam. Alexander Hoghton expressed the hope, in his will of 3 August 1581, that Sir Thomas Hesketh of nearby Rufford would be 'friendly' to William Shakeshafte. Dr William Allen, notorious founder of the English colleges in Europe, was the brother-in-law of one William Hesketh of Lancashire. The wife of Thomas Hesketh was also a cousin by marriage to Thomas Savage, a successful London goldsmith. Born at Rufford, near Preston, Thomas Savage would be named by Will Shakespeare in 1599 as one of two trustees for his interest in the ground lease of the Globe Theatre.

There is, then, a strong chance that Will followed or even accompanied Father Edmund Campion up to Lancashire, where he found employment as a tutor, musician and 'player' in the Catholic household of Alexander Hoghton. But the date of Hoghton's will indicates that Shakespeare's time in Lancashire was cut short.

On 4 August 1581 – the day after Alexander drafted his will – the Privy Council in London ordered a search for 'certain books and papers which Edmund Campion has confessed he left at the house of one Richard Hoghton in Lancashire'.

Campion's travels had brought him to Lyford Grange in Oxfordshire. Anxious to return to Hoghton Hall to retrieve his papers, the Jesuit was persuaded to hold another Mass at Lyford on 16 July 1581. The government's agents swooped. Campion was discovered hiding with two other priests in a secret chamber.

The capture of Campion sent a tidal wave of panic through the recusant community. Richard Hoghton and Bartholomew Hesketh were arrested in Lancashire. Sir William Catesby of Lapworth was also apprehended. A watch was placed on Edward Arden of Park Hall and his Throckmorton relations at Coughton Court.

Alexander Hoghton hastily drew up his will and died, in suspicious circumstances, on 12 September.

Another Campion contact who quickly made his will before his arrest on 4 August was Henry Wriothesley, Second Earl of Southampton and father to Will Shakespeare's future patron. The earl would be found dead in the Tower of London on 4 October 1581.

Father Robert Persons fled the country. John Cottam, whose brother was now a prisoner in the Tower of London, resigned his teaching post in Stratford and returned to his native Lancashire; his replacement, Alexander Aspinall, was yet another Lancastrian schoolmaster.

With so many Catholics running for cover, it is hardly surprising that 'William Shakeshafte' decided he would be better off at home. But Stratford was in turmoil. The Earl of Leicester's supporters – chief among them Sir Thomas Lucy of Charlecote – were clamping down on anyone suspected of having trafficked with the Jesuits. Will Shakespeare had little choice but to disappear until the storm had passed.

THE HAMLET of Earl's Common lies 16 miles west of Stratford in the rolling countryside of the ancient Forest of Feckenham.

Roy Palmer, in *The Folklore of Worcestershire*, noted that Shakespeare is said to have spent eight months hiding at Earl's Common 'while waiting for some trouble to blow over at home'. Reputedly, Will stayed at The Drainers' Arms, a half-timbered inn which burned down in 1892. 'Drainer' was almost certainly a corruption of 'Dragoner' – the village inn was probably named after George, the dragon-slaying patron saint of England.

Like its Warwickshire sister, the Forest of Arden, Feckenham was recusant country. At Temple Broughton, barely a mile to the north of Earl's Common, the future martyr and saint, Arthur Bell, would be born in 1590. A mile to the south-east of Earl's Common stood Huddington Court, the home of a Catholic family named Wintour. Robert Wintour was then 13 years old; his brother Thomas was 10. Their sister Dorothy would marry John Grant of Snitterfield, and all three men would join with Robert Catesby of Lapworth in the Gunpowder Plot of 1605.

Shakespeare left hints that he had indeed gone to ground in the Forest of Feckenham. In his *History of Henry the Fourth*, he created one of his most popular comic characters by lampooning the early Protestant martyr, Sir John Oldcastle. William Brooke, Lord Cobham, was one of Oldcastle's descendants. Cobham served as Lord Chamberlain to Queen Elizabeth from 1596 to 1597. He objected to Will's portrayal of his ancestor, causing Shakespeare to change the name of his larger-than-life character from Oldcastle to Falstaff.

A legend first recorded in 1702 holds that Elizabeth herself commanded Shakespeare to write a play showing Falstaff in love, giving Will fourteen days to come up with the script. The result was *The Merry Wives of Windsor*, which appeared in 1597 – the year in which Lord Hunsdon, Cobham's successor as Lord Chamberlain, was installed as a Knight of the Garter at Windsor. The queen did not attend this event, but she was present at the Garter Feast on 23 April, and so Will's new play was probably performed at Westminster on his thirty-third birthday.

Under pressure, Shakespeare had fallen back on familiar ground. He presented Sir John Falstaff as a penniless guest at the Garter Inn – Windsor's answer to The Drainers' Arms at Earl's Common – foolishly trying to woo two married women at the same time. The frothy comedy made light of the terrifying experience of having to hide from government agents in chimneys and laundry baskets.

Another hiding place for a recusant on the run is suggested during Falstaff's final attempt at seduction, which takes place at Herne's Oak in Windsor Great Park.

Herne is a demonic figure in British folklore. It is probable, though, that Shakespeare singlehandedly invented the tradition that Herne the Hunter haunts an ancient oak tree in the grounds of Windsor Castle. Herne's earlier associations were with the Forest of Feckenham in Worcestershire: it was said that Herne had killed a sacred stag belonging to the Abbess of Bordesley, for which he was condemned to ride the night sky with his pack of spectral hounds.

Charlotte Carmichael Stopes wrote in 1901 that one Roger Shakespeare, who was buried in 1558, was 'by some supposed to be the old monk of Bordesley'. Given the family connection, Will Shakespeare must have known of the tale of Herne the Hunter and the 'sacred stag' of Bordesley Abbey. In *The Merry Wives*, he transferred the legend from Feckenham Forest to Windsor.

At Broughton Green, a few fields away from Earl's Common, stands the Temple Oak, 11 metres in girth and entirely hollow. Estimates of its age put it at more than 1,000 years old. The Temple Oak was ancient – and quite possibly hollow – in Shakespeare's day.

It is to the hollow oak that Falstaff makes his way by night, disguised as Herne, for the climax of *The Merry Wives of Windsor*. There, he is beaten and whipped by the Fairy Queen and her elves. Behind the comedy, there was a harsh message for Elizabeth, the 'Fairy Queen'.

The last Catholic Abbot of Westminster had been John de Feckenham. Born in the Forest of Feckenham, a few miles from Earl's Common, he had served as chaplain to the Bishop of Worcester, John Bell of Temple Broughton – home of the Temple Oak – and, later, as chaplain to the Worcestershire clergyman Edward Bonner, Bishop of London. In the time of Queen Mary, John de Feckenham interceded on behalf of the Princess Elizabeth when she was sent to the Tower of London in the wake of the Kentish rebellion; risking the wrath of the queen, Feckenham pleaded for Elizabeth's life and liberty. He sat in the first Parliament of Elizabeth's reign but refused to alter his religion as the new queen demanded, and so he was committed to the Tower in 1560.

Feckenham spent the rest of his life as a prisoner, ending up in the internment camp for Catholics at Wisbech Castle in Cambridgeshire, where he died in October 1585. During this time he was subjected to persistent attempts to convert him by the ultra-Protestant reformer and priest-hunter, Robert Horne.

Horne had been appointed Bishop of Winchester by Queen Elizabeth, replacing John White who, at the funeral for Queen Mary, had warned that the 'Wolves' were emerging from their German exile to spread their Protestant doctrines in England. But it was as the persecutor of John de Feckenham that Will invoked Horne the priest-hunter in the diabolical form of Herne.

Robert Horne occasionally spelt his name 'Herne'. A 1602 pirated copy of *The Merry Wives* even replaced 'Herne' with 'Horne'.

> There is an old tale goes that Herne the hunter,
> Sometime a keeper here in Windsor Forest,
> Doth all the winter time at still midnight
> Walk round about an oak with great ragg'd horns:
> And there he blasts the trees, and takes the cattle,
> And makes milch-kine yield blood, and shakes a chain
> In a most hideous and dreadful manner.
> You have heard of such a spirit, and well you know
> The superstitious idle-headed eld
> Received, and did deliver to our age,
> This tale of Herne the hunter for a truth.

During the eight months that Will spent lying low at The Drainers' Arms, he might well have escaped from the Horne-like pursuivants by clambering inside the Temple Oak as the search for Edmund Campion's fellow Jesuits, and those who had given them shelter, dragged on through the winter of 1581–82. The shameful treatment of the idol-worshipping Catholic elder, John de Feckenham, prompted the nightmarish image of the remorseless Herne, rattling his chains in 'a most hideous and dreadful manner'.

Whatever Queen Elizabeth might have hoped for when she required Shakespeare to show Falstaff in love, this was not it. Recalling the fearful aftermath of Campion's capture, Will gave Elizabeth a stark reminder of the 'superstitious' cleric who had stepped in to save her life, and whom she subsequently imprisoned for twenty-five years.

Invited to laugh at those Catholics who hid in hollow oaks and baskets of dirty linen, the 'Fairy Queen' was then encouraged to lead the whipping and pinching of a reprobate posing as her very own priest-hunter, Robert Horne or 'Herne'.

IN THE Tower of London, the 'Seditious Jesuit' Edmund Campion was tortured and all his fingernails 'dragged out'. On the morning of 1 December 1581, he and two other priests were strapped to wicker hurdles and hauled slowly through the streets to Tyburn, near today's Marble Arch. There, in the icy rain, the three priests were hanged by the neck, cut down while they were still breathing, and systematically hacked into pieces.

Thomas Cottam was executed in like fashion on 30 May 1582. He had been carrying a letter and some trinkets for the family of Robert Debdale when he was apprehended. Debdale, a former pupil at the King's New School in Stratford, had returned to England in late June 1580, but he was promptly caught and held in the Gatehouse prison next door to Westminster Abbey.

Debdale was discharged on 10 September 1582, and by the following March he was back at the English College in Rheims, where he was later ordained. Using the alias 'Palmer', he made his way back to England and was arrested again. On 8 October 1586, Robert Debdale of Shottery was hanged, drawn and quartered at Tyburn.

Sometime between the execution of Thomas Cottam on 30 May 1582 and the release of Robert Debdale from the Gatehouse in September, Will Shakespeare emerged from his eight months in hiding at Earl's Common. It was also towards the end of this period that John Shakespeare put in his last appearance at a meeting of the Stratford Corporation. On Wednesday 2 September 1582, John walked to the guild hall on Church Street to vote for a new mayor.

There were three candidates. Adrian Quiney lived almost directly opposite the Shakespeares on Henley Street; his grandson would eventually marry Will's daughter. John Sadler was one of the wealthiest property owners in Stratford; his son and daughter-in-law would stand as godparents to Will Shakespeare's twins. And then there was George Whateley, a prosperous woollen draper who lived a few doors down from the Shakespeare family.

John Shakespeare cast his vote for Sadler, who declined the office on the grounds of ill health. Adrian Quiney became bailiff by default. George Whateley received just two votes – one from Quiney's son, Richard, and the other from William Smith, haberdasher, of Henley Street.

Will's father had not attended a single meeting of the council since January 1577. His decision to be present at the meeting of 2 September 1582 appears to have been motivated, as much as anything, by the desire to be seen to be voting *against* his near-neighbour, George Whateley.

Less than three months later, on 27 November, the consistory court of the Diocese of Worcester issued a licence permitting 'Willelmum Shaxpere' to marry 'Annam Whateley de Temple Grafton'. The licence was needed because Will and Anne Whateley were anxious to get married in a hurry.

The very next day – Wednesday 28 November – two Stratford farmers rode the 20-odd miles to Worcester and laid down a bond of £40, indemnifying the bishop against any repercussions arising from the hasty marriage of Will Shakespeare to 'Anne Hathwey of Stratford in the Diocese of Worcester, maiden'.

The term 'maiden' was a trifle optimistic. Anne Hathaway was already pregnant.

Somehow, Will Shakespeare had received the bishop's permission to marry two women. The bond laid down by Fulke Sandells and John Richardson ensured that, rather than marrying 'Annam Whateley' of Temple Grafton, Will wed 'Anne Hathwey' of Shottery.

IT IS routine procedure for scholars to aver that 'Anne Whateley' did not exist: she was simply a scribal error, a slip of the pen. But in the Worcestershire County Archive there is an eight-and-a-half page document headed '*Ultimo Testamentii John Whateley de Hendeley in Ardena*'. Probated in 1554, John Whateley's will proves that there was an 'Anne Whateley' in the vicinity of Stratford-upon-Avon.

John Whateley, a draper of Henley-in-Arden, 8 miles north of Stratford, had married a woman from Lapworth. His will named their four daughters and five sons, including George Whateley, whose bid for the mayoralty of Stratford was opposed by John Shakespeare in 1582. Also named in Whateley's will was 'Agnes my daughter'.

The names Anne and Agnes (the 'g' was not pronounced) were interchangeable. Shakespeare's other Anne – Anne Hathaway – was named in *her* father's will as 'Agnes'. It is most likely that John Whateley's daughter Agnes was also known as Anne Whateley.

There was a strong streak of Catholicism in the Whateley family. George Whateley sponsored two of his brothers, John and Robert, to serve as secret priests in their hometown of Henley-in-Arden. This alone might account for John Shakespeare's decision to vote against his fellow alderman in September 1582, for by then Will's father was trying to distance himself from the 'papists' of the district. It is also probable that Agnes Whateley, like her brothers, remained true to the Catholic cause.

She would have been at least a dozen years older than Will Shakespeare. Local tradition associates her with 'haunted Hillborough', a sixteenth-century manor house 4 miles downriver from Stratford. Hillborough lay in the parish of Temple Grafton – the Bishop's court in Worcester referred to 'Annam Whateley' as being of Temple Grafton – and belonged to the Huband family, whose seat was at Ipsley in the Forest of Feckenham; Will Shakespeare would purchase a significant investment from Ralph Huband of Ipsley in 1605. The Hubands were intermarried with the influential Throckmortons of Coughton and the ultra-Catholic Sheldons of Beoley, near Ipsley. Hillborough Manor was almost certainly a Catholic safe-house. Anne – or Agnes – Whateley continued to haunt the isolated manor after her death in the form of a ghostly White Lady.

Two of Agnes Whateley's brothers functioned as underground priests, supported by their brother, George. Agnes, it would seem, served as a nun – an Augustinian 'White Lady'. Nuns were forbidden in Elizabethan England, and yet Shakespeare would later boast that one of his early sexual conquests was a 'sacred nun', a 'sister sanctified of holiest note'. In his strikingly personal poem 'A Lover's Complaint' (see Chapter 12), he devoted several stanzas to this mysterious 'sister' who had rejected many a suitor, only to fall for the honey tongue of the 18-year-old poet:

> 'O, pardon me, but that my boast is true!
> The accident which brought me to her eye
> Upon the moment did her force subdue,
> And now she would the cagèd cloister fly ...

'Religious love put out religion's eye', wrote Will. An 'accident' brought him to her, and as she nursed him back to health, Agnes' vow of chastity was undermined.

In his sonnets, Will would allude to his lameness – 'So I, made lame by Fortune's dearest spite'; 'And strength by limping sway disablèd'; 'Speak of my lameness, and I straight will halt' – while theatrical tradition has him specialising in playing older characters, such as Adam in *As You Like It*, for which a limp might have been appropriate. Perhaps, as Will flitted between Earl's Common and Stratford in 1582, evading the government's priest-hunters and Sir Thomas Lucy's men, he suffered an accident from which he recuperated at Hillborough Manor.

John Frith, the vicar of Temple Grafton, was described as an 'old priest and Unsound in religion' whose 'chiefest trade is to cure hawks that are hurt or diseased, for which purpose many do repair to him'. Frith had previously been reported for solemnising marriages outside the times stipulated by the authorities and without the regulation reading of the banns. The reason why Will had required a special licence to marry Agnes Whateley was because Advent was fast approaching, when nuptials were proscribed.

If a secret wedding did take place in the private oratory at Clopton House, as Stratford tradition would have it, then who better to perform the rites than the 'Unsound' old priest and bird-mender, John Frith of Temple Grafton?

SO MANY years his senior, Agnes Whateley would have been a mother-substitute and a reminder of Will's family past; she compares with those Shakespeare women who belonged to the Benedictine priory at Wroxall. Theirs was a love born of shared beliefs, a meeting of minds in a time of terror.

John Aubrey, writing in about 1681, disclosed that Shakespeare 'was wont to go to his native Country once a year'. He added: 'I think I have been told that he left 2 or 300 pounds per annum there and thereabout to a sister.' This cannot have been Shakespeare's only surviving sibling, Joan Hart, who was left much less than that in his will. Maybe it was to his beloved 'sister sanctified of holiest note' that Will made the more generous bequest.

There is also the remark of Will's earliest biographer, Nicholas Rowe, who stated in 1709 that Shakespeare 'had three daughters, of which two lived to be married'.

The Stratford records indicate that Will Shakespeare had two daughters and a son by Anne Hathaway. Rowe's reference to Will's third daughter is a mystery. It is notable, though, that Shakespeare's later plays, written when his thoughts were turning towards retirement, feature several long-lost daughters finally reunited with their errant fathers.

LOOKING BACK on his months on the run in the Forest of Feckenham, Will amused himself in *The Merry Wives of Windsor* by showing Falstaff's attempts to seduce two mature women. To one of these women, Mistress Page, he gave two children, William and Anne. The other, Mistress Ford, has two servants, John and Robert – which were also the names of Agnes Whateley's priestly brothers.

Agnes was an orphan. So was Anne Hathaway, whose father died in September 1581. Richard Hathaway had asked in his will to be 'honestly buried'. His son Bartholomew went further, expressing his hope to 'arise at the Latter Day and to receive the reward of His elect'. These were extreme Protestant sentiments. The Hathaways might have shared the tiny village of Shottery with the Catholic Debdale family, but their religious proclivities seem to have tended towards Puritanism.

Shottery was a little closer to Stratford than Temple Grafton. Quite what brought Will to Shottery in the summer of 1582 is unclear – perhaps it had something to do with the family of Robert Debdale, then a prisoner in the Gatehouse in London.

At 26, Anne Hathaway was eight years Will's senior. Her family apparently belonged to the hard-line Protestant faction. It could be that by impregnating her, Will Shakespeare was seeking some form of revenge for the deaths of the Jesuits, Campion and Cottam.

If that was the plan, it backfired. William Whateley, vicar of Crowle, was present at the consistory court in Worcester on 27 November 1582, when the licence was granted allowing Will Shakespeare to marry 'Annam Whateley'. The parish of Crowle lay adjacent to Earl's Common. William Whateley took over as vicar of Crowle after the Reverend John Whateley – Agnes' brother – left the Church of England to work secretly as a priest in his hometown of Henley.

It seems likely that William Whateley raised the alarm: word got back to Stratford that the 18-year-old Shakespeare boy was about to marry his 'sacred nun'. The next day, two friends of the late Richard Hathaway arrived in Worcester and laid down their £40 surety. Young Will was dragooned into a shotgun marriage with his Protestant Anne.

John Shakespeare, it is to be hoped, was satisfied with the arrangement. In the parlance of the time, his eldest son had become 'honest' – a loyal Protestant. Will's new wife moved into the family home on Henley Street, and in late May 1583, Anne gave birth to a baby girl. She was baptised Susanna, a name with Puritan connotations.

The question of Will's marriage to Anne Hathaway – was it a loveless match? – has been endlessly debated. The discovery of John Whateley's will adds another dimension to the problem. The marriage was surely haunted by the presence of a 'White Lady', Will's other Anne, whom he had jilted by marrying his 'second best bed'.

But Will's misfortune was literature's gain. His early comedies revolve around the theme of young lovers' confusion when faced with a choice of partners. *The Taming of the Shrew* is perhaps the most apposite. Opening with a sequence set in Will's native Warwickshire, the plot requires an evil-tempered harpy to be forcibly domesticated before her saintly sister can be wed.

Now that Agnes Whateley's existence can no longer be denied, we might wonder whether Shakespeare would rather have married his fair, heavenly 'Bianca' – the White lady of *The Taming of the Shrew* – instead of the dark and difficult 'Kate'.

8

Hall the Priest

FOUR MILES north of Stratford lay the manor of Edstone. John Somerville, the 23-year-old heir to the Edstone estate, had married Margaret, the daughter of Edward Arden of Park Hall.

On 25 October 1583, John Somerville set out for London, accompanied by a page from Edward Arden's household. He was going to assassinate Queen Elizabeth with a 'dag' – a primitive pistol – because 'she was the bane of the Catholic Church'.

Just south of the town of Banbury, the page deserted his young master, who was then apprehended by local officials at a wayside inn near the village of Aynho. Interrogated at Oxford and tortured in London, Somerville named others involved in his crazy scheme. He was condemned to a traitor's death.

Somerville was moved to Newgate prison on the eve of his execution. Within two hours of his arrival he was dead from strangulation.

Edward Arden was arrested at the London residence of the juvenile Earl of Southampton – Will Shakespeare's future patron. Denying that he was guilty of anything other than being a Catholic, Arden was hanged, drawn and quartered on 20 December 1583. His head, along with that of his Somerville son-in-law, was stuck on a pole over the southern gateway to London Bridge.

Also taken into custody were Arden's wife Mary, née Throckmorton, and Hugh Hall, a Catholic priest who masqueraded as a gardener while ministering to the Arden family. Strangely, the priest – who, it was claimed, had prompted John Somerville's suicide mission – was released after questioning. There can be little doubt that he was 'turned'; he next appears in the household of the Lord Chancellor and royal favourite, Sir Christopher Hatton.

Father Hugh Hall's knowledge of the Catholic network in the Midlands was pretty comprehensive. He had previously served Sir John Throckmorton of Coughton, Lord Windsor of Hewell Grange and the Sheldon brothers, Ralph and William, of Beoley. When the news broke of Somerville's arrest, Father Hall had fled to Idlicote, south of Stratford, where he sought refuge with William Underhill before eventually being apprehended. In 1597, Underhill would sell a 'pretty house of brick and timber' to Will Shakespeare, who made it his home for the rest of his days.

WHAT HAD happened, precisely, is as clear as pitch. The Arden family would insist that since Midsummer, John Somerville had been 'affected with a frantic humour grown of jealousy conceived of his wife'. There had been no conspiracy – only the ravings of a young man who was temporarily deranged.

Whatever the circumstances, Somerville's capture allowed the authorities to move against a number of prominent Catholics whose aim, it was rumoured, had been to rescue Mary, Queen of Scots, from her long-term imprisonment and topple the regime of Elizabeth I. The plot was exposed when Edward Arden's close relative, Francis Throckmorton (son of Sir John, cousin of Lord Windsor), was arrested. Francis had been acting as an intermediary between the Catholic exiles (especially Dr William Allen, to whom he was related by marriage) and Mary's supporters at home. The government argued that Throckmorton, in collaboration with Henry Percy, Eighth Earl of Northumberland, had been conspiring with Mary's powerful French relations to mount an invasion of England.

Francis Throckmorton later retracted the confession which had been racked out of him in the Tower of London, but he was executed all the same in July 1584. The Earl of Northumberland was found dead in his cell in the Tower in June 1585. He had been shot through the heart.

The Stratford region had barely recovered from the backlash which followed the capture of Edmund Campion in 1581. Now, the rage of the local Puritans was unleashed once again. Those with connections to the Arden, Somerville and Throckmorton families were minutely scrutinised. On 31 October 1583 a warrant was issued for the seizure of 'such as shall be in any way akin to all touched, and to search their houses'.

The clerk to the Privy Council, Thomas Wilkes, moved into the Charlecote home of the magistrate, Member of Parliament and fanatical persecutor of Catholics, Sir Thomas Lucy, for fifteen days to supervise the clampdown. Wilkes wrote to the queen's spymaster, Sir Francis Walsingham, from Charlecote on 7 November:

Unless you can make Somerville, Arden, Hall the priest, Somerville's wife and his sister, to speak directly to those things which you desire to have discovered, it will not be possible for us here to find out more than is found already, for that the papists in this county greatly do work upon the advantage of clearing their houses of all shows of suspicion.

One of those 'shows of suspicion' would have been John Shakespeare's copy of the 'Testament of the Soul', which he had received from Campion in 1580. The testament, minus its front page, was prudently hidden among the rafters of the Shakespeare home on Henley Street, not to see the light of day again for 175 years.

'I WOULD there were no age between ten and three-and-twenty, or that youth would sleep out the rest,' wrote Will many years later, 'for there is nothing in the between but getting wenches with child, wronging the ancientry, stealing, fighting – hark you now, would any but these boiled-brains of nineteen and two-and-twenty hunt this weather?' These words come from one of his last plays, *The Winter's Tale*. They are spoken by an Old Shepherd just before he finds a baby girl who has been abandoned during a storm. The Old Shepherd's speech immediately follows Shakespeare's most famous stage direction: '*Exit, pursued by a bear.*'

The puritanical Earl of Leicester had adopted Warwickshire's emblem of the Bear and Ragged Staff, so that *Exit, pursued by a bear* could be interpreted as 'Vamoose, chased by Lord Leicester's henchmen.'

By the time Will wrote *The Winter's Tale*, he was himself an old poet or 'shepherd' reflecting on his troubled youth. The image of the Storm occurs frequently in his works, to the extent that it became the staple Gothic symbol of chaos and horror. But in Shakespeare's writings, the Storm plays a specific role: it is the defining metaphor for the Reformation as a cosmic crisis.

England was a ship tossed on a stormy sea. As Clare Asquith asserted in her study of *The Hidden Beliefs and Coded Politics of William Shakespeare*, the image of 'The Tempest' was as loaded in Shakespeare's day as 'The Blitz' was after the Second World War, or 'The Troubles' in the context of Northern Ireland.

The Storm was no generalised image of supernatural mischief – it was a recognised metaphor for sectarian madness and religious strife.

The English Reformation did not begin and end with Henry VIII's assault on the monasteries. It was an ongoing process which required the disenfranchisement and merciless extirpation of those who refused to adopt the State-imposed creed. Though there were some who advocated reform out of disgust with the complacency of the medieval Church, there were others for whom the Church of England was simply an expression of national identity, differentiating England from the mighty Spanish empire. And there were many for whom the Reformation meant little more than the chance to transfer wealth from the old aristocracy to the Protestant parvenus. The latter group was the most powerful of all, for they accrued their fortunes by picking over the carcase of the Church and squeezing the Catholics dry. The Storm might have begun as a genuine spiritual movement, but its violence was sustained by self-interest, greed and bigotry.

The Storm could strike at any moment. One reading of *The Winter's Tale* suggests that Will had abandoned his 'sacred nun' and baby daughter when he got caught up in a storm of his own. He married a Protestant and, like his father, made every effort to be seen to be conforming. This was Will's conflict: his personal Reformation; his spiritual 'tempest'.

As we have just seen, in *The Winter's Tale* he would remark that only 'these boiled-brains of nineteen and two-and-twenty' would go hunting in such a storm. Will was indeed 19 years old when his Somerville kinsman was arrested. John Somerville himself was 23.

We do not know what Will was up to at this time. But we do have the statement of John Aubrey, who gathered some information about the youthful Shakespeare from the people of Stratford. 'His father was a Butcher,' wrote Aubrey in his *Brief Lives*, 'and I have been told heretofore by some of the neighbours, that when he was a boy he exercised his father's Trade, but when he killed a Calf he would do it in a high style, and make a Speech.'

John Aubrey also noted, 'There was at this time another Butcher's son in this town that was held not at all inferior to him for a natural wit, his acquaintance and coetanean, but died young.'

Will's father was many things – a glover and whittawer, an alderman, a money-lender, a 'brogger' dealing illicitly in wool – but there is no evidence that he practised butchery as a trade. The townsfolk, however, told the inquisitive Aubrey that Will as a boy had been a 'Butcher', like his father, and that another 'Butcher's son', who was Will's friend and contemporary, had 'died young'.

Maybe the confusion arose from a mistake: the inability of Aubrey's informants to tell the difference between the Latin for 'wool-merchant' (*lanarius*) and 'butcher' (*lanius*). There is, though, another tradition which cast Will in the role of a poacher.

The story was told by Nicholas Rowe, Shakespeare's first biographer, in 1709. Will had fallen into 'ill Company', some of whom 'made a frequent practice of Deer-stealing'. The hot-headed Will Shakespeare was caught poaching a deer from Sir Thomas Lucy's manor of Charlecote, near Stratford. 'For this,' wrote Rowe, 'he was prosecuted by that Gentleman, as he thought, somewhat too severely; and in order to avenge that ill Usage, he made a Ballad upon him.'

Two versions of that ballad survive. In one, published in 1790 by Edmond Malone, Will mocked Sir Thomas Lucy as a cuckold:

Sir Thomas was too covetous
    To covet so much deer,
When horns enough upon his head
    Most plainly did appear.

The second version was heard sung in Stratford in the eighteenth century:

A parliament member, a justice of peace,
At home a poor scarecrow, at London an ass,
    If lousy is Lucy, as some folk miscall it,
    Then Lucy is lousy, whatever befall it ...

According to Nicholas Rowe, Will's alleged authorship of the ballad 'redoubled the Prosecution against him to that degree, that he was obliged to leave his Business and Family in *Warwickshire*, for some time, and shelter himself in *London*.'

There was no deer park at Charlecote in Shakespeare's day. The ballads need not have been written by Shakespeare at all. They simply reflect the local resentment towards a Puritan who empowered himself by hounding Catholics. But the legend of Shakespeare the deer poacher cannot be wholly dismissed.

WHEN A buck was killed, its penis and testicles were cut off and then its stomach was opened and its entrails removed. The head was often kept as a trophy while the rest of the body was chopped up.

Exactly the same treatment was meted out to convicted enemies of the State: they were hanged by the neck (sometimes for just a few seconds), then cut down from the rope and stripped naked. Their genitals were hacked off and thrown into a fire. Their stomachs were ripped open and their innards pulled out. The victim was expected to live long enough to see his still-beating heart held up by the executioner. Then his head was chopped off, parboiled, and mounted on a spike. His body was butchered and the four quarters displayed in different parts of the kingdom.

Many Catholic priests were hunted, caught and executed in this manner. We are reminded of the Feckenham tradition of Herne the hunter, forever damned for having slaughtered a sacred stag belonging to the Abbess of Bordesley.

Another word for an older male deer is a 'hart'. The 'sacred stag' of Bordesley – perhaps that 'old monk', Roger Shakespeare – was also, by way of a simple pun, a Sacred Heart.

Shakespeare made use of the imagery of the deer and its hunter in *The Merry Wives of Windsor* ('Divide me like a bribed buck, each a haunch'). In his *Tragedy of Julius Caesar*, Mark Antony apologises to the bleeding carcase of the assassinated Roman for being 'meek and gentle with these butchers': 'Pardon me, Julius. Here wast thou bayed, brave hart; / Here thou didst fall, and here thy hunters stand / Signed in thy spoil and crimsoned in thy lethe.' But it was in *As You Like It*, written at about the same time as *Julius Caesar*, that Shakespeare most clearly remembered his kinsman Edward Arden, hanged and butchered, his head stuck on a pole. In the Forest of Arden, the exiled Duke Senior is told of how the 'melancholy' Jaques came across a 'poor sequestered stag / That from the hunter's aim that ta'en a hurt' beneath an ancient oak:

> The wretched animal heaved forth such groans
> That their discharge did stretch his leathern coat
> Almost to bursting, and the big round tears
> Coursed one another down his innocent nose
> In piteous chase.

The moralising Jaques watched as a 'careless herd' hurried by, ignoring the dying beast, much as the traffic across London Bridge paid little heed to Arden's head:

> 'Ay,' quoth Jaques,
> 'Sweep on, you fat and greasy citizens,
> 'Tis just the fashion. Wherefore should you look
> Upon that poor and broken bankrupt there?'

Jaques then railed against 'the body of the country, city, court', swearing 'that we / Are mere usurpers, tyrants, and what's worse, / To fright the animals and kill them up / In their assigned and native dwelling place.' As if it were not bad enough that the usurpers and tyrants of Elizabeth's England savaged these 'poor and broken' bankrupts, they did so even in their 'native dwelling place' – Will's mother-forest of Arden.

TWO LOCAL traditions recall that, in his youth, Will Shakespeare was a 'Butcher' who made a speech when he 'killed a Calf' and a poacher who stole a deer from Sir Thomas Lucy, for which 'he was prosecuted by that Gentleman, as he thought, somewhat too severely'.

In addition, we have the testimony of the Old Shepherd in *The Winter's Tale*, who remarks that the 'boiled-brains of nineteen and two-and-twenty' have 'scared away two of my best sheep, which I fear the wolf will sooner find than the master'.

Will's 23-year-old kinsman, John Somerville, was said to have been 'out of his mind' when he set out from Arden to shoot Queen Elizabeth, hoping 'to see her head set on a pole, for that she was a serpent and a viper'. Somerville claimed to have heard his father-in-law, Edward Arden, arguing that 'the Queen would not suffer the Catholic religion and doth execute all good Catholics'. He explained that 'the idea of murdering the Queen struck him after what his wife had said at Park Hall in the presence of Edward Arden and his brother that touched very greatly on her honour' – a reference, perhaps, to the gossip surrounding the queen's relationship with Arden's enemy, the Earl of Leicester. There is also evidence that Somerville had conferred with the MP for Coventry, Sir Henry Goodere, who had been imprisoned for his involvement with Mary, Queen of Scots.

The unnamed page, attached to Edward Arden's household, who accompanied Somerville on the road as far as Banbury, later testified that Somerville had seemed 'tormented of mind'. On the Continent, Father Robert Persons heard a different version of the story. As far as Edmund Campion's former companion was aware, the young squire of Edstone had drawn attention to himself on the road to Oxford when he 'happened to thrash a certain butcher, for the reason that he would not lend him some money'. Persons noted that Somerville had attacked the butcher like a 'raging lunatic'. When questioned about the assault, Somerville 'answered in the maddest way that he had done it because he imagined this butcher to be the Queen'.

Where this altercation might have taken place was hinted at by Shakespeare in one of his earliest history plays, *The True Tragedy of Richard Duke of York and the Good King Henry the Sixth* – commonly known as *3 Henry VI*. The start of the fifth act finds the Earl of Warwick on the walls of Coventry with a couple of messengers. There follows an exchange which has no real connection with the historical events being depicted:

WARWICK:	Say, Somerville – what says my loving son?
	And, by thy guess, how nigh is Clarence now?
SOMERVILLE:	At Southam did I leave him with his forces,
	And do expect him here some two hours hence.
	A march afar off
WARWICK:	Then Clarence is at hand – I hear his drum.
SOMERVILLE:	It is not his, my lord. Here Southam lies.
	The drum your honour hears marcheth from Warwick.

The only explanation for this passage is that Shakespeare was channelling his late kinsman Edward Arden, onetime High Sheriff of Warwickshire, and his son-in-law, John Somerville.

The Southam road ran south to Banbury, where it intersected with the road from Stratford-upon-Avon. Banbury was a Puritan stronghold. Agnes Whateley's nephew had married and settled there: Richard Whateley would serve on the town's council and be instrumental in tearing down the festive Maypole and the ornamental High Cross. The family name is preserved in the seventeenth-century Whateley Hall Hotel at Banbury Cross.

Shakespeare was said to have stolen a deer from Sir Thomas Lucy. The manor of Edstone, near Stratford, fell under Lucy's jurisdiction. Banbury did not.

The uproar which followed Somerville's arrest must have caused Sir Thomas no end of embarrassment – he had to play host to the clerk to the Privy Council while the investigations proceeded. In his fury, Lucy victimised the local community, causing John Shakespeare to hide his Jesuit 'Testament' in the roof of his Henley Street home.

John Somerville's Edstone estate was held in trust until his twenty-fourth birthday, which he never reached; among the trustees were two Puritans, Sir Fulke Greville and Sir Thomas Lucy, and two Catholic brothers, Ralph and William Sheldon. It is likely that Somerville was considered 'not at all inferior' to Shakespeare 'for a natural wit', for he had been educated at Hart Hall, Oxford. Could Somerville, then, have been the other 'Butcher's son', Will's 'acquaintance and coetanean', who 'died young'?

The term 'butcher' seems to have been contemporary slang, with the obvious meaning of 'assassin' or 'executioner' and a shadow meaning derived from the French *boucher*, which as a noun meant a 'butcher', but as a verb could mean to 'stop up' or 'plug'. The latter sense can be glimpsed in those telling phrases used of Christopher Marlowe ('the mouth of so dangerous a member may be stopped') and Will Shakespeare ('it sometime was necessary he should be stopped').

Somerville was unquestionably stopped: betrayed by his page or a 'certain butcher', he was strangled in his Newgate cell before he could disclose any secrets in his scaffold speech.

John Aubrey heard from the people of Stratford that Will Shakespeare was the magniloquent son of a 'Butcher' who, in his youth, 'exercised his father's Trade'. It seems probable that, in an effort to save his own hide, John Shakespeare had turned informant: in the summer of 1582 he sought legal protection against four of his fellow citizens 'for fear of death and mutilation of his limbs'. The fact that John Somerville's father – also called John – had made two local Puritans trustees of his son's estate suggests that he, too, was minded to stay on the right side of the ruthless Protestant elite.

When he 'killed a Calf', the neighbours told John Aubrey, Will did so 'in a high style, and made a Speech.' A young deer is known as a 'calf'. The 'Speech' that Will made might have been his deposition to the authorities or the loud argument he raised at the Banbury crossroads, giving the local officials time to put together a posse and chase down Somerville at Aynho.

The guilt for having stopped his 'tormented' cousin would have stayed with Will for the rest of his life. In his later years he formed a close friendship with John Somerville's brother, Sir William Somerville of Edstone. But the real pain came from having ruined his 'old religious uncle', Edward Arden.

In 1599, the Ardens of Park Hall were finally stripped of their right to bear arms, along with their estate, which was forfeited to the Crown. Will Shakespeare responded with his *As You Like It* homage to his 'native dwelling place' and its description of the 'poor sequestered stag', broken and bankrupt.

Part of the inspiration for *As You Like It* came from *The Book of Prayer and Meditation*, composed by the Dominican friar Luis de Granada in 1554. The book exhorted Catholics to 'suffer all calamity, affliction, persecution, imprisonment and torment of the world' rather than be bullied into converting to Protestantism.

An English-language copy of Luis de Granada's book had been smuggled out of the Marshalsea prison by John Somerville's uncle, Edward Grant of Snitterfield. It was found in Somerville's pocket after his arrest.

WILL WAS presumably still in Stratford in the early summer of 1584. His non-identical twin children, Hamnet and Judith, were baptised the following February. But the aftermath of the Somerville scandal made life in Arden uncomfortable. As Nicholas Rowe reported in 1709, Will's brush with Sir Thomas Lucy obliged him to 'leave his Business and Family in *Warwickshire* ... and shelter himself in *London*'.

Whether or not Will settled immediately in London is not clear. These are his 'lost years', when he vanishes from the records. It is conceivable that he went to sea – not as a mariner, but as a musician. Sir Walter Raleigh put together an epoch-making expedition which sailed two months after Shakespeare's twins were baptised. Commanded by Sir Richard Grenville, who liked to have music played raucously while he dined, the venture aimed to plant a colony of settlers on the coast of Virginia.

If Will did sail with Grenville on the *Tiger*, he would have learnt the art of building fortifications in Puerto Rico and the horrors of a sea-storm and near-shipwreck on the Outer Banks; he would have empathised with the colonists, abandoned to their fate on Roanoke Island, and engaged in a little piracy in Bermuda.

The *Tiger* returned to England in October 1585, laden with Spanish booty. One of the investors in the mission was the queen's spymaster, Sir Francis Walsingham, who no doubt had a couple of observant eyes and ears aboard Grenville's flagship.

Sooner or later, though, Will took up residence in London. He already had a friend there. Richard Field was the son of a tanner who lived close to the Shakespeare family home in Stratford. A couple of years older than Will, Field had moved to London in 1579 to train as a printer, spending the first six years of his apprenticeship with Thomas Vautrollier, a French-born printer based at the old monastery precinct of Blackfriars. Vautrollier fell foul of John Whitgift, Archbishop of Canterbury, in 1584 and fled to Scotland. He returned to London in 1586 and died a year later. Richard Field then went into business with, and subsequently married, Vautrollier's widow, Jacqueline. He would publish Shakespeare's two long narrative poems, 'Venus and Adonis' and 'Lucrece', in 1593 and 1594 respectively.

Field was able to introduce Will Shakespeare to the world of the London booksellers, concentrated in the churchyard of St Paul's Cathedral. He achieved his independence as a printer in 1587, the year in which Christopher Marlowe's *Tamburlaine* plays took the theatre world by storm.

Earlier that year, nearly two decades of plots and counterplots, real or imagined, culminated in the beheading of Mary, Queen of Scots. She had blundered into a trap laid for her by Sir Francis Walsingham, who had founded the fledgling secret service, and his ally Sir William Cecil, First Baron Burghley, who had grown immensely rich on the proceeds of power and persecution. Lord Burghley had also mounted the first major intelligence operation of Elizabeth's reign – the kidnapping of the Catholic agitator Dr John Story in Antwerp and his public execution in 1572.

By disposing of Mary Stuart, the Protestant faction removed a Catholic claimant to the throne. But for Elizabeth's erstwhile brother-in-law, King Philip of Spain, the execution of the Queen of Scots was the last straw. Relations between England and Spain had been deteriorating, partly because English pirates kept plundering the Spanish fleet and partly because Elizabeth's advisers had persuaded her to support the Dutch rebels against Spanish rule in the Netherlands and to prosecute a vicious war in Catholic Ireland. Finally spurred into action, Philip of Spain despatched his Great Armada in the summer of 1588.

The Armada was defeated by bad weather and English pluck. The queen's penny-pinching, and the corruption of her ministers, ensured that the sailors who had defended her realm went unpaid; thousands of them died of hunger and disease. More effort went into terrorising Catholics.

The first proper theatre in London had opened in 1576 on the site of the dissolved priory of Holywell in Shoreditch, north of the City. After the Armada scare, two priests were left hanging from a gibbet outside the theatre. One of them, Father William Hartley, had run an illegal printing press for Edmund Campion.

THE MOST powerful person in the country, after the queen, was the Lord High Treasurer, Lord Burghley. Will Shakespeare had probably come to Burghley's notice – as well as that of Sir Francis Walsingham – over the Somerville affair. Somerville had apparently confided in Sir Henry Goodere, who most likely passed on the details of their conversation to Lord Burghley (Goodere attributed his rehabilitation, after his suspicious dealings with Mary Stuart, to Burghley's 'great favour').

Burghley knew that the best weapon against Catholics, both in England and overseas, was other Catholics who were prepared to betray their co-religionists. Shakespeare's intimate knowledge of the Catholic network in the Midlands made him useful to Lord Burghley.

Another leading figure who found employment for Will Shakespeare was John Whitgift. As Bishop of Worcester, Whitgift had effectively granted Will his two marriage licences, one permitting him to marry Agnes Whateley, the other stipulating that he would wed Anne Hathaway. In August 1583, John Whitgift became Archbishop of Canterbury, the most senior post in the English Church.

It is through Whitgift that we first come across a mysterious individual named William Hall. On 17 June 1592, 'Will Hall' was paid £10 for services rendered to the Archbishop's Pursuivant, Anthony Munday, a playwright and polemicist who was also collaborating in 1592 with William Shakespeare.

In *The Shakespeare Conspiracy*, Graham Phillips and Martin Keatman argued that 'William Hall' was a codename used by Shakespeare whenever he did the State some service.

Shakespeare certainly possessed the right qualities for espionage – a plausible manner, an eye for detail, an actor's flightiness – and few poets of the time remained aloof from intelligence work.

The name he chose as a cover had connotations of ambition and grandeur, as if Will saw spying as a route to riches. The dissolute Petruchio of *The Taming of the Shrew* woos the puritanical Katherine as 'Kate of Kate Hall, my super-dainty Kate'. Shakespeare perhaps liked to think of himself as a 'Will of Will Hall' and eventually achieved such a quasi-baronial status when, in 1597, he acquired the title of 'gentleman' and the Great House in Stratford from William Underhill.

Underhill was the man to whom the gardener-priest Hugh Hall had run after the arrest of John Somerville. To save his own life, Father Hall incriminated Edward Arden. Thus, by calling himself 'Will Hall', Shakespeare made a grim nod towards the turncoat priest. He might even have chosen the pseudonym as an echo of Dr William Allen, the Catholic thorn in the government's side, who became Cardinal Allen in 1587.

The cover name was, in fact, an open secret. In the late summer of 1592, just after 'Will Hall' had been paid for his services to Whitgift's playwright-cum-priest-hunter Anthony Munday, an entertainment was staged at the archbishop's residence in Croydon. Penned by the diminutive satirist Thomas Nashe, who also worked for Archbishop Whitgift in his war of words with the Puritan extremists, the 'pleasant comedy' was entitled, *Summer's Last Will and Testament*.

It opened with a flustered fool bursting onto the stage, spouting Latin quips from Horace and hastily buttoning up his coat. 'Will Summer's ghost I should be', proclaimed the fool, before gabbling his way through the Prologue and then hassling the actors with constant instructions.

This was probably a skit on Will Shakespeare, who oversaw the death of Summer – 'Must needs he fall, whom none but foes uphold' – and, in a joke which appears in response to a morris dance, with its ritual re-enactment of a sacrifice, suddenly exclaimed:

WILL SUMMER: O brave Hall! O, well-said, butcher.
      Now for the credit of Worcestershire ...

Ostensibly, the Will Summer character was based on King Henry VIII's jester, William Somer. But the name also alluded to Will Shakespeare's ill-fated kinsman, John Somerville, whose surname was pronounced 'Sommer-will'.

The Archbishop of Canterbury, John Whitgift, would have known that 'brave Hall' was the talkative 'butcher' who had stopped John Somerville and ruined the house of Arden.

9

The Primrose Way

BY 1592, Will's theatrical career was sufficiently established for him to have attracted the envy of his rivals. One of these was a university-educated writer who, on his deathbed, composed an open letter to his fellow University Wits.

Robert Greene warned his friends to beware of actors:

> Yes trust them not: for there is an upstart Crow, beautified with our feathers, that with his *Tiger's heart wrapped in a Player's hide*, supposes he is as well able to bombast out a blank verse as the best of you: and being an absolute *Johannes fac totum*, is in his own conceit the only Shake-scene in a country ...

There would be no prizes for guessing who this 'upstart Crow' might have been. Greene's reference to a 'Tiger's heart wrapped in a Player's hide' was a steal from Shakespeare's *3 Henry VI*, which had done good business when it was performed by Lord Strange's Men at the Rose Theatre. In the first act, Queen Margaret, the 'She-wolf of France', is berated by her prisoner, the Duke of York: 'O tiger's heart wrapped in a woman's hide!'

Robert Greene made a point about Shakespeare that Thomas Nashe made at the same time in *Summer's Last Will and Testament* (Katherine Duncan-Jones even suggested that Nashe was the real author of Greene's pamphlet; Nashe had fervently denied this, so it might well be true): Will fussed over everything – writing, acting, costumes, direction. He was, in Greene's words, a *Johannes fac totum* – a Jack of all trades.

Will was one of two poets who complained when Greene's *Groatsworth of Wit* was published after Greene's death in September 1592. The other complainant was Christopher Marlowe. The publisher, Henry

Chettle, issued a partial apology: 'With neither of them that take offence was I acquainted,' wrote Chettle, 'and with one of them I care not if I never be' – this, it is generally assumed, was Marlowe. As for the other:

> I am as sorry as if the original fault had been my fault, because myself have seen his demeanour no less civil than he excellent in the quality he professes: besides, divers of worship have reported the uprightness of his dealing, which argues his honesty, and his facetious grace in writing, which approves his Art.

We can only guess at who these 'divers of worship' were: Lord Burghley and Archbishop Whitgift spring to mind. Evidently, though, Shakespeare had influential patrons who could vouch for his character and put the frighteners on a publisher.

WILL HAD hit pay dirt with his first batch of history plays, the *Henry VI* trilogy. But shortly after the success of *3 Henry VI*, the bubonic plague returned, forcing the closure of the theatres in June 1592. The acting companies took to the road and, apart from a short spell when the theatres reopened that winter, remained on tour for the next two years.

Shakespeare was spared the lot of the strolling player. If he was the 'Will Hall' paid £10 for services rendered to Whitgift's servant, Anthony Munday, in 1592, then he could already earn more running errands for men of high standing than he would from selling a play. He also had the good fortune to befriend a young nobleman.

Henry Wriothesley was an exquisite youth, nearly ten years younger than Shakespeare. Pale, thin and effeminate looking, he wore his long, curling brown hair over one shoulder in a style seemingly inspired by the American Indians of Virginia.

His father, the Second Earl of Southampton, had died in 1581. Wriothesley (pronounced 'Rosely') then became a Ward of Court, his fate and fortune entrusted to Lord Burghley, who held the lucrative post of Master of the Court of Wards and Liveries. By the age of 16 he had graduated from St John's College, Cambridge. Presented at Court the following year, Henry Wriothesley, Third Earl of Southampton, quickly became a noted recipient of royal favours.

Lord Burghley had plans for the handsome and wealthy young earl. He was intent on marrying Southampton to his granddaughter, Lady Elizabeth de Vere. The marriage would have cemented Burghley's position as one of the leading dynasts of his age. If Southampton rejected the match, he would be liable for a massive payment in compensation to Burghley when he turned 21. Either way, the sly Burghley could not lose.

Southampton did in fact refuse to marry Burghley's granddaughter, a decision which cost him £5,000. His determination to avoid being completely ensnared by the queen's most trusted adviser was probably due to his Catholic background. His father had perished in the Tower of London soon after Campion the Jesuit was captured. His mother, Mary Browne, was the daughter of the defiantly Catholic Viscount Montagu. As recently as 1591, Swithin Wells, the first tutor employed by the Southamptons, had been hanged in London; his crime, attending a celebration of the Mass.

Shakespeare's kinsman Edward Arden had been arrested at the London residence of the orphaned Earl of Southampton. Lord Burghley would have been fully aware of this connection between Will Shakespeare and the headstrong young earl and knew how to turn it to his advantage. He set the poet the task of persuading Southampton to give serious thought to the question of marriage.

The first seventeen of Shakespeare's sonnets, as they were published in 1609, are formulaic entreaties to a fair youth to marry and reproduce: 'Is it for fear to wet a widow's eye, / That thou consum'st thy self in single life?' The tone changes with the eighteenth sonnet in the sequence:

Shall I compare thee to a Summer's day?
Thou art more lovely and more temperate.
Rough winds do shake the darling buds of May,
And Sommer's [sic] lease hath all too short a date ...

The original brief – to argue in favour of marriage – had been forgotten. Shakespeare had found himself a 'Master Mistress'.

The sonnets chart the course of an intense relationship, though not a homosexual affair, as has often been claimed. Sonnet 18, which compared Southampton with a short-lived 'Sommer', hints at the true nature of the bond.

The conceit was much the same as in *Summer's Last Will and Testament*, which Thomas Nashe wrote at about the same time. In the young Catholic earl, Will had identified an 'eternal Sommer' – a second Somerville – more 'lovely and more temperate' than the first.

IF THE earliest sonnets advised Southampton to cheat death through sexual reproduction, 'Venus and Adonis' explored the probable consequences of defying Queen Elizabeth and her chief minister, Lord

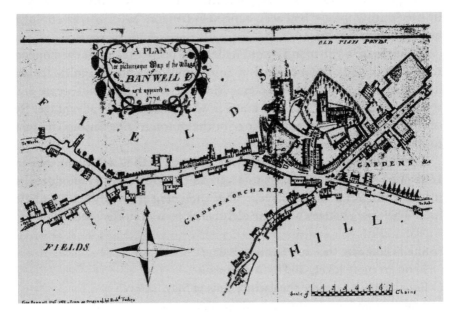

8 Banwell, Somerset, 'as it appeared in 1770'.

Burgley. Southampton became the 'Rose-cheeked Adonis'; the queen 'Sick-thoughted Venus'. Just as Elizabeth had showered the earl with royal favours, so her alter ego endeavoured to seduce the prim youth.

The warning note is sounded when Venus cautions Adonis to fear her 'disturbing jealousy' which 'Gives false alarms, suggesteth mutiny, / And in a peaceful hour doth cry, "Kill, Kill!" ... This sour informer, this bate-breeding spy ... / That sometime true news, sometime false doth bring'. Adonis spurns her advances, denouncing her 'love' as 'full of forgèd lies'. The fate which Venus had predicted overtakes him. An 'angry chafing boar' gores the youth. Venus finds his body; beside it, a 'purple flower sprung up, chequered with white, / Resembling well his pale cheeks, and the blood / Which in round drops upon their whiteness stood.' The goddess plucks the flower, places it between her breasts and, 'weary of the world', returns to heaven.

The message was clear: if Southampton opposed the queen, she would set her boar-like ministers on him. All that would be left of the young earl would be something stained with his blood.

'Venus and Adonis' was dedicated 'To the Right Honourable Henry Wriothesley, Earl of Southampton and Baron of Titchfield' and entered in the Stationers' Register by the printer Richard Field on 28 April 1593. It drew a response from an unlikely quarter.

Father Robert Southwell was a Jesuit priest. Distantly related to Shakespeare, via the Arden bloodline, he had been acting as 'spiritual adviser' to the Earl of Southampton – another reason for Lord Burghley to have attached his poet to the royal ward.

Father Southwell took exception to Will's choice of subject matter. In a poem of his own, entitled 'St Peter's Complaint', he criticised Shakespeare's preference for profane love stories over more sacred material:

Christ's thorn is sharp, no head his garland wears,
Still finest wits are 'stilling Venus' rose,
In paynim [pagan] toys the sweetest veins are spent,
To Christian works few have their talents lent.

Southwell's poem was published in 1595, the year of his death, and reissued in 1616 – the year of Shakespeare's death – with a prefatory letter 'To my worthy good cousin, Master W.S.' from 'Your loving cousin, R.S.'

'License my single pen to seek a peer', wrote Robert Southwell, punning on his distant cousin's name. 'Favour my wish, well-wishing works no ill; / I move the suit, the grant rests in your will.' Southwell felt that Shakespeare was misusing his poetic gifts. There was nothing wrong with 'well-wishing', argued the Jesuit. Properly targeted, a talent like Will's could do much good for the Catholic cause: 'Sweet flights you shoot, learn once to level right.'

Father Southwell had given his own demonstration of the brutality at the heart of the Elizabethan regime. He was in London when he bumped into a Catholic named Thomas Bellamy, whose sister, Anne, was anxious to receive the Jesuit at Uxendon Hall, the home of the Bellamys near Harrow-on-the-Hill. On the morning of Sunday 25 June 1592, Southwell rode with Thomas Bellamy to Uxendon. At the same time, a spy named Nicholas Jones set off in the opposite direction.

The Bellamys were well known for their Catholic activism. Back in January, their house had been raided. Richard Topcliffe, the queen's chief interrogator, had imprisoned Anne Bellamy in the Gatehouse. The 29-year-old Anne soon fell pregnant. Her family had no doubt that she had been raped by Richard Topcliffe.

Anne was released and moved into lodgings in Holborn. Ashamed and desperate, she wrote to Topcliffe for help. He offered her a quid pro quo.

Southwell walked into a trap. Anne Bellamy had provided Topcliffe with a map of Uxendon, indicating where the Jesuit would be hiding. The house was stormed. The slim, auburn-haired priest gave himself up and vanished into the torture chambers of London, not to reappear until his trial in January 1595. Anne Bellamy was quickly married off to Topcliffe's agent, Nicholas Jones. As Mrs Jones, she was the only material witness to give evidence against Father Southwell.

On Friday 21 February 1595, Will Shakespeare's 'loving cousin' was strapped to a hurdle and dragged to his place of execution. Witnesses claimed that when his severed head was brandished by the hangman, 'no one was heard to cry "Traitor, traitor!" as before times they were wont to do'.

SOUTHWELL'S CAPTURE informed one of Shakespeare's bloodiest plays. *The Most Lamentable Roman Tragedy of Titus Andronicus* is often dismissed as an immature piece by critics who refuse to acknowledge the violence of the times. In fact, *Titus Andronicus* is a sustained howl of rage, its grotesque horrors merely a reflection of Elizabeth's England.

The title character represented those gentlemen whose families – like the Ardens and the Bellamys – had suffered for their allegiance to Rome. Queen Elizabeth was portrayed as Tamora, Queen of the Goths (a nod towards her 'Gothic' Lutheran creed). Tamora plots her revenge on Titus with the help of her black servant and lover, Aaron, whose unrepentant wickedness and unusually close relationship to the queen, along with the fact that he ends up holding an illegitimate baby, identify him with the psychopathic Topcliffe, one who could speak of:

> ... murders, rapes, and massacres,
> Acts of black night, abominable deeds,
> Complots of mischief, treason, villainies,
> Ruthful to hear yet piteously performed ...

In an echo of 'Venus and Adonis', Aaron compares himself with the 'chafèd boar'.

Besides her scheming lover, the Queen of the Goths has two quarrelsome sons, Chiron and Demetrius, whose names betray their origins as two of Elizabeth's favourites. Chiron, the centaur, was the queen's Master of Horse, Robert Devereux, Second Earl of Essex and stepson to her former favourite, the Earl of Leicester. Demetrius, named after the Greek goddess of the harvest, was the poet, soldier and explorer Sir Walter Raleigh, obsessed with establishing plantations in Virginia.

Under the queen's supervision, Chiron and Demetrius rape Lavinia, the daughter of Titus Andronicus. They then chop off her hands and cut out her tongue to secure her silence.

Lavinia's shocking treatment in the play was a dramatic rerun of Anne Bellamy's fate. Violated and impregnated by Queen Elizabeth's torturer-in-chief, Anne was deprived of any opportunity to denounce her assailant. Topcliffe used his victim as a weapon against Father Southwell, turning her mute appeals for justice into the accusation that the Jesuit was the real liar. (Topcliffe also wrote to Anne's father, demanding that the family make over their farm at Preston to Nicholas Jones; Richard Bellamy refused, and so his entire family was imprisoned.)

Viewed in its contemporary context, *Titus Andronicus* is an unbearably bleak and painful tragedy. Will, who was distantly related to Father Southwell, was the same age as Anne Bellamy – who perhaps reminded him of Agnes ('Anne') Whateley, the Catholic mother of his own illegitimate child. He carried her dreadful example forward into the poem that followed 'Venus and Adonis'.

'The Rape of Lucrece' was dedicated to the Earl of Southampton and published in 1594. The poem relates that, while besieging Ardea (shades of 'Arden'), the tyrannical Tarquin overhears another Roman nobleman boasting about the 'incomparable chastity' of his wife, Lucrece. Overcome with lust, Tarquin steals into Lucrece's chamber. He ignores her pleas:

'No more,' quoth he, 'by heaven, I will not hear thee.
Yield to my love. If not, enforcèd hate
Instead of love's coy touch shall rudely tear thee.
That done, despitefully I mean to bear thee
    Unto the base bed of some rascal groom
    To be thy partner in this shameful doom.'

And so he rapes her. But unlike Anne Bellamy, married off to 'some rascal groom', Lucrece does not lose her voice. She gives a full account of her violation and then stabs herself to death. Tarquin, for his crimes, is banished.

The narrative poems, 'Venus and Adonis' and 'Lucrece', along with *Titus Andronicus*, suggest that Will was having grave doubts about the regime he was forced to serve. The persecution of Catholic priests and the families which protected them had reached a new pitch of severity, as favourites like Essex and Raleigh squabbled for precedence and Richard Topcliffe rode roughshod over the law. At the centre of it all stood the vain and brittle queen, a 'lovesick' Venus who was also the 'dread Fury' Tamora and the mistress of the 'angry chafing boar' which rampaged through her kingdom, leaving a trail of shattered bodies.

In his sonnets, meanwhile, Will was keen to stress that, though fear had taught him not to say his catechism, his writings expressed the Catholic 'love' that he dared not declare openly:

As an unperfect actor on the stage,
Who with his fear is put beside his part,
Or some fierce thing replete with too much rage,
Whose strength's abundance weakens his own heart;
So I for fear of trust, forget to say,
The perfect ceremony of love's right [or 'rite'],
And in mine own love's strength seem to decay,
O'er-charg'd with burden of mine own love's might:
O let my books be then the eloquence,
And dumb presagers of my speaking breast.
Who plead for love, and look for recompense,
More than that tongue that more hath more expressed.
    O learn to read what silent love hath writ,
    To hear with eyes belongs to love's fine wit.

THE SONNETS were never intended for publication. They were first mentioned by Francis Meres in 1598 as Shakespeare's 'sugared Sonnets among his private friends'. When two of the sonnets appeared the following year, in a volume suggestively entitled *The Passionate Pilgrim*, Will was 'much offended'. *The Passionate Pilgrim* ascribed various poems to Shakespeare which were not his work and exposed two of his private sonnets – 'When my love swears that she is made of truth' and 'Two loves have I of comfort and despair' – to the public gaze.

Another poem pirated in *The Passionate Pilgrim* was Christopher Marlowe's 'The Passionate Shepherd to his Love' ('Come live with me, and be my love, / And we will all the pleasures prove'), to which was added 'Love's Answer':

If that the world and love were young,
And truth in every shepherd's tongue,
Those pretty pleasures might me move
To live with thee and be thy love.

This was, in fact, the first stanza of 'The Nymph's Reply to the Shepherd', Sir Walter Raleigh's tongue-in-cheek answer to Marlowe.

One of the most complex and restless personalities of his day, Sir Walter Raleigh had climbed his way into the queen's favour a decade earlier. He wrote fawning poems in which Elizabeth was 'Cynthia' and he was her 'Ocean' (his name sounded like 'Water'). But his star had fallen.

Late in 1591, Raleigh had secretly married one of the queen's maids of honour, Elizabeth ('Bess') Throckmorton. The queen invariably reacted with fury whenever one of her courtiers married without her permission – they were meant to have eyes only for her – and by the summer of 1592 Raleigh was in disgrace. Both he and Bess were confined to the Tower of London. Released shortly before Christmas, they were debarred from the Court. Raleigh settled, rather bitterly, on his Sherborne estate in Dorset.

He had gathered around him an elite circle of philosophers, including the brilliant astronomer and mathematician Thomas Hariot, who had sailed to Virginia on the *Tiger* in 1585; the scientists Walter Warner and Robert Hues; and the poets George Chapman, Matthew Roydon and Christopher Marlowe. Quite possibly, the occultist Dr John Dee was part of the circle, as were, perhaps, Henry Percy, Ninth Earl of Northumberland, and Ferdinando, Lord Strange, whose acting company performed Will's *Titus Andronicus*. This loose group of intellectuals was branded, late in 1591, 'the school of atheism of Sir Walter Raleigh' by the Jesuit Father Robert Persons.

George Chapman's two-part poem of 1594, 'The Shadow of Night', is thought to glance at Raleigh's philosophical circle. It was Shakespeare, though, who gave Raleigh's group its familiar name.

Love's Labour's Lost was written at about this time, with the character of Don Armado seemingly based on Raleigh. The play opens with a quartet of men committing themselves to intellectual pursuits along the lines of the 'Academy' founded by the future King of France, Henri de Navarre. The men forswear female company but immediately fall in love with the Princess of France and her maidens.

Biron, or Berowne, the most Shakespeare-like of the characters, addresses his love poems to Rosalind, whose colouring is unfashionably dark. 'No face is fair that is not full so black,' protests Biron. The King of Navarre replies, 'O paradox! Black is the badge of hell, / The hue of dungeons and the school of night.' Thus, Raleigh's circle of freethinkers became the School of Night – a combination of Father Persons' 'school of atheism' and Chapman's 'Shadow of Night'.

Almost certainly, in the spring of 1593, just before Kit Marlowe was killed at Widow Bull's house on Deptford Strand, Will Shakespeare and his patron travelled to Dorset, not very far from Southampton's Titchfield estate in Hampshire, to spend time with Sir Walter Raleigh and his 'compeers by night'. The occasion provoked a fit of jealousy in Shakespeare, who grumbled in his sonnets that another poet – a 'better spirit' and a 'worthier pen' – was vying for Southampton's attention:

> Was it the proud full sail of his great verse,
> Bound for the prize of (all too precious) you,
> That did my ripe thoughts in my brain inhearse,
> Making their tomb the womb wherein they grew?

The maritime imagery points to Raleigh having been the 'Rival Poet' of the sonnets:

> But since your worth (wide as the Ocean is)
> The humblest as the proudest sail doth bear,
> My saucy barque (inferior far to his)
> On your broad main doth wilfully appear.
> Your shallowest help will hold me up afloat,
> Whilst he upon your soundless deep doth ride,
> Or (being wracked) I am a worthless boat,
> He of tall building, and of goodly pride.

Raleigh, the seasoned mariner, 'damnable proud', was then rebuilding his four-storey Sherborne Lodge in a manner befitting his 'goodly pride'. His wife, Bess Throckmorton, was related to Shakespeare. A visit to

Sherborne in 1593 would account for Will's knowledge of the School of Night, his sulky response to Sir Walter's poetry and his image, in 'Venus and Adonis', of 'poor Wat, far off upon a hill' with ears pricked to 'hearken if his foes pursue him still'.

FROM SHERBORNE, Shakespeare and Southampton travelled further west, following the old Roman road which ran from Old Sarum to the Mendip Hills. They were going to visit another property which Raleigh had in his covetous sights.

The manor of Banwell in Somerset belonged to the Bishop of Bath and Wells. Thomas Godwin had been appointed to the bishopric in 1584. Despite being 'aged and diseased, and lame of the gout', Godwin took for his third wife a 20-year-old London widow. In an attempt to deprive Godwin of the manor of Banwell, Raleigh informed the queen of the bishop's inappropriate match. Elizabeth's response was to criticise both Raleigh and Godwin.

The see had fallen vacant between 1590 and 1592. Then, in 1593, Dr John Still was raised to the bishopric. He had formerly been the Master of Southampton's old Cambridge college, and perhaps Raleigh hoped that the new Bishop of Bath and Wells might be persuaded to relinquish the manor of Banwell.

The visit to Banwell would have repercussions for both Shakespeare and his youthful patron. For a hint of what happened, we must turn to a poem first published in 1594.

'Willobie his Avisa' was probably written by Matthew Roydon, one of Raleigh's School of Night poets. Subtitled 'The true Picture of a modest Maid, and of a chaste and constant wife', it concerned a woman with the 'feigned name' of Avisa. Will Shakespeare was invoked in a prefatory verse: 'Yet Tarquyne pluckt his glistering grape, / And Shake-speare, paints poore Lucrece rape.' The poem gave directions to the place where 'Avisa' had been found. 'At wester side of Albions Ile, / Where Austine pitcht his Monkish tent' points towards the west of England, where Bristol Cathedral stands on the site of St Augustine's Abbey. Fishermen's huts along the coast south of Bristol were called Auster Tenements, after St Augustine or 'Austin':

Not farre from thence there lyes a vale,
A rosie vale in pleasant plaine ...

At East of this, a Castle stands,
By auncient sheepheards built of olde,

And lately was in shepheards hands,
Though now by brothers bought and solde,
    At west side springs a Christall well;
    There doth this chast *Avisa* dwell.

About 14 miles south-west of Bristol, the village of Banwell sits on the alluvial plain, immediately to the north of the Mendips, 5 low-lying miles from the shore. A poem appended to the 1596 edition of 'Willobie his Avisa' noted that 'Avisa' dwelt on '*Sea-bred* soyle' and 'flowrie bancks'.

In *The Sea-Board of Mendip*, published in 1902, Francis A. Knight remarked that the vale in which Banwell lies was once known as Primrose Valley. This was due to the prevalence of the Primrose peerless, *Narcissus melioluteus*, a double-headed daffodil which flowers between March and May, hence its alternative name, 'April Beauty'.

The vale where 'Avisa' lived was sprinkled with primroses. Entering this 'rosie vale' by way of Churchill Gate presented Shakespeare with one of his enduring metaphors. It became his personal road to perdition: his 'primrose path of dalliance' (*Hamlet*); the 'primrose way to th'everlasting bonfire' (*Macbeth*); 'the flow'ry way that leads to the broad gate and the great fire' (*All's Well That Ends Well*).

South-east of the village stood Banwell Castle. An Episcopal palace built for the bishops of Bath and Wells, it had been sold to Edward Seymour, First Duke of Somerset and Lord Protector of England, during the reign of his nephew, Edward VI, whose half-sister Mary later restored it to the Church. In the village itself, a clear spring, one of the largest in the region, famous for its curative properties, gave Banwell its name. Here, according to Matthew Roydon's poem, the 'chast *Avisa*' dwelt 'in publique eye'.

The term 'shepherds', as used by Roydon, had several meanings. There were indeed shepherds tending their flocks on the down. The bishops who owned Banwell Castle were also shepherds, in the ecclesiastical sense of the word, while pastoral poetry frequently classed poets as 'shepherds'.

There were also many people named Sheppard in the Banwell area, and one of them was Shakespeare's lover.

HER NAME was Jane Sheppard. Baptised at St Margaret's, Westminster, on 1 November 1568, she was almost exactly halfway in age between the 29-year-old poet and his patron.

An unreliable pedigree created for her great-grandson ('late his Majesty's Envoy Extraordinary to the Italian Princes') referred to her as 'Jana filia ... Shepherd de Durham'. The likelihood is that Jane's father

Robert Sheppard came not from Durham in the north-east of England but from Dyrham, east of Bristol, which was also spelled 'Durham'.

The family had moved to London, where several of them were employed at Court: two of Jane's brothers were glovers, embroiderers and perfumers for the royal household; a third brother worked for the royal catering department. The Sheppards seem, however, to have maintained their West Country links, and with the plague rife in London, Jane was sent away to the safety of Banwell.

Roydon alluded to her family background in 'Willobie his Avisa' and in the prefatory poem for the second edition of 1596, remarking that '*Avisa*, both by Syre and spouse, / Was linckt to men of meanest trade'. Her 'Sire' was also 'the Mayor of the towne'. Jane's father died intestate and was buried at Westminster on 19 August 1574, when Jane was not quite 6 years old. There is nothing to indicate that he was the 'Mayor' of Banwell, but the church records show a payment of £18 to John Sheppol or 'Sheppod' of Wolvershill in 1521. The manor of Wolvershill lay within the parish of Banwell, and this John 'Sheppod' might have been the Sir John Shyppard or Shepperd who witnessed three wills in the adjacent parish of Worle in 1540.

Jane Sheppard was linked to 'men of meanest trade'. In about 1593, she married John Davenant, a wine merchant of Thames Street in London. There are indications that her family had been involved in the same trade. The Churchwarden's Accounts for Banwell reveal that in 1530, 'Rychard Scheppard' paid 1s. 12d 'for the Brewing House' which stood just west of the church, beside the 'Christall well'.

One thing that Matthew Roydon made clear in 'Willobie his Avisa' is that the 'modest Maid' worked at an inn: 'Seest yonder howse, where hanges the badge / Of Englands Saint.' The oldest known inn at Banwell was The George on the High Street, west of the church.

As Jane Sheppard and, later, Mistress Davenant, Jane spent most of her life in taverns and inns, and was long remembered as 'a very beautiful woman, & of a very good wit and of conversation extremely agreeable'.

'Willobie his Avisa' detailed various attempts by 'Ruffians, Roysters, young Gentlemen, and lustie Captaines' to seduce the maid, both in London and in 'countrie hills', before and after her wedding. Part of the poem concerns a youth identified as *Henrico Willebego* or 'H.W.'. At his 'first sight' of the maid, H.W. was 'sodenly affected'. He 'bewrayeth the secresy of his disease unto his familiar frend W.S.', who had only just recovered from his own infatuation with the maid.

Cruelly, 'the old player' – W.S. – persuaded 'this new actor', H.W., that it was possible to charm the delightful hostess: 'She is no Saynt, she is no Nonne, / I thinke in tyme she may be wonne.' 'But at length this Comedy was like to have growen to a Tragedy,' wrote Roydon, 'by the weake and feeble estate that H.W. was brought unto.' This happened between March and May, when the Primrose peerless was in bloom.

Whether or not 'W.S.' really did encourage his 'frend Harry' – Henry Wriothesley – to pour out his heart to Jane Sheppard, Will and the young Earl of Southampton were undoubtedly caught up in a love-triangle. Shakespeare tells us as much in his sonnets: 'Take all my loves, my love, yea take them all, / What hast thou then more than thou hadst before?' Matthew Roydon stated in 'Willobie his Avisa' that 'W.S.' had been in love with the maid. Shakespeare confirms this: 'That thou hast her it is not all my grief, / And yet it may be said I lov'd her dearly ...'

At times, he felt so close to his patron that sharing a lover presented no difficulties: 'But here's the joy, my friend and I are one, / Sweet flattery, then she loves but me alone.' At others, he accused Jane and Southampton of breaking a 'two-fold truth': 'Hers by thy beauty tempting her to thee, / Thine by thy beauty being false to me.' Suspicion and jealousy were never far away:

> To win me soon to hell my female evil,
> Tempteth my better angel from my sight [or 'side'],
> And would corrupt my saint to be a devil,
> Wooing his purity with her foul pride.
> And whether that may angel be turn'd fiend,
> Suspect I may, yet not directly tell,
> But being both from me both to each friend,
> I guess one angel in another's hell.

Like Biron's beloved Rosalind in *Love's Labour's Lost*, Jane was attractively dark-eyed. When the going got tough, Will used her complexion as a stick to beat her with: 'For I have sworn thee fair, and thought thee bright, / Who art as black as hell, as dark as night.' He was readier to forgive Southampton: 'No more be griev'd at that which thou hast done, / Roses have thorns, and silver fountains mud ...'

In April 1593, when Shakespeare and Southampton were competing for Jane's affections, 'Venus and Adonis' was going to press. The poem implies that Will and Jane were already lovers.

The 'lovesick' Venus has made her first determined attempt to woo Adonis, who fails to get away because his horse is distracted:

But lo, from forth a copse that neighbours by
A breeding jennet, lusty, young, and proud,
Adonis' trampling courser doth espy,
And forth she rushes, snorts, and neighs aloud.
    The strong-necked steed, being tied unto a tree,
    Breaketh his rein, and to her straight goes he.

The stallion puts on an energetic display. The jennet plays it cool: 'Being proud, as females are, to see him woo her, / She puts on outward strangeness, seems unkind.' But when the master moves to control his steed, 'the unbacked breeder, full of fear, / Jealous of catching, swiftly doth forsake him, / With her the horse, and left Adonis there.'

Southampton – 'Adonis' – had already lost his 'strong-necked steed' once to a 'breeding jennet'.

A jennet is a small Spanish horse.

We know from the will of Jane's uncle, William Sheppard, that Jane was familiarly known as 'Jennet'.

10

The More Fool I

LATE IN the summer of 1593, 'William Hall' was on the move. He was despatched to Prague on 28 August with a letter from the Lord High Treasurer, Lord Burghley, to Edward Kelly.

Kelly was a curious figure. Originally from Worcester, he had been caught digging up a corpse in a churchyard near Preston, Lancashire, in the early 1580s. This brought him to the attention of Ferdinando, Lord Strange, who perhaps introduced Edward Kelly to Dr John Dee, the occultist and spy with whom Kelly would spend much of the 1580s travelling around Europe.

Edward Kelly finally settled in Prague, under the protection of the Holy Roman Emperor. There, he was contacted by Lord Burghley, who wanted information on the Catholic exiles in the city. One of the couriers who flitted between Burghley and Kelly was the poet Matthew Roydon; another was the poet and diplomat Sir Edward Dyer.

Also in Prague at the time was Richard Hesketh, a 'yellow-haired' man of about 50. He was almost certainly the son of Sir Thomas Hesketh of Rufford in Lancashire, to whom 'William Shakeshafte' had been bequeathed by Alexander Hoghton in his will of 3 August 1581.

The contents of the letter carried by 'William Hall' from Lord Burghley to Kelly in Prague are unknown, but they appear to have set in motion a tragic chain of events. Soon after the letter was sent, Richard Hesketh returned to England and showed up at the Lancashire home of his friend, Lord Strange.

Ferdinando, Lord Strange, was the son of Henry Stanley, Fourth Earl of Derby, and Margaret Clifford, named in the will of King Henry VIII as the successor to Elizabeth I. On the death of his father in September 1593, Lord Strange became the Fifth Earl of Derby. His theatre company, which produced Shakespeare's *Henry VI* trilogy and *Titus Andronicus*, duly changed its name to Derby's Men.

The Protestant regime was concerned about the newly elevated earl. He stood to inherit the throne from Elizabeth, but his family was besmirched with Catholicism. His kinsman, Sir William Stanley, had defected to the Spanish side in the Netherlands. There were noises coming from the Continent that, on the death of Elizabeth, Sir William Stanley 'would go to Scotland with his regiment' and 'make it strong' before siding with the Earl of Derby, 'as would all the English'. Derby was, therefore, a threat to the interests of Protestant arrivistes such as Lord Burghley.

Richard Hesketh brought Derby a letter purporting to come from the Catholic exiles in Prague, promising their support for a *coup d'état* against Elizabeth. The earl informed the authorities. Hesketh was arrested, interrogated, and executed on 29 November 1593.

Derby, however, was not yet off the hook. He was summoned to appear before the Privy Council on 10 March 1594, apparently to answer charges of blasphemy. At much the same time an inquiry was convened at Cerne Abbas in Dorset to investigate accusations of atheism which had been levelled at Sir Walter Raleigh and his School of Night. The Cecil faction, led by Lord Burghley and his devious son Robert, was moving against its enemies, using allegations of 'atheism' as its excuse to strike.

On 29 March 1594, Lord Burghley received a letter from the Earl of Derby, who had evidence of a new conspiracy. The earl did not live to go into detail. He began vomiting on 5 April, and by the sixteenth of the month he was dead, probably from arsenic poisoning.

The government spread the rumour that Derby had been poisoned by the Jesuits. The Catholics, meanwhile, were wise to Lord Burghley's game plan: he wanted Derby out of the way so that he could marry his granddaughter, Lady Elizabeth de Vere – she whom Southampton had declined to marry – to Derby's weak-minded brother, who became the Sixth Earl of Derby.

The death of the Fifth Earl eliminated a contender for the throne who, if not a Catholic, was supported by Catholics in England and overseas. The process had started with a letter from Lord Burghley, which 'William Hall' had taken to Edward Kelly in Prague, and ended with the poisoning of Shakespeare's theatrical patron. This might be why, in a sonnet to the Earl of Southampton, Shakespeare wrote archly of taking a vinegar cure for a stomach ailment:

Thence comes it that my name receives a brand,
And almost thence my nature is subdu'd
To what it works in, like the Dyer's hand,

Pity me then, and wish I were renew'd,
Whilst like a willing patient I will drink,
Potions of Eisel 'gainst my strong infection,
No bitterness that I will bitter think,
Nor double penance to correct correction.

ON 2 MAY 1594, Southampton's widowed mother married the vice-chamberlain of the royal household, Sir Thomas Heneage. Will Shakespeare provided an entertainment for the occasion.

A Midsummer Night's Dream opens with two ageing lovers – Theseus, Duke of Athens, and Hippolyta, Queen of the Amazons – bemoaning the slow passage of the 'old moon': 'She lingers my desires / Like to a stepdame or a dowager, / Long withering out a young man's revenue.'

As a government insider, Sir Thomas Heneage had persecuted the Catholic kindred of the dowager Countess of Southampton, and so Theseus admits that he won his bride-to-be's love 'doing thee injuries'. Heneage had also been a favourite of Queen Elizabeth, who flirted with him, arousing the jealousy of the Earl of Leicester. Accordingly, Will reminded his audience of Leicester's failure to win the queen's hand during the 'princely pleasures' held at Kenilworth in 1575.

The 'princely pleasures' helped to inspire the fairyland element of *A Midsummer Night's Dream*, as well as the subplot involving a group of artisans who offer to perform an interlude for the nuptials of Theseus and Hippolyta. Led by a carpenter named Peter Quince, these 'rude mechanicals' endeavour to rehearse their *Most Lamentable Comedy and Most Cruel Death of Pyramus and Thisbe*, and it is Quince – a part possibly played by Shakespeare himself – who introduces the 'very tragical mirth': 'If we offend, it is with our good will. / That you should think, we come not to offend / But with good will.'

Good Will had reason to fear causing offence. The play was interwoven with references to the courtly world of Sir Thomas Heneage and the government of Elizabeth I.

The poet Edmund Spenser had characterised Elizabeth as the Faerie Queen. She retained that guise in *A Midsummer Night's Dream*, becoming Titania, Queen of Fairies. Titania quarrels with Oberon, King of Fairies, whom Spenser had identified as Elizabeth's father, Henry VIII, but for whom Shakespeare probably had in mind Lord Burghley. A true father figure to the queen, Burghley was now an old man; he had been training up his second son, Robert Cecil, to succeed him as the power behind the throne.

The younger Cecil was short, hunchbacked and splay-footed. Shakespeare ascribed the same deformities to Richard 'Crookback', the 'elvish-marked, abortive, rooting hog' of his *Tragedy of King Richard the Third*. In *A Midsummer Night's Dream*, though, he played on Robert Cecil's mischievous streak. The queen had nicknamed him 'elf' and 'pygmy' (his father was her 'Spirit'), and so Shakespeare turned him into 'Robin Goodfellow', the meddling imp who serves the King of Fairies.

The play also lampooned one of the spies in Sir Thomas Heneage's service. The 'Dream' of the title belongs to Nick Bottom, an egotistical idiot who fancies playing all the parts in the interlude by himself. The character of 'bully Bottom' owed much to Will's fellow playwright, Anthony Munday.

At the age of 18, Munday had travelled to Italy. From there, he sent back information to Lord Burghley about the Jesuit mission, which was then preparing to send its first priests into England. A year later, Munday published his own account of the capture of Edmund Campion. The Catholics dubbed him 'Judas'.

Munday had been impressed by the improvisational skills of the Commedia dell'Arte in Italy, and when he returned to London in 1580 he gave a demonstration of their techniques by performing '*extempore, like the Italian comedians*'. He was booed off the stage. In retaliation – and with funding from the Puritans of the Corporation of London – Munday wrote his *Blast of Retreat from Plays and Theatres*, claiming that actors were 'brawlers, roisterers, loiterers and ruffians' and the playhouses 'chapels of Satan'. Such propagandist efforts secured him a post as messenger to the queen's chamber in 1584. Irrespective of his earlier outburst, he also maintained a career as a playwright; Francis Meres would describe him in 1598 as 'our best plotter'.

Will mocked Munday's chaotic behaviour in *A Midsummer Night's Dream*. As Bottom the weaver – 'the shallowest thickskin of that barren sort' – he was both the 'best plotter' (in weaving terms, the 'bottom' was the core upon which the thread was wound) and a limelight-hogging ham whom the carpenter Peter Quince finds difficult to control.

The satire reached its sharpest point when Bottom was 'translated'. The interfering Robin Goodfellow – 'Puck' – transforms Bottom's head into that of an ass. The Fairy Queen then falls in love with the ass-headed actor.

Like Bottom, 'Judas' Munday had become a member of the queen's household when he donned an ass' head and turned from acting to writing anti-Catholic propaganda.

BY 1594, ANTHONY Munday was working for Sir Thomas Heneage. Previously, he had served as a priest-hunter for the Archbishop of Canterbury; 'Will Hall' had been paid £10 for helping Munday in 1592. Also in 1592, or thereabouts, Will Shakespeare had been one of several playwrights who attempted to rescue Munday's play, *The Book of Sir Thomas More*, from oblivion.

The misbegotten venture of *The Book of Sir Thomas More* echoes throughout Will's comedy of 'Bottom's dream'. Shakespeare's principal contribution to the revisions of Munday's script was the scene in which More, as the Under-Sheriff of London, calms a riotous mob. The Londoners had been growing increasingly hostile towards foreigners. An uprising was planned for 1 May 1517 – as one character remarks: 'Ay, for we may as well make bonfires on May Day as at Midsummer. We'll alter the day in the calendar.'

The wedding of Sir Thomas Heneage and Southampton's mother, for which Will wrote *A Midsummer Night's Dream*, took place on 2 May 1594. Like the rioting Londoners, Will had altered the day in the calendar, transposing May Day to Midsummer. The inspiration for doing so might well have come from the fact that Sir Thomas Heneage was known to one of his spies, Michael Moody, by the codename 'Thomas Moore'.

Sir Thomas More had earned plaudits for his handling of the London mob in 1517: 'And whensoe'er we talk of Ill May Day / Praise More, whose honest words our falls did stay.' He was promoted to Lord Chancellor by Henry VIII, but More harboured no illusions about worldly success: 'And let this be thy maxim: to be great / Is, when the thread of hazard is once spun, / A bottom great wound up, greatly undone.'

Historically, King Henry's determination to divorce his Catholic queen and declare himself head of the Church of England was More's undoing. Sixty years after More's martyrdom, the subject was still too contentious to make it onto the stage. Even the revisions of Will Shakespeare and others could not get Munday's play past the censor, although that did not stop Shakespeare making use of the material.

In *The Book of Sir Thomas More*, the statesman hosts a banquet and engages a meagre troupe of players to perform a morality play, *The Marriage of Wit and Wisdom*. When one of the players goes missing, frantically searching around London for the right kind of beard, Sir Thomas More himself takes the part of Good Council in the interlude. This odd episode was probably written by Anthony Munday, who as Bottom the weaver in *A Midsummer Night's Dream* is likewise obsessed with prop beards.

Munday's play-within-a-play – *The Marriage of Wit and Wisdom* – became, for the occasion of the Heneage-Southampton marriage, a 'tedious brief scene' based on a Babylonian legend.

As told by the Roman poet Ovid, the legend concerned two neighbours, Pyramus and Thisbe, who were forbidden by their parents to see each other. They managed to communicate through a chink in the wall and arranged to meet one night at the tomb of Ninus, over which grew a 'tall mulberry, hung thick with snowy fruits'.

Thisbe arrived first but was frightened off by a ravenous lion. Pyramus found her discarded veil and assumed the worst. He plunged his own sword into his ribs, his blood splashing onto the white fruits of the mulberry. Thisbe returned to find her lover dying under the tree. She took up his sword and called on the mulberry always to 'have fruit of a dark and mournful hue, to make men remember the blood we two have shed!' With that, she fell on the sword, and the fruits of the mulberry have been a dark purple colour ever since.

Shakespeare had already used the image of a bloodstained flower in 'Venus and Adonis', which concluded with a blood-spattered 'purple flower ... chequered with white'. *A Midsummer Night's Dream* also features a 'little western flower – / Before, milk-white; now, purple with love's wound', which maidens call 'love-in-idleness'. The juice of this flower, when dripped onto the eyelids, causes the sleeper to fall madly in love with the first creature he sees upon waking, which is how Robin Goodfellow tricks the Fairy Queen into falling for a bad actor with the head of an ass.

'Idleness' was a derogatory term for the worship of sacred idols. The Elizabethan regime had helped to provide a multitude of these relics – bloodstained handkerchiefs, human remains – by sacrificing so many Catholic priests. Much of the plot of *A Midsummer Night's Dream* revolves around the effect of these relics on the eyes of their beholders. One of the most potent of them all was the bloodstained shirt of Sir Thomas More, beheaded for his loyalty to the Church of Rome.

The mulberry was also known as the 'more tree', its purple fruits emblematic of More's blood-sacrifice. It was customary in Warwickshire to pair a mulberry with a quince. Shakespeare's use of Peter Quince to introduce the legend of the mulberry suggests that he was eager to stress the relevance of the 'more tree'.

In a play performed for the marriage of the spymaster Sir Thomas Heneage to the dowager Countess of Southampton, Will daringly highlighted the martyrdom of Catholics and the queen's 'love-in-idleness' for her asinine priest-hunter, 'Judas' Munday.

IT WAS probably around the time of *A Midsummer Night's Dream* that the Earl of Southampton fell in love with Elizabeth Vernon, one of the queen's ladies-in-waiting and a cousin to Southampton's friend, the Earl of Essex. They eventually married on 30 August 1598, when the bride was already pregnant. The queen found out and flew into one of her trademark rages. Both bride and groom were sent to the Fleet prison.

Things had cooled by then between Shakespeare and his 'familiar friend'. The theatres had reopened late in 1594. The Earl of Derby's Men found a new patron, in the form of the Lord Chamberlain, Henry Carey, and it was as 'servants to the Lord Chamberlain' that Shakespeare and his fellows were paid for two 'comedies or Interludes' performed at Christmas before the queen.

Will's parting gift to Southampton was surely his *Most Excellent and Lamentable Tragedy of Romeo and Juliet*, which dates to the time of Southampton's twenty-first birthday in October 1594. The much-loved tale of love across the sectarian divide was clearly pitched at Southampton, whose mother was, like Romeo, a Montagu. Southampton also presented Will with a gift – one which has foxed scholars ever since.

The tradition was handed down by Sir William Davenant and recorded by Nicholas Rowe in 1709. Davenant 'was probably very well acquainted with his [Shakespeare's] affairs,' wrote Rowe, who revealed that 'my lord *Southampton* at one time gave him a thousand pounds, to enable him to go through with a purchase which he heard he had a mind to. A bounty very great, and very rare at any time.'

Rev. John Ward heard from the people of Stratford in 1662 that Shakespeare 'spent at the rate of a thousand a year'. Where he got that sort of money from is uncertain. The sonnets might offer a clue.

For a time, Shakespeare seems to have thought his days were numbered: 'But be contented when that fell arrest, / Without all bail shall carry me away.' Now the poet took his leave of the fair youth:

> Farewell thou art too dear for my possessing,
> And like enough thou know'st thy estimate,
> The Charter of thy worth gives thee releasing:
> My bonds in thee are all determinate.

This sonnet – the eighty-seventh in the published sequence – is unique. Every line has a feminine ending. It appears to mark the end of the affair:

> For how do I hold thee but by thy granting,
> And for that riches where is my deserving?

The cause of this fair gift in me is wanting,
And so my patent back again is swerving.

What this 'fair gift' might have been is hinted at:

Thy self thou gav'st, thy own worth then not knowing,
Or me to whom thou gav'st it, else mistaking,
So thy great gift upon misprision growing,
Comes home again, on better judgement making.

Southampton's 'great gift' had grown upon 'misprision'. The term survives in English law as the offence of misprision of treason – the foreknowledge of an act of treason and the failure to report it.

Had Will been guilty of misprision? There were treasons galore at this time, most of them emanating from the power struggle between, on the one hand, Lord Burghley and Robert Cecil, and, on the other, the Earl of Essex and his followers. Shortly after the Earl of Derby's death in April 1594 another plot came to light. This had supposedly involved a planned uprising in North Wales which, it was claimed, would be part-funded by Ralph Sheldon of Beoley, Worcestershire. Sheldon was related to Will Shakespeare.

Not for the first time, Shakespeare's network of Catholic contacts had placed him in jeopardy. The publication in 1594 of 'Willobie his Avisa', penned by Lord Burghley's man, Matthew Roydon, suggests that the knives were out. Will's name was being blackened – as Christopher Marlowe's had been before his murder. His best hope would have been to appeal to Burghley's avarice.

A few years earlier, the Catholic patsy Anthony Babington had offered the Lord High Treasurer £1,000 in exchange for his life. Will's 'great gift upon misprision growing' might have represented a similar gambit. Bribery was rife. Everyone had their price. The sum of £1,000 was perhaps just enough to buy off Lord Burghley, or his stunted son, and save Will Shakespeare from the consequences of misprision.

It also required W.S. and H.W. to go their separate ways. Southampton could no longer be Will's noble Catholic figurehead: 'Thus have I had thee as a dream doth flatter, / In sleep a King, but waking no such matter.'

ON 19 MARCH 1596, the Chamber treasurer paid 'Hall and Wayte' £15 for conveying messages from the Netherlands to the Secretary of State, Sir Robert Cecil. Later that same year, the Sheriff of Surrey issued a 'writ of attachment': 'Be it known that William Wayte seeks sureties of the peace against William Shakespeare, Francis Langley, Dorothy Soer wife of John Soer and Anna Lee for fear of death and so forth.'

Wayte was the thuggish stepson of a Southwark judge; he was described in 1592 as a 'certain loose person of no reckoning or value'. That Will Shakespeare was involved with Francis Langley comes as no surprise: Langley owned the Swan Theatre in Southwark. As for why Shakespeare's quarrel with William Wayte should have come to the attention of the justices, we can only guess that it was somehow connected to the business conducted by 'Hall and Wayte' in the Netherlands, where Wayte was perhaps Will's minder and, like Kit Marlowe and Richard Baines before them, they had fallen out.

The year 1596 was a difficult one. The second edition of 'Willobie his Avisa' was published and the plague returned, forcing the theatres to close in July. This was followed by a hammer blow. The register of Holy Trinity Church, Stratford-upon-Avon, records the burial on 11 August of 'Hamnet, filius William Shakspere'. Will's son and heir had died at the age of 11.

Hamnet's early death drew Shakespeare back to his family. On 20 October 1596, just a few weeks after his son was buried, Will revived his father's application for a coat of arms.

John Shakespeare had made his application to the College of Arms some thirty years earlier. It had been quietly overlooked. Will's renewed application survives in two drafts. He claimed that his father's grandparents had been 'advanced and rewarded' by the 'most Prudent Prince King Henry the seventh of famous memory'. A senior officer at the College of Arms also noted that, in addition to his service as bailiff and 'chief of the town of Stratford upon Avon', John Shakespeare held 'land and tenements, of good wealth and substance, £500'.

The coat of arms was granted. It depicted a spear 'of the first steeled argent' on a 'Bend Sable' against a gold background. The motto Will had chosen was *Non Sanz Droict* – 'Not Without Right'. Shakespeare had bought himself the status of a gentleman. The Garter King of Arms would soon be criticised for having sold coats of arms to twenty-three 'mean persons', one of whom was 'Shakespear yᵉ Player'. But whether or not Shakespeare was an acceptable recipient of the title of 'gentleman', he had acquired the privilege.

He also bought a property in Stratford. The 'pretty house' on the corner of Chapel Street was in 'great ruin and decay'. Will paid 'sixty pounds in silver' for it in May 1597 and then 'repair'd and modell'd it to his own mind'.

The vendor, William Underhill, was the 'subtle, covetous and crafty man' to whom the gardener-priest Hugh Hall had fled after the arrest of John Somerville in 1583. Two months after he sold New Place to Shakespeare, Underhill was dead; he had been poisoned by his eldest son.

Underhill's estate eventually passed to his second son and, in the autumn of 1602, Will was finally able to complete his purchase of New Place.

He now possessed the largest private dwelling in Stratford and the right to call himself a gentleman. It was small compensation for the loss of his only son.

BEN JONSON'S earliest surviving play, *The Case is Altered*, was probably performed by the Earl of Pembroke's Men in the summer of 1597. It is notable for containing 'the most grossly scatological scene in all of Elizabethan drama'. A miser named Jaques de Prie hides his ill-gotten gold in a bucket of horse manure, wondering 'Who will suppose that such a precious nest / Is crown'd with such a dunghill excrement?' The name Jaques was itself a joke – a 'jakes' being an Elizabethan privy or toilet.

Jonson then collaborated with Thomas Nashe on *The Isle of Dogs*, the satire which landed Ben in prison and nearly caused the permanent shutdown of the theatres. His next offering, *Every Man in his Humour*, was performed by Shakespeare's company in September 1598.

A tradition set down by Will's first biographer, Nicholas Rowe, has Shakespeare giving the younger playwright a much-needed break:

> Mr Jonson, who was at that time altogether unknown to the world, had offered one of his plays to the players in order to have it acted, and the persons into whose hands it was put … were just upon returning it to him with an ill-natured answer … when Shakespeare luckily cast his eye upon it, and found something so well in it to engage him first to read it through, and afterwards to recommend Mr Jonson and his writings to the public.

If Will had indeed helped to kick-start Ben Jonson's career, he was to be poorly rewarded. 'After this they were professed friends,' wrote Nicholas Rowe, 'though I don't know whether the other ever made him [Shakespeare] an equal return of gentleness and sincerity.'

As the Lord Chamberlain's Men were presenting Jonson's *Every Man in his Humour* on the stage, the playwright was arrested for killing the actor Gabriel Spenser. While awaiting trial, Ben was converted to Catholicism by a priest who visited him in Newgate prison. 'Thereafter', noted William Drummond, 'he was 12 years a Papist.'

In the circumstances, being 'almost at the gallows', this had the trappings of a deathbed conversion. At his trial, though, Jonson calmly admitted his guilt and asked for 'the book'. He read out the neck-verse 'like a clerk' and, as mentioned earlier, was branded on the base of his thumb with a letter T, for Tyburn.

Ben's timely conversion should be considered a sham. He had bought his life and freedom by agreeing to pose as a Catholic. Ben then returned to London's theatrical underbelly as an informer working for Sir Robert Cecil – a man who, as Jonson told William Drummond, 'never cared for any man longer nor he could make use of him'.

THREE DAYS after Christmas 1598, a gang of workmen trudged through the snow to the Theatre in Shoreditch. The landowner would later accuse them of 'pulling breaking and throwing down the said Theatre in very outrageous violent and riotous sort'. By the beginning of January, the playhouse had been dismantled.

The timbers were transported across the river to a plot of land in Southwark, where the original Theatre was rebuilt. Will Shakespeare owned one-tenth of it.

The Globe, as the new playhouse was known, opened at the summer solstice, 12 June 1599, with a performance of Shakespeare's *Julius Caesar*. The spectators found themselves inside a 'wooden O', a polygonal structure, with a thrust stage raised on trestles, 5 feet off the ground, and an open roof. There were three tiers of seating, covered by a canopy of thatch, taking the theatre's capacity up to a little over 3,000. The population of London was about 200,000, so that in relative terms the Globe was a huge stadium, identified by the image of Hercules holding the Earth on his shoulders and the motto *Totus mundus agit histrionem* – 'The whole world plays the actor'.

Jonson resented the success of Will's *Julius Caesar*, partly because he had wanted his own play to open the new theatre. His *Every Man Out of his Humour* was presented at the Globe later that year, with Shakespeare in the cast.

Every Man Out of his Humour was the first salvo in what became an increasingly acrid rivalry between Jonson and Shakespeare. In the third act of the play, a yokel named Sogliardo boasts that he has acquired a coat of arms: 'I can write myself gentleman now; here's my patent, it cost me thirty pounds.' His crest – a 'boar's head proper' – is ridiculed as signifying 'a swine without a head, without brain, wit, anything indeed, ramping to gentility'. One character quips, 'Let the word be, "Not without mustard".'

The 'Not without mustard' gag was borrowed from Thomas Nashe. In his *Pierce Penniless* of 1592, Nashe told the story of a 'mad Ruffian' who 'being in danger of shipwreck by tempest' prayed for deliverance, vowing 'never to eat haberdine [dried salted cod] more whilst I live'. The tempest abated, and the ruffian mocked his own prayer by adding 'not without mustard, good Lord, not without mustard.'

If, as was suggested earlier, Will Shakespeare had taken part in the Virginia expedition of 1585, then he would have weathered the Atlantic storm which nearly sank the *Tiger*. Ben's veiled reference, via his 'Not without mustard' jibe, to Will's family motto – *Non Sanz Droict* – lends weight to the possibility that Shakespeare was onboard the *Tiger* when it ran aground on the Outer Banks.

Will could have taken this ribbing with a pinch of salt, were it not for the more pointed barbs in *Every Man Out of his Humour*. The 'essential Clown' Sogliardo models himself on Fastidious Briske, a 'neat, spruce, affecting Courtier' who keeps a pageboy for sexual purposes. Fastidious also has a mistress. Fallace is her name; she happens to be Sogliardo's niece, and her husband, a 'good doting citizen', is as besotted with her as she is with the effeminate Fastidious: 'I have heard of a citizen's wife has been beloved of a courtier; and why not I?'

'Willobie his Avisa' was reissued – and suppressed – that year, reminding the citizens of London that 'H.W.' had told the witty 'Avisa' that her husband was 'a worthlesse thing, / That no way can content your mind, / That no way can that pleasure bring, / Your flowring yeares desire to find ...' *The Passionate Pilgrim* was also published in 1599, bringing two of Will's love-triangle sonnets to public attention alongside several verses which follow a similar pattern to 'Willobie his Avisa'. The old gossip would not go away. Jonson's sly hints in *Every Man Out of his Humour* about Southampton the effeminate courtier, Shakespeare the 'essential Clown' and Jane Davenant, the 'proud mincing' wife, merely fanned the flames.

SHAKESPEARE STRUCK back. He was then attempting to have his coat of arms quartered with that of his Arden kinsmen. *As You Like It* was a homage to his native region, and he welcomed Ben Jonson to the Forest of Arden as the moody philosopher Jaques.

The sylvan world of *As You Like It* is a Catholic retreat. This is indicated by Touchstone, the jester who accompanies the banished Rosalind (pronounced 'Rose-aligned', with a hint at the rosary) and her friend Celia into exile: 'Ay, now am I in Arden; the more fool I.' The Woodland folk were more fools – 'fools' of Sir Thomas More, whose name betokened 'folly' and 'Rome'.

Jaques is quickly caught up in the foolishness:

JAQUES: A fool, a fool, I met a fool i'th' forest,
           A motley fool – a miserable world! –
           As I do live by food, I met a fool ...

Jonson had indeed met a 'fool' – the priest who had converted him in prison. Jaques resolves to become a 'noble fool, / A worthy fool' and to 'moral on the time':

> Invest me in my motley. Give me leave
> To speak my mind, and I will through and through
> Cleanse the foul body of th'infected world,
> If they will patiently receive my medicine.

He is allowed to deny his insinuations about Southampton and Jane Davenant:

> What woman in the city do I name
> When I say that the city-woman bears
> The cost of princes on unworthy shoulders?
> Who can come in and say that I mean her
> When such a one as she, such is her neighbour?

Shakespeare had given Jonson a 'purge that made him bewray his credit', joked the students at Cambridge. This was it: as Jaques, Ben had become his own toilet or 'jakes'. At the end of *As You Like It* he elects to stay in the forest with those who have 'put on a religious life': 'Out of these convertites / There is much matter to be heard and learned.'

The ghost of another poet stalks the Woodland. Touchstone remarks: 'When a man's verses cannot be understood, nor a man's good wit seconded with the forward child, understanding, it strikes a man more dead than a great reckoning in a little room.' Celia picks up the theme: '"Was" is not "is". Besides, the oath of a lover is no stronger than the word of a tapster. They are both the confirmer of false reckonings.' Even a sloe-eyed shepherdess gets in on the game:

> PHOEBE (*aside*): Dead shepherd, now I find thy saw of might:
>   'Who ever loved that loved not at first sight?'

The line came from 'Hero and Leander', the poem that Christopher Marlowe was working on when he was killed. Officially, Marlowe had died during an argument in a little room over the 'reckoning'.

In the fantasy Arden of *As You Like It,* Will felt free to question the government's version of events. The newly opened Globe seemed to offer him the liberty to challenge the cynical assumptions of the State: 'Yet your mistrust cannot make me a traitor … Treason is not inherited, my lord, / Or if we did derive it from our friends, / What's that to me? My father was no traitor.'

Now all the world was Shakespeare's stage. He would use it to show the world a true reflection of itself.

11

Remember Me

ROBERT DEVEREUX, Second Earl of Essex, was the petulant favourite of the queen; his stepfather, the Earl of Leicester, had been Elizabeth's beloved 'eyes'. On 14 April 1599, the Earl of Essex landed in Ireland and took command of the largest expeditionary force the English had ever sent into that stricken land.

Essex craved military glory. But, as he wrote to his cousin, Sir Fulke Greville, early in 1599, the queen had 'destined me to the hardest task that ever gentleman was sent about'. He was required to suppress an Irish rebellion, spearheaded by Hugh O'Neill, Earl of Tyrone, which had received support from Scotland and Spain.

Will Shakespeare referred to the mission in one of the first plays performed at the Globe, his *Life of Henry the Fifth*:

> Were now the General of our gracious Empress –
> As in good time he may – from Ireland coming,
> Bringing rebellion broachèd on his sword,
> How many would the peaceful city quit
> To welcome him!

No one welcomed Essex on his return. His campaign had been a disaster. One of his first disobedient acts had been to appoint the Earl of Southampton his General of Horse, despite having been expressly forbidden to do so. Essex then marched his troops off in the wrong direction. By mid-July, barely one-third of his force was fit for battle.

The earl began to suspect that he had been set up: Ireland would be his ruin, while his enemies at home prospered. This was indeed a favourite tactic of the Cecils, who had competed with Essex for control of the intelligence services. Lord Burghley had died in August 1598, leaving his dwarfish son, Robert Cecil, to continue serving the queen as her chief minister.

On 7 September 1599, Essex held a private conference with the rebel O'Neill. What he learned from this meeting alarmed him. He resigned his post on 24 September and took ship for England, accompanied by his most trusted followers. They rode hard, reaching the palace of Nonsuch on the morning of 28 September.

Covered with mud, Essex burst into Elizabeth's bedchamber. The queen was 'newly up, her hair about her face'. Without her red wig and white make-up, her advancing age was all too apparent. She listened calmly while Essex gabbled and then asked him to come back when he had cleaned himself up.

As of that moment, his career was over. His enemies cast 'libels abroad in his name against the state' and set 'paper upon posts, to bring his innocent friends in question'. The source of these rumours masqueraded as the wounded party: 'At court upon the very white walls, much villainy hath been written against Sir Robert Cecil.'

Essex was banished from Court and became a magnet for those malcontents – survivors of his Irish expedition, blighted Catholics – who had suffered at the hands of Elizabeth and the 'little men' who served her.

EARLY IN 1601, supporters of the Earl of Essex approached the leading members of Shakespeare's theatre company, wishing 'to have the play of the deposing and killing of King Richard the second to be played the Saturday next'.

Will's colleague Augustine Phillips testified a few days later that the players had demurred; the *Tragedy of King Richard the Second* was 'so old & so long out of use' that they could expect little profit from it. The Essex delegation offered an inducement of 40 shillings and Will's play was quickly restaged on Saturday 7 February.

They might as well have lit a warning beacon. The play was notorious for its scene in which a king is forced to abdicate. Even Elizabeth recognised the message: 'I am Richard II, know ye not that?' she is reported to have said. The performance galvanised the authorities. Essex was promptly summoned to appear before the Privy Council.

The next morning – Sunday, 8 February – the earl assembled a force of about 300 men and marched them to the City of London, hoping to spark an uprising. The entrance to the city was barred. Essex was proclaimed a traitor. He returned to his house on the Strand, where he threw various documents on the fire, including a letter from King James VI of Scotland, but when he was threatened with an artillery bombardment he gave himself up.

Essex believed that he had uncovered a conspiracy to plant Isabella Clara Eugenia, daughter of King Phillip II of Spain and now Queen of the Spanish Netherlands, on the throne after Elizabeth's death. Desperately, he pointed out that certain individuals 'being principally loved by the principal Secretary, Sir Robert Cecil' had been placed in key strategic positions, enabling Cecil – who had secretly commissioned portraits of Isabella and her husband – to take control of England on behalf of the Spanish Infanta.

However he had heard about Cecil's machinations – from O'Neill in Ireland or King James in Scotland – Essex had been thoroughly outwitted. Cecil ensured that he was disgraced, marginalised, and finally provoked into mounting his abortive rebellion. The earl was beheaded on Ash Wednesday, 25 February. His close ally Southampton was committed to the Tower of London under sentence of death.

The final act of the tragedy had been triggered by the performance of Shakespeare's *Richard II*. Augustine Phillips was subjected to a cursory examination and the players were commanded to perform before the queen on the eve of Essex's execution.

But the rebellion had not yet run its course. Among those penalised for their part in the foiled coup were William Parker, John Grant, Robert Catesby, Francis Tresham, John and Christopher Wright and two brothers of Henry Percy, Ninth Earl of Northumberland.

The seeds of the Gunpowder Plot had been sown.

SIR ROBERT Cecil's clerk noted on 6 October 1601 that 'Willm Halle' had returned with messages from Denmark. At about the same time, Will Shakespeare started work on his tragedy of a Prince of Denmark.

A month earlier, Will's father had died in his seventies. John Shakespeare was buried at Holy Trinity Church, Stratford-upon-Avon, on 8 September.

The authorities reserved the right to insist that Catholics were buried not in consecrated ground but in a hole by a crossroads. Many were buried in secret, their official graves occupied by stone-filled coffins. Thus, in 1614, the Archbishop of Canterbury demanded that the tomb of Sir George Browne – a son of the Catholic Lord Montagu and kinsman of the Earl of Southampton – be opened so that 'the churchwardens might assure him that the body was there'. Browne's remains were then reburied 'neither in church nor churchyard' but beside the highway.

Conceivably, John Shakespeare's friends on the Stratford Corporation intervened to secure him a Christian burial. Richard Quiney, Will Shakespeare's 'Loving good Friend', had just commenced his second term as bailiff of Stratford; within months, he would be dealt a fatal head injury by thugs employed by the puritanical Greville family.

The death of Will's father must have put him in mind of the 'Spiritual Testament' which John Shakespeare had signed in 1580:

> Item, I John Shakespear do ... pray and beseech all my dear friends, parents and kinsfolk, by the bowels of our Saviour Jesus Christ ... notwithstanding least by reason of my sins I be to pass and stay a long while in Purgatory, they will vouchsafe to assist and succour me with their holy prayers and satisfactory works, especially with the holy sacrifice of the Mass, as being the most effectual means to deliver souls from their torments and pains ...

Celebrating Mass was forbidden. Honouring the terms of his father's 'Testament of the Soul' would have required Will Shakespeare to put his life on the line, along with everything he owned.

This gave him something to brood on when, as 'Willm Halle', he made his trip to Denmark. He had been 16 in the summer of 1580, when John Shakespeare received his 'Testament' from a Jesuit priest. A short while before, on 17 December 1579, a teenage girl had drowned in the Avon. Her body was laid to rest at Alveston, across the river from Stratford, but was then exhumed and an inquest held to determine whether the poor girl had committed suicide.

The town clerk of Stratford presided over the inquest in February 1580. To the relief of the young woman's family, it was found that she had merely slipped on the weed-strewn riverbank and been swept away by the current. Her death was *per infortunium* – 'an accident' – and so she was spared the fate of the suicide, which was to be buried at a crossroads, where passers-by could hurl stones and broken crockery at the grave.

Suicides and Catholics suffered the same posthumous indignities.

Will Shakespeare had not forgotten the drowned girl. Her name was Katherine Hamlet.

A DISTRACTED young woman drowns in a 'weeping brook'. Unaware that she is dead, her lover watches her funeral procession and is shocked at the 'maimèd rites' that attend her burial. The girl's brother, equally dismayed, demands, 'What ceremony else?' The 'churlish' priest replies:

> Her death was doubtful,
> And but that a great command o'ersways the order
> She should in ground unsanctified have lodged
> Till the last trumpet.

The suspicion of suicide meant that the drowned girl should have 'Shards, flints and pebbles' thrown at her, rather than 'charitable prayers'.

Will wrote his *Tragedy of Hamlet, Prince of Denmark* during the winter months following his father's death. Katherine Hamlet was resurrected as Ophelia, whose death by drowning was similarly 'doubtful'.

The play opens with Prince Hamlet in mourning for his father and disturbed by the fact that the Danish Court has moved on. Hamlet's uncle, Claudius, has married Hamlet's mother and usurped the throne. The narrative is impelled by the appearance of Hamlet's father as a ghost, demanding vengeance.

The ghost functions like a spectral reminder of John Shakespeare's illicit 'Testament of the Soul'. In terms which challenged the Protestants' dismissal of the doctrine of Purgatory, the ghost informs Hamlet:

> I am thy father's spirit,
> Doomed for a certain term to walk the night,
> And for the day confined to fast in fires
> Till the foul crimes done in my days of nature
> Are burnt and purged away.

He calls on Hamlet to avenge his 'most unnatural murder'. A false account of his death has been spread about and the murderer has seized the throne:

> Brief let me be. Sleeping within mine orchard,
> My custom always in the afternoon,
> Upon my secure hour thy uncle stole
> With juice of cursèd hebenon in a vial,
> And in the porches of mine ear did pour
> The leperous distilment ...

The poison worked like the drip-drip effect of Protestant sermonising, curdling the lifeblood and coating the body with a 'thin, white crust', like the layer of whitewash which had been used to deface the images in Stratford's Guild Chapel. Hamlet's father died – presumably, like

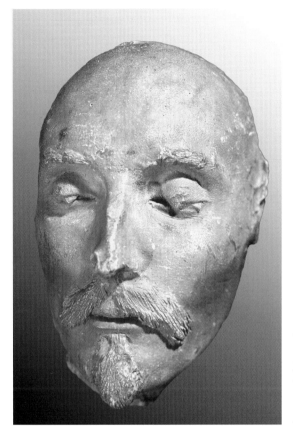

1 The death mask of
Shakespeare. *Reproduced
with kind permission of
the Universitäts- und
Landesbibliothek Darmstadt*

2 Droeshout engraving and
Jonson's commendation 'To
the Reader'. *First Folio (1623),
copy held in Victoria & Albert
Museum*

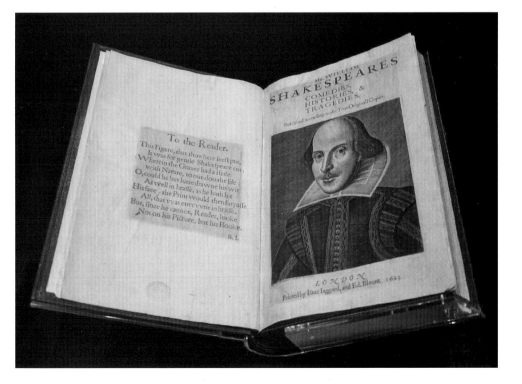

3 *The Chess Players*, attributed to Karel Van Mander, *c.* 1603.

4 *A Sculptor's Workshop, Stratford-upon-Avon, 1617,* by Henry Wallis (1830–1916). *Reproduced by kind permission of the Royal Shakespeare Company*

6 The Davenant bust, credited to Louis Francois Roubillac, *c. 1702–62. Courtesy of The Art Archive, Garrick Club*

5 The Chandos Portrait. *National Portrait Gallery*

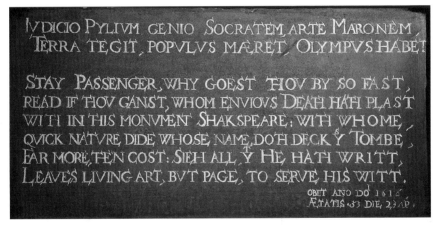

7 Detail of Shakespeare funerary monument.

8 Inscription on Shakespeare's grave, Holy Trinity Church, Stratford-upon-Avon.

9 Shakespeare
monument, Holy Trinity
Church, Stratford-upon-
Avon. *Copyright John
Cheal 'Inspired Images'
2012*

10 Engraving of Shakespeare's
funerary monument, by
Wenceslaus Hollar. Taken
from the pre-Civil War sketch
of the monument made by
Sir William Dugdale, 1636.
*Published in 'The Antiquities of
Warwickshire', 1656*

11 Ben Jonson. Engraving by George Vertue (1684–1786).

12 Sir William Davenant (1606–68).

13 Ben Jonson. Engraving by Robert Vaughan, *c.* 1627.

14 Shakespeare. Engraving by William Marshall, *c.* 1640.

15 Hillborough Manor, Temple Grafton in 1938. Reputedly the home of Anne (or 'Agnes') Whateley. *Warwickshire County Record Office, PH137/5*

16 Christ Church Meadow, Oxford; scene of Jane Davenant's confession to Father Henry Garnet, 1605. *Courtesy of Tejvan Pettinger, www.oxfordlight.co.uk*

17 Will of John Whateley, draper, of Henley-in-Arden. Probated in 1554, the will names 'Agnes my daughter'. *Worcestershire Archive and Archaeology Service*

18 The Painted Room of the Taverne run by John and Jane Davenant, 3 Cornmarket, Oxford. A Catholic 'IHS' symbol over the fireplace; a later Protestant text to the left. *With kind permission of the Oxford Preservation Trust*

19 Father Henry Garnet, SJ (1555–1606). Falsely accused of having masterminded the Gunpowder Plot, Father Garnet's execution inspired the murder of King Duncan in Shakespeare's *Tragedy of Macbeth*.

20 This copy of Garnet's 'Confession' was bound in his skin. It sold at auction in 2009. *Image courtesy of Wilkinsons' Auctioneers*

21 The Executions of the Gunpowder Plotters.

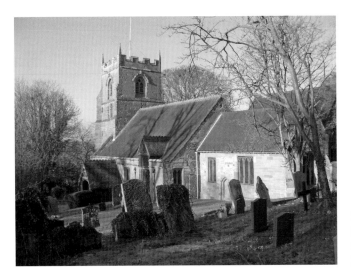

22
St Leonard's
Church,
Beoley.

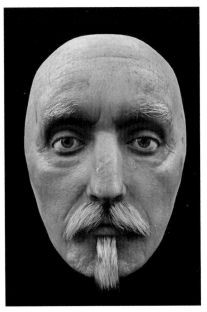

23 The Beoley skull. *With kind permission of R.H. Richardson, churchwarden, St Leonard's Church, Beoley*

24 Computer-generated image of Shakespeare's face, from the Darmstadt death mask. Created by the University of Dundee's Craniofacial Identification Division. Close inspection reveals features in common with the Beoley skull and Shakespeare portraiture, including damage to the forehead, eye socket and cheekbones. *Copyright Exclusivepix*

Shakespeare's – without making his confession or receiving the benefits of last communion and extreme unction:

> Thus was I, sleeping, by a brother's hand
> Of life, of crown, of queen at once dispatched,
> Cut off even in the blossom of my sin,
> Unhouseled, dis-appointed, unaneled,
> No reck'ning made, but sent to my account
> With all my imperfections on my head.
> O horrible, O horrible, most horrible!

The ghost presents the prince with a dreadful dilemma: 'Adieu, adieu, Hamlet. Remember me.' Like the shade of John Shakespeare, taunting his son with the promises made in his Jesuit will, Hamlet's father spoke with the voice of those Catholics who cried out for justice. And like Prince Hamlet, Will vowed to 'wipe away all trivial fond records' and reflect on his father's requests, especially in the theatre: 'Remember thee? / Ay, thou poor ghost, while memory holds a seat / In this distracted globe.'

ELIZABETH WAS fast approaching the end of her life. She had refused to name her successor. All discussion of the topic was banned. Few, though, were in any doubt as to who would succeed her.

James VI of Scotland was the son of Elizabeth's cousin, Mary, Queen of Scots. Crowned at the tender age of 13 months, James had ruled over a fractious country for thirty-five years. The English, who had been ruled for the past half-century by two women and a boy, were pleased to note that King James was a married man with two male heirs. He was also learned and erudite, having been raised and tutored in the frigid air of the Scottish Reformation.

Several leading figures secretly opened up channels of communication with King James in Scotland. The most pressing issue to be thrashed out was the king's stance on religion. For his part, James was eager for insights into the state of the kingdom he would soon inherit.

King James disliked long plays. At around 4,000 lines, *Hamlet* is far and away Shakespeare's longest. Two versions of the play survive. The first, published in 1603, is considerably shorter than subsequent editions and was probably a slimmed-down text used in performance. The version printed in 1604 was 'enlarged to almost as much again as it was, according to the true and perfect copy'. At its fullest length, *Hamlet* was perhaps not meant to be watched but to be read – specifically, by a man who was himself a 'Prince of Denmark'.

On 23 November 1589, James VI of Scotland had married the 14-year-old Anne, daughter of Frederick II of Denmark, at the Old Bishop's Palace in Oslo. The couple had then stayed at Elsinore, the setting for Will's *Tragedy of Hamlet*.

Like the fictional Prince of Denmark, King James had received a sound Protestant education. But the certainties implanted by Hamlet's tutors begin to unravel when the ghost of his father appears. Hamlet has discovered that there are 'more things in heaven and on earth ... Than are dreamt of in our philosophy.'

Both of James' parents had been Catholics. His mother had been executed in England as a threat to the Protestant ascendancy. His father, Henry Stuart, Lord Darnley, had also had a claim to the English throne.

Early in the morning of 10 February 1567, Lord Darnley was murdered in Edinburgh. The house in which he had been staying was blown to smithereens by gunpowder. But the explosion had not killed him. His body was discovered, along with that of a servant, in a nearby garden, wearing only a nightshirt. Darnley had been strangled.

A contemporary sketch, prepared for Queen Elizabeth's long-serving minister, Lord Burghley, shows how similar Darnley's death was to the murder of Hamlet's father. Lord Darnley was a tall man, but in the Burghley sketch he is enormous, a partially denuded giant lying beside a huge tree, as if he had lain down to sleep in an orchard.

The man behind the murder plot was James Hepburn, Fourth Earl of Bothwell. Although Queen Mary was a confirmed Catholic, she had worked hard not to alienate the Scottish Calvinists, and Bothwell had become one of her most trusted Protestant advisers.

Having killed her husband, Bothwell abducted Mary, Queen of Scots. They were married just three months after Darnley's murder.

King James showed no love towards his Catholic mother. He had been brought up and schooled by her enemies, who blamed Mary herself for Lord Darnley's death. Like Prince Hamlet, James VI had cause to accuse his late mother of 'honeying and making love' with the murderer of her husband.

The arrival of a troupe of players allows Hamlet to deploy a trick used time and again by Shakespeare to prick the conscience of the spectator:

> I have heard that guilty creatures sitting at a play
> Have by the very cunning of the scene
> Been struck so to the soul that presently
> They have proclaimed their malefactions ...

Hamlet persuades the players to perform an old tragedy – the 'murder of Gonzago', or, as the Prince calls it, *The Mousetrap* – to test the guilt of his father's murderer. In a preliminary dumb show, the players mime the plot:

> *Enter a King and a Queen very lovingly, the Queen embracing him ... He lays him down upon a bank of flowers. She, seeing him asleep, leaves him. Anon comes in a fellow, takes off his crown, kisses it, and pours poison in the King's ears, and exits ... The dead body is carried away. The poisoner woos the Queen with gifts. She seems loath and unwilling a while, but in the end accepts his love. Exeunt the Players.*

Hamlet's play-within-a-play was an extraordinary moment in Will's work, coming so soon after the revival of his tragedy of *Richard II* on the eve of the Essex revolt. He had revealed his technique by explicitly stating that a play could be more than mere entertainment and by instructing the Scottish king to read the text as a sort of psychodrama designed to prompt a reconsideration of past crimes.

Will personalised the allegory by drawing on the iconography of Darnley's death. After Mary's hasty marriage to Bothwell, the earl's opponents – including the guardians of the infant James – rode out from Edinburgh to take the queen away from her new husband. They marched under a banner which depicted Lord Darnley's corpse lying beneath a tree, his young son kneeling beside him, and bore the words: 'Judge and avenge my cause, O Lord'.

Mary, Queen of Scots, was held captive and forced to renounce the throne in favour of her son. She then escaped to England, where Elizabeth kept her prisoner for two decades before signing her death warrant.

The Earl of Bothwell fled to Scandinavia. On the orders of King Frederick of Denmark, he was cast into a dungeon in Dragsholm Castle where, chained to a pillar, Bothwell went out of his mind and died in April 1578. In November 1579, King James of Scotland married King Frederick's youngest daughter, Anne of Denmark.

The parallels between Hamlet, Prince of Denmark, and James VI were obvious. Shakespeare used his *Tragedy of Hamlet* to shake the Scottish king's Protestant convictions and remind him of his father's murder. With the ghostly voice of his own father whispering in his ear, Will implored King James to consider the plight of the English Catholics who would soon be his subjects.

Hamlet prevaricates. He seeks proofs of the ghost's claims, like a man unwilling or unable to credit the terrible stories he's been hearing. Friends are sent to spy on him. He refuses to slay his murderous uncle while the latter is trying to pray, thereby mistaking a show of piety for the real thing.

The tragedy ends in a bloodbath, the royal family dead and the country delivered into the hands of its enemies. This, Will implied, might be the outcome if King James ignored the sufferings of the Catholics and allowed himself to be snared in the plots laid for him by Protestant ministers, whose professions of piety were mere cloaks for their ruthless ambition.

THE 21ST DAY of March 1603: a hush descended over London.

'Not a bell rang out,' remarked a Jesuit prisoner. 'Not a bugle sounded – though ordinarily they were often heard.'

Queen Elizabeth was dying in her palace at Richmond. As a precaution, some sixty 'principal Papists' were rounded up and interned.

The Virgin Queen passed away, aged 69, in the early hours of 24 March, the last day of the old year. Rumours abounded that she had died insane or, more remarkably, a Catholic, like her father. The Venetian ambassador reported that 'in her private chapel she preserved the altar with images, the organs, the vestments which belong to the Latin rite, and certain ceremonies which are loathed by other heretics'.

The government swiftly proclaimed the accession of King James I. Masterminded by Sir Robert Cecil, the transition went smoothly. 'Great fears were,' wrote Father Henry Garnet, the Jesuit superior in England, to Father Robert Persons in Rome, 'but all are turned into greatest security; and a golden time we have of unexpected freedom.'

The funeral for Elizabeth took place at Westminster Abbey on 28 April 1603. There was, predictably, a 'great outpouring of poetry'.

An unknown versifier called upon Shakespeare and others to compose elegies: 'You poets all, brave Shakespeare, Jonson, Greene, / Bestow your time to write for England's Queen.' There is nothing to suggest that Will did 'set forth sweet Elizabeth's praise', as the author of the 'Mournful Ditty' had demanded. His reticence was noted by the part-time playwright, Henry Chettle:

Nor doth the silver-tonguèd Melicert
Drop from his honeyed Muse one sable tear
To mourn her death who gracèd his desert,
And to his lays opened her royal ear.
    Shepherd, remember our Elizabeth,
    And sing her rape, done by that Tarquin, death.

Shakespeare was not going to reinvent Elizabeth's reign as an idyllic Golden Age. In public, he remained tight-lipped, preferring to express his thoughts in a private sonnet:

Not mine own fears, nor the prophetic soul,
Of the wide world, dreaming on things to come,
Can yet the lease of my true love control,
Supposed as forfeit to a confin'd doom.

As the superior of the Jesuits had intimated, England's Catholics were enjoying a 'golden time' of 'unexpected freedom':

The mortal Moon hath her eclipse endur'd,
And the sad Augurs mock their own presage,
Incertainties now crown themselves assur'd,
And peace proclaims Olives of endless age.

Sonnet 107 contains Will's only reference of the time to the passing of Elizabeth, the 'mortal Moon' whose changeability had been a recurring motif in his writings.

'Now with the drops of this most balmy time, / My love looks fresh,' he wrote, echoing the thoughts of Father Garnet in a letter to Rome: 'Great hope is of toleration ... All sorts of religions live in hope and suspense; yet the Catholics have great cause to hope for great respect ... and have good promise thereof from his majesty.' King James' personal motto was *Beati pacifici* – 'Blessed are the peacemakers'. With his accession, peace had been proclaimed. And after years in hiding, Will's true faith looked 'fresh', and would still do so 'When tyrants' crests and tombs of brass are spent.'

CROWDS FLOCKED to greet King James on his five-week journey from Edinburgh to London. What they glimpsed was a 37-year-old of medium height, with aquatic blue eyes, thin brown hair, a square-cut beard and a hangdog expression. As the cheering crowds pressed forward to meet His Majesty, an 'honest plain Scotsman' was heard presciently to mutter, 'This people will spoil a good king.'

James entered London on 7 May 1603, 'greatly moved by the zeal and affection expressed towards him by all sorts of people'. His new subjects were 'admonished that if they shall find cause to seek anything at his hands' they should 'resort by way of petition, and they shall receive favourable answer if their complaints be just.'

The king soon found his subjects' attentions trying: the 'access of the people made him so impatient that he often dispersed them with frowns, that we may not say curses'. When told that they only wanted to see his face, he responded with characteristic vulgarity – 'God's wounds! I will pull down my breeches and they shall also see my arse!'

There were just two kinds of people with whom James enjoyed spending time. The first was attractive young men. He was often to be seen leaning against a male favourite, one hand caressing their neck while the other fiddled with his codpiece.

James was also stimulated by the presence of fine minds. His table was 'a trial of Wits' – 'he collected Knowledge by variety of Questions' and was 'ever in chase after some disputable Doubts, which he would wind and turn about with the most stabbing Objections'. Those 'understanding Writers' who were privileged to engage in table talk with King James also witnessed his startling table manners. Sir Anthony Weldon observed that the king's tongue was 'too large for his mouth, which ... made him drink very uncomely, as if eating his drink'. The king's drunken slovenliness, his habit of dropping food and drink onto his shabby clothes, would only increase with age. So too would his 'terrifying insomnia, turbulent nights, laboured breathing, palpitations' and what his physician described as 'frank delirium with hallucinations'.

At the age of 18, it had been remarked of James that he was 'too lazy and indifferent about affairs ... allowing all business to be conducted by others.' Scotland, he had once observed, was a 'wild unruly colt'. He expected England to be more 'towardly'.

He was delighted to find that he had, in Sir Robert Cecil, a devoted secretary. To James, the hunchbacked Cecil was like a 'little beagle that lies by the fire when all the good hounds are running in the fields.'

The hunting metaphors betrayed the king's foremost interest in life. Though Sir John Oglander would claim in his *Royalist's Notebook* that 'James was the most cowardly man that ever I knew', when riding to hounds the king was fearless and indefatigable.

With Cecil happy to shoulder the burdens of government, James soon took to disappearing for weeks on end, chasing animals relentlessly and corresponding with his 'little beagle' by letter.

PLAGUE SWEPT through the capital in the hot summer of 1603, claiming over 30,000 lives by the end of the year. The public theatres, closed in March, would not reopen for at least another twelve months. The coronation ceremonies for King James and Queen Anne, scheduled for St James' Day, 25 July, were scaled back to limit the spread of infection, and the king's triumphant procession from the Tower of London to Westminster Abbey was postponed until 15 March 1604.

That early spring morning, a magnificent train paraded through the city streets. The king rode a white jennet. His Gentlemen of the Privy Chamber walked alongside, holding a rich canopy over the king's head. The Venetian ambassador noted that the canopy was borne aloft by 'twenty-four gentlemen, splendidly dressed, eight of whom took it, turn and turnabout'. One of these gentlemen was Will Shakespeare.

'Were't aught to me I bore the canopy,' wrote Will, 'With my extern the outward honouring, / Or laid great bases for eternity, / Which proves more short than waste or ruining?'

His company were now the King's Servants, made so by letters patent issued on 19 May 1603. The first name on the list of those players who now enjoyed the king's patronage was that of Lawrence Fletcher, an actor who had spent several years in Scotland. The next name on the list was William Shakespeare.

As a newly appointed Gentleman Groom of the Most Honourable Privy Chamber, Will had been presented with a length of scarlet-red cloth by the Master of the Great Wardrobe, so that he could be 'splendidly dressed' when he outwardly honoured the king in his procession. Also sporting red livery in the royal train that day was the king's perfumer, Thomas Sheppard, the brother of Will's 'Dark Lady', Jane.

Along the route, seven 'great gates' had been erected for the occasion. These elaborate edifices were the 'great bases' which, as Will suggested in one of his sonnets, had been laid for an illusory eternity. The wood-and-plaster gates were topped with obelisks or 'pyramids', to which Shakespeare referred in another sonnet:

> No! Time, thou shalt not boast that I do change,
> Thy pyramids built up with newer might
> To me are nothing novel, nothing strange,
> They are but dressings of a former sight ...

Of the two sonnets written in reaction to the king's progress of 15 March 1604, one – Sonnet 125 – is addressed to a 'suborn'd *Informer*', a telltale who mocked Shakespeare's 'obsequious' role in the procession, leading Will to protest that a 'true soul / When most impeach'd, stands least in thy control.' This suborned informer was probably Ben Jonson, who had penned three of the pageants performed at the 'great gates' that day.

The second sonnet – Sonnet 123 – spoke out against the guiding hand which had raised the ceremonial arches. The citizenry imagined that they were seeing something 'novel', but the grim fact was that nothing had changed:

> Thy registers and thee I both defy,
> Not wond'ring at the present, nor the past.
> For thy records, and what we see doth lie,
> Made more or less by thy continual haste ...

It was as if Elizabeth, the 'English Jezebel', had never died. At its heart, the regime remained the same, employing the same devious methods in the headlong pursuit of its agenda. The gulf between the official records and the visible reality was as great as ever as Sir Robert Cecil resumed his attacks on the Catholics.

Shakespeare, however, refused to be cowed: 'This I do vow and this shall ever be, / I will be true despite thy scythe and thee.'

True to his conscience and his father's memory, Will took up his quill again.

12

Chaos is Come Again

AMONGST THOSE who had corresponded with King James before the death of Queen Elizabeth was the Ninth Earl of Northumberland, Henry Percy, nicknamed the 'Wizard Earl' on account of his scientific interests.

In the latter days of Elizabeth's reign, Northumberland sent his kinsman, Thomas Percy, to meet secretly with King James. The earl's aim was to prepare James for his imminent accession. Where the 'papists' were concerned, Northumberland advised the king that 'their faction is strong, their increase is daily, and their diffidence in your Majesty is not desperate.' 'It were pity,' wrote Northumberland, 'to lose so good a kingdom for the not tolerating a Mass in a corner.'

James seemed happy with Northumberland's choice of messenger and insisted that the earl should 'employ hereafter none other Mercury in your dealing with me'. In a premonitory aside, the king remarked that 'princes make sometimes use of treason, yet they ever hate the traitor'.

Northumberland gathered from Thomas Percy that James was being misinformed about the state of England. He suspected that Sir Robert Cecil was at least partly responsible, and warned the king that his every move was being watched. The earl again pleaded the cause of the 'papists', to which the Scottish king responded: 'As for the Catholics I will neither persecute any that will be quiet, and give but an outward obedience to the law, neither will I spare to advance any of them that will by good service worthily deserve it.' It would not be long before James was pretending that no such undertaking had been given. He revealed his real attitude in letters to Sir Robert Cecil. England, he felt, was 'already too much infected' with 'Jesuits, seminary priests, and that rabble'.

The king had found a fellow spirit in Cecil, who detested 'that generation of vipers (the Jesuits)'. Referring, presumably, to Northumberland's man, Thomas Percy, Cecil advised King James 'to deliberate how you should deal with the messenger from Antichrist'. James answered Cecil:

> I will never allow in my conscience that the blood of any man shall be shed for diversity of opinions in religion, but I would be sorry that Catholics should so multiply as they might be able to practise their old principles upon us ... I only wish that some order might be taken as the land might be purged of such great flocks of them that daily diverts the souls of many from the sincerity of the gospel, and withal that some means might be found for debarring their entry again.

Cecil had heard what he wanted to hear.

The 'little beagle' also turned King James against his own rivals, the 'diabolical triplicity' of Northumberland, Lord Cobham (Cecil's brother-in-law) and Sir Walter Raleigh. Within weeks of the king's accession, Raleigh and Cobham were locked up in the Tower. Northumberland, however, became a Privy Councillor and captain of the royal bodyguard.

On 18 November 1603, Northumberland reminded King James of his kinsman's previous service: 'This ancient Mercury of mine, my cousin Percy, who could not before time look you in the face but by owl-light, would be glad to see your Majesty by daylight.' He assured James that Thomas Percy would 'ever be found your Majesty's most loyal and devoted servant.' With that, the Wizard Earl put his neck on the block.

WILL SHAKESPEARE had also communicated with King James, imploring him – via *Hamlet* – to take heed of the Catholics' plight. This might have occasioned the 'amicable Letter to Mr. Shakespeare' which the king had been pleased to write 'with his own Hand'. First mentioned in 1710, this letter, 'tho now lost, remain'd long in the Hands of Sir William D'avenant', as a 'credible Person' could then testify.

It has been doubted that this 'amicable Letter' ever existed, although there are no firm grounds for believing that it didn't. Within two weeks of his arrival in London, King James had raised Shakespeare's company to the status of the King's Men. Like many others, Will had formed the impression that James was not averse to the idea of religious toleration. If the king was as good as his word, then the renewed persecution of Catholics must have been the work of Sir Robert Cecil.

Will Shakespeare suggested as much in *Measure for Measure*. The title referred to one of the king's publications. James had written his treatise on good government, *Basilikon Doron*, for the benefit of his son and heir, Prince Henry. It included an injunction not to concentrate too much power in the hands of self-serving subordinates: 'And above all, let the *measure* of your love to everyone be according to the *measure* of their virtue.' By entrusting Cecil with the business of government, King James had shown that he was not inclined to follow his own guidance.

Measure for Measure opens with the Duke of Vienna preparing to leave the city and investing all his power and 'terror' in a couple of deputies – a wise old lord named Escalus and Angelo, a man of 'stricture and firm abstinence'. By making the 'precise' Angelo his 'secondary', the duke mirrored King James, whose reliance on Cecil was also in contravention of his advice to Prince Henry: 'Take heed therefore, my son, to such Puritans ... whom no deserts can oblige.'

Angelo instantly revives a number of old laws, with the consequence that a young gentleman named Claudio is arrested and sentenced to death.

The duke, meanwhile, disguises himself as a friar and tours the city's underbelly to monitor the impact of his deputy's hard-line policies.

Duke Vincentio was clearly modelled on King James. In her secret correspondence with the Scottish king, Penelope Rich, the exquisite sister of the Earl of Essex, had given James the codename 'Victor'. Shakespeare altered this to Vincentio – from *vincere*, to 'conquer' – which meant the same thing.

The duke shared the king's ambivalence towards his subjects:

I'll privily away. I love the people,
But do not like to stage me to their eyes.
Though it do well, I do not relish well
Their loud applause and *aves* vehement ...

Outwardly, the play deals with sexual morality. However, the laws reintroduced by Angelo had little to do with sex. An intriguing anomaly in *Measure for Measure* reveals what the play was really about.

Awaiting execution, Claudio complains that he has fallen foul of a rusty old statute:

But this new governor
Awakes me all the enrollèd penalties
Which have, like unscoured armour, hung by th' wall
So long that nineteen zodiacs have gone round
And none of them been worn ...

In the very next scene, the duke, in conversation with a friar, remarks, 'We have strict statutes and most biting laws, / The needful bits and

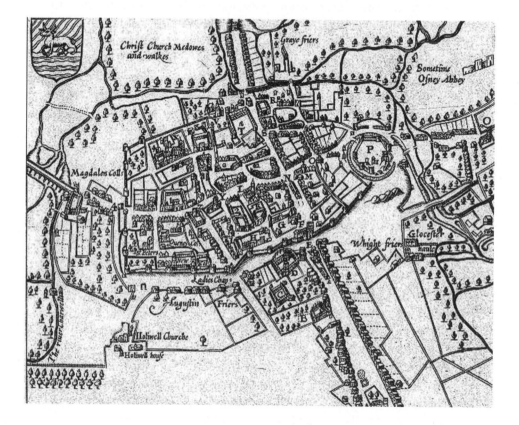

Christ Church Medowes and walkes

Graye friers

Sometime Ofney Abbey

Magdalen Coll:

Wright friers

Glocester houfe

Ladies Chap:

Augustin Friers

Holiwell Churche

Holiwell house

9 John Speed's map of Oxford, 1605 (north at the bottom, south at the top).

curbs to headstrong weeds, / Which for these fourteen years we have let slip.' Claudio's 'nineteen zodiacs' referred to English law and the Act Against Jesuits and Seminarists passed by the Elizabethan Parliament in 1585, which gave all priests working in England forty days to leave the country, on pain of death.

The duke, as a representation of King James, referred to Scottish law, and the proclamation issued by the General Assembly of the Kirk of Scotland on 3 March 1590, which allowed all 'Jesuitis or Seminarie Priestis' one month to leave the country before the death penalty was imposed.

Shakespeare was unaware that King James had, in a letter to Cecil, expressed his desire to see 'the last edict against Jesuits and priests put in execution'. Misled by Cecil over the strength of English Catholicism, the king had reacted angrily, reinstating the swingeing fines for recusancy which he had previously suspended. Shakespeare assumed that the revival of the harsh laws against Catholic priests was solely Cecil's doing.

The first Parliament of King James' reign reinforced the laws which had been introduced nineteen years earlier in England and fourteen years earlier in Scotland. Jesuit and seminary priests were given until 19 March 1604 to 'depart out of the Realm'.

The deadline fell just four days after Will Shakespeare walked in King James' triumphant procession through London, holding the canopy over the king's head.

BARELY A year after Shakespeare wrote *Measure for Measure*, the Venetian ambassador questioned Cecil in March 1605 over 'the cause of this extraordinary movement against the Catholics', for he could see 'no reason which justified the persecution'. Cecil's response was bureaucratic. 'My Lord, it cannot be helped: there are laws that must be observed.'

The words could have come straight from the mouth of Angelo: 'Be you content, fair maid, / It is the law, not I, condemn your brother.' The 'fair maid' is Isabella, Claudio's sister, who is about to enter a convent dedicated to St Clare of Assisi. To his surprise, the reptilian Angelo finds himself attracted to Isabella. He makes her an offer: if she sleeps with him, he will spare her brother's life.

This odd scene was intended to remind King James that his 'little beagle' had once favoured the claim of the Spanish Infanta, Isabella Clara Eugenia, to the English throne. In James' exchange of letters with the Earl of Northumberland he had quizzed the Wizard Earl about Cecil's preferences, while the discovery of Cecil's plans had led to the failed uprising and the execution of the Earl of Essex in 1601.

The duke hears about Angelo's treachery. He recalls that the deputy had once been betrothed to a woman named Mariana. The duke arranges for Angelo to sleep with Mariana in the mistaken belief that he is bedding Isabella. Angelo then goes back on his word and orders that Claudio be put to death.

Mariana lives in a 'moated grange' called St Luke's. The name compares with that of Lucio, the 'fantastic' who supports Isabella when she pleads with the 'outward sainted' Angelo for her brother's life.

Lucio is one of a succession of Shakespearean characters whose names are derivatives of Luke – they range from Lucentio, a scholar from the Catholic college at Rheims, in *The Taming of the Shrew* to Caius Lucius, the General of the Roman forces in *Cymbeline*. Each one of these 'Luke' characters displays Jesuit credentials. Shakespeare's distant cousin, Robert Southwell, had joined the Society of Jesus on St Luke's Day, 18 October 1578. Father Southwell and his colleague, Father Garnet, later adopted Luke the Evangelist as the patron saint of their English mission.

The Jesuits had gathered to celebrate St Luke's Day in October 1591 at the moated manor house of Baddesley Clinton, a field or two away from Shakespeare Hall in Warwickshire, close to the ruins of Wroxall Abbey, where Isabella Shakespeare had served as a prioress. Father Southwell and Father Garnet narrowly escaped capture when the house was raided. They gave thanks to St Luke for their deliverance.

Shakespeare almost certainly had Baddesley Clinton in mind for Mariana's 'moated grange' of St Luke's. The name Mariana also hinted at an alternative treatise on good government, for if the *Measure for Measure* title was drawn from King James' *Basilikon Doron*, the jilted Mariana recalled *De rege et regis institutione* ('The King and the Education of the King'). Commissioned by Phillip II of Spain for his son, Phillip III, the treatise had been composed by the Spanish Jesuit, Juan de Mariana. Like James' *Basilikon Doron*, it was first printed in 1599.

The Spanish treatise argued that if a ruler 'is destroying the state, considers public and private fortunes as his prey, is holding the laws of the land and our holy religion in contempt', then that 'Prince must be warned and invited to come to his senses'. If the ruler refused to mend his ways, he could be declared a public enemy and put to the sword.

King James had betrayed his own principles by investing too much power in his deputy, who had previously preferred another claimant – the Spanish Infanta, whose brother was King Phillip III of Spain – to the throne. The result of the king's laxity had been a crackdown driven by Cecil's contempt for 'the laws of the land and our holy religion'.

If James failed to heed Will's warning in *Measure for Measure*, he could be cast as a public enemy, a tyrant.

All works out well in *Measure for Measure*. Angelo's hypocrisy is exposed and he is compelled to marry Mariana. Vincentio, the 'old fantastical duke of dark corners', offers himself in marriage to Isabella – politically, an alliance of England and the Spanish Netherlands. The only sour note is the punishment meted out to Lucio for 'slandering a prince'.

Will's play had been passed to another playwright, Thomas Middleton, whose revisions drew much of the sting from Shakespeare's text. Lucio's priestly attributes are still visible: a conscientious prison-visitor, he praises Isabella as a 'thing enskied and sainted'; he also dismisses the duke as a 'fool, a coward', a 'very superficial, ignorant, unweighing fellow' and 'one of all luxury, an ass, a madman'.

In the hands of Thomas Middleton, Lucio the Jesuit became a dirty-minded pimp whose penalty for maligning the king is to marry a 'punk'.

HOPES WERE fading for the Catholics. Few could afford the monthly fine of £20 for avoiding Protestant church services (for good measure, the government decided that there were thirteen months in the year). The king's Scottish hangers-on were encouraged to help themselves to the livestock, land and possessions of practising 'papists'.

The Venetian ambassador was not alone in expressing concern. In the spring of 1604, the French ambassador presented King James with a *Supplication to the King's Most Excellent Majesty*, written by a secular priest. 'When the King began to read it,' states a contemporary report, 'he fell into a great passion and with many oaths trod it under his feet.'

Such fits of passion to which the king gave vent whenever the Catholics were mentioned formed the basis for Shakespeare's next play.

The Tragedy of Othello the Moor of Venice was performed before King James on 1 November 1604. Again, Shakespeare referenced something that James himself had written – in this case, 'Lepanto', an epic poem concerning a famous naval victory against the Turks in the Mediterranean.

The play was also designed to appeal to the king's fascination with black skin. When James married Anne in Norway, he ordered four young Africans to dance naked in the snow for his bride's amusement. But Othello's blackness is also a sign of his otherness. King James had been baptised a Catholic but raised by Calvinists. At heart, Shakespeare felt, James was a Catholic 'More' adrift in a venal State.

Queen Anne had almost certainly converted to Catholicism; Queen Elizabeth had even written to her, demanding to know who had counselled her to embrace the Church of Rome. The issue became a source of friction between King James and Queen Anne, and *Othello* reflected this. 'The hearts of old gave hands,' says the Moor to his bride, 'But our new heraldry is hands, not hearts.'

The Sacred Heart had been supplanted by the emblem of the Red Hand, a device associated with the O'Neills of Ulster, which now represented those who had surrendered their lands to the English Crown and then had them 'regranted' in return for renouncing Catholicism.

Detached from his Catholic roots, symbolised by the relic of a spotted handkerchief which Othello received from his dying mother, the Moor's conflict is entirely within himself. He has rejected the Sacred Heart and adopted the Red Hand.

Late in 1604, the Archbishop of Canterbury denounced Rome as 'the purple harlot and seat of anti-Christ'. Othello's wife is similarly branded: 'Was this fair paper, this most goodly book, / Made to write "whore" upon?' The assumption that his wife has been converted – 'She turned to folly, and she was a whore' – causes Othello to demand that she swear she is 'honest' (a Puritan term) and then to kill her. Like so many a priest, the innocent Desdemona dies a 'guiltless death' so that she cannot 'betray more men'.

Just weeks before *Othello* was first performed, the Treaty of London brought an end to two decades of war between England and Spain. Will Shakespeare had been well placed to keep tabs on the negotiations: the King's Men were paid to act as courtiers to the Spanish ambassador Juan Fernández de Velasco, the Constable of Castile, from his arrival at Dover until after the peace deal was concluded on 18 August 1604.

The Spaniards bribed the English delegates, including Sir Robert Cecil, with huge pensions (Cecil's greed is noted by the 'most villainous knave', Iago, in *Othello*: 'These Moors are changeable in their wills – fill thy purse with money'). But for the Catholics of England, the Anglo-Spanish treaty was a disaster. No effort was made by the Spanish ambassador to alleviate their sufferings. The treaty gave King James and Cecil – who was awarded the title of Viscount Cranborne immediately after the conference – carte blanche to continue their unrelenting persecution.

The king's love for his subjects was conditional: 'Excellent wretch! Perdition catch my soul / But I do love thee, and when I love thee not, / Chaos is come again.' By killing them for their consciences, James was destroying the most precious thing he had – his immortal soul.

ON 24 JULY 1605, Will invested £440 in 'one half of all tithes of corn and grain arising within the towns, villages and fields of Old Stratford, Bishopton and Welcombe'. He did not have all the money to hand – a year later, he still owed £20 to the vendor, Ralph Huband, who also owned Hillborough Manor, traditionally the home of Agnes Whateley. The purchase established Shakespeare as something of a grandee. He had already bought many acres of land around Stratford for £320 from John and William Combe in May 1602. What is not clear is where he found the capital for these investments.

By the end of August 1605, Will was in Oxford. On the warm afternoon of Tuesday 27 August, the king and his retinue rode into the city, accompanied by civic dignitaries and leading figures from the university. They approached from Woodstock, north of Oxford, and halted at the gates of St John's College, where three youths 'in habit or attire like nymphs or sibyls' addressed the king in Latin. Their words recalled a legendary prophecy uttered by three 'fatal sisters' to the king's supposed ancestor, Banquo:

Hail, whom Scotland loves!
Whom England, hail!
Whom Ireland serves, all hail!
... Hail, mighty Lord of Britain, Ireland, France!

Onwards the procession moved, through the North Gate and along Corn Market towards Carfax crossroads. Scholars lined one side of the street, the townsfolk cheering from the other. The royal party finally came to Christ Church, where there were more orations and, in the evening, a tedious comedy entitled *Alba* ('Scotland').

Number 3, Corn Market, was known in Shakespeare's day as the Taverne. Adjoining it to the north was the Crosse Inn, which offered stables and lodging. On Will's journeys between Stratford and London, he would stay at the Crosse Inn, taking his refreshments next door at the Taverne, where he was on friendly terms with the owners.

John and Jane Davenant had spent the first years of their married life in London, burying five children there between Christmas 1593 and Christmas 1597. In January 1598, Jane turned in desperation to the astrologer-physician Simon Forman. 'She supposeth herself with child,' wrote Forman in his casebook, 'but it is not so.'

An Oxford scholar would later report that John Davenant was 'an admirer of plays and play-makers, especially Shakespeare'. It is likely, though, that the continuing gossip surrounding his wife, the old player

'W.S.' and the Earl of Southampton – which had resurfaced in 1599 with the latest edition of 'Willobie his Avisa' and Jonson's *Every Man Out of his Humour* – got too much for him. The Davenants moved to Oxford, taking on the lease of the Taverne. Like the Crosse Inn next door, the Taverne belonged to relatives of William Underhill, who sold New Place in Stratford to Will Shakespeare.

The Taverne was large: four storeys high, with more than twenty rooms and a shared garden at the rear. Jane was an experienced hostess, her husband a professional wine merchant, and together they ran a thriving business. A child, named after her mother, Jane, was baptised at the Church of St Martin, Carfax, on 11 February 1602.

John Davenant rode in the official train which accompanied King James and his entourage into Oxford in August 1605. Will Shakespeare was also present to witness the performance of *Tres Sybillae* by three youths in crude make-up on the edge of the town. What he saw there would inspire his most blistering attack on the king.

THE DARK-EYED Jane – 'Jennet' to her friends – had been on his mind when he wrote *Othello*. Iago quips about having jennets for 'germans' ('siblings', with the shadow meaning of 'Lutherans' or Protestants) and remarks, 'If she be black and thereto have a wit, / She'll find a white that shall her blackness fit.' The pun on the word 'wight' made Iago's couplet mildly obscene: a witty, black-haired woman would soon find a man to fill her darkest recess.

A poem, part of which was published with *Shake-speares Sonnets* in 1609, places Will with Jane in Oxford in the late summer of 1605.

The poem is set beside a river. A distraught woman is tearing up letters and tossing them, along with love tokens, into the stream. Her face, shaded by a sunhat of plaited straw, reveals a beauty not yet ravaged by time.

Her sobs attract the attention of a 'reverend man' who happens to be grazing his cattle nearby. He demands to know the 'grounds and motive of her woe'.

The 'fickle maid full pale' addresses him as 'Father' and unfolds her tale.

Years before, she had been seduced by a young man, a serial womaniser with curly brown hair, a soft, patchy beard and an irresistible way with words. He had used his 'craft of will' on many a susceptible female – including a 'sacred nun' – but he insisted that the maid was his first and last, his 'origin and ender'. Overwhelmed by his 'subduing tongue', the woman had succumbed: 'Who, young and simple, would not be so lovered? / Ay me! I fell, and yet do question make / What I should do again for such a sake?' That was in the past. But the affair had been rekindled. Once again, the 'fickle maid' had allowed herself to be seduced:

'O that infected moisture of his eye,
O that false fire which in his cheek so glowed,
O that forced thunder from his heart did fly,
O that sad breath his spongy lungs bestowed,
O all that borrowed motion, seeming owed,
    Would yet again betray the fore-betrayed,
    And new pervert a reconcilèd maid.'

And there, 'A Lover's Complaint' – as it was published in 1609 – ends. Whatever the 'reverend man' had to say to the maid has been lost to posterity.

With his customary precision, Shakespeare indicated where the scene was set:

From off a hill whose concave womb re-worded
A plaintful story from a sistering vale,
My spirits to attend this double voice accorded,
And down I laid to list the sad-tuned tale ...

The hill with the 'concave womb' recalled the ancient legend of King Lludd. A dreadful plague had smitten the land. Lludd consulted his wise men, who told him that the cause of the pestilence was the constant fighting of two dragons, one red and one white. Following their counsel, Lludd measured out his kingdom, the exact centre of which was at Carfax in Oxford. There, he dug a pit, in which he placed a cauldron filled with mead, and covered it with a satin sheet.

The dragons appeared, wrestling in the sky. They landed in the pit on Carfax hill, drank the sweet mead, and fell asleep. Lludd gathered up both dragons in the satin sheet and transported them into deepest Wales, where they were buried inside a mountain.

The legend of King Lludd had a curious echo in events which had taken place a short distance from Carfax. Jane Clifford, better known as Fair Rosamund, was the mistress of King Henry II, who installed her in his hunting lodge at Woodstock. When their affair came to an end in about 1176, Jane Clifford retired to the nearby nunnery at Godstow, where she died and was buried.

A few years later Hugh, Bishop of Lincoln, demanded that her remains be removed from the chapel and reburied outside as an example to lewd and adulterous women. The nuns did as they were told, but as soon as the bishop was gone they disinterred Fair Rosamund's bones again and carried them back inside the church.

Jane Clifford's family crest featured two red dragons or 'wyverns gules'. Like the red and white dragons of Carfax, carried away in a satin sheet, Fair Rosamund's bones had been transported for reburial in a 'silken scented bag'. The legend of Carfax hill, with its concave pit, 're-worded' the sorry tale of Jane Clifford's remains in the 'sistering vale' of Godstow.

The Rosamund story was well known. Shakespeare's contemporary, Samuel Daniel, had published his 'Complaint of Rosamond' along with a cycle of sonnets in 1592, reissuing the poem two years later with his *Tragedy of Cleopatra*. Arguably, Fair Rosamund and Cleopatra were connected: the River Thames, which flows past Godstow, becomes the Isis as it winds through Oxford – a new Nile, as it were, named after the goddess of the Egyptian river.

Inspired by Daniel's 'Complaint of Rosamond', Shakespeare had hinted at Fair Rosamund's grave in *Romeo and Juliet*: 'What's in a name? That which we call a rose / By any other name would smell as sweet.'

Those with a fondness for sacred relics believed that Rosamund's mortal remains were 'sweet-smelling'. And, as Shakespeare knew, the 'Rose of the World' was, by any other name, called Jane.

Will copied the rhyme scheme and stanza form of Daniel's 'Complaint of Rosamond' in his own 'Lover's Complaint', implicitly suggesting that the 'poor afflicted ghost' of Jane Clifford had risen from her grave – as she did in Daniel's poem – to bemoan her fate. The subject of Will's poem was another Jane. She, too, was an adulteress, and he had first seduced her in 1592, the year in which Daniel's 'Complaint of Rosamond' appeared.

Like the 'fickle maid' of 'A Lover's Complaint', Jane Davenant was neither young nor old: she was 36 at the time. She made her complaint on the bank of the Thames, where the river was known as the Isis.

Will Shakespeare had walked from Carfax hill to Christ Church College to hear the cathedral bell, the 'loudest thing in Oxford'. The bell had been known as 'Mary' when it belonged to Oseney Abbey, but when the monasteries were dissolved under Henry VIII it had been moved to Christ Church and renamed 'Great Tom'.

The bell sounded awful. Its clapper was worn out. The 'double voice' of Mary, now Tom, was 'sad-tuned'.

To the south of Christ Church College lay a triangular meadow bounded by the river. It was here that Will lay down on the grass to watch the middle-aged beauty who was weeping on the riverbank.

Her hair fascinated him: 'For some, untucked, descended her sheaved hat, / Hanging her pale and pinèd cheek beside; / Some in her threaden fillet still did bide ...' The 'folded schedules' which she was tearing and tossing into the river were 'sadly penned in blood'. They were computations of nativity. Jane Davenant was two months pregnant.

Local farmers grazed their cattle on Christ Church Meadow. The 'reverend man' who sat beside Jane to hear her confession used the alias 'Farmer'.

He was the superior of the Jesuits in England.

THE CONFESSION recorded in 'A Lover's Complaint' took place in the summer of 1605. The poem also harked back to the start of the affair, drawing on two poems from 1592. One was Samuel Daniel's 'Complaint of Rosamond'; the other, 'St Peter's Complaint', by Father Robert Southwell.

Southwell's poem examined the moment when St Peter was challenged at the door to the chamber in which Jesus was on trial. A maid asked him, 'Art thou not also one of this man's disciples?' to which Peter replied, 'I am not.'

English Catholics faced a similar challenge – the 'Bloody Question' devised by Lord Burghley. Much hinged on the answer to the question, 'who would you support if the Pope invaded England, the Queen or the Bishop of Rome?' Many felt compelled to answer in the manner of the first Bishop of Rome, St Peter, by denying their faith.

'Favour my wish,' wrote Southwell to his 'worthy good cousin, Master W.S.', 'well-wishing works no ill'. Father Southwell implied that, by penning 'lovers' lays' instead of devotional poetry, Will Shakespeare was as guilty of betraying his Saviour as St Peter had been.

Southwell was betrayed by a pregnant woman in 1592; he died a traitor's death in 1595. Ten years would go by before Shakespeare responded to the Jesuit's criticisms. Will's answer to 'St Peter's Complaint' featured a conversation between a pregnant woman and an apostle of the Bishop of Rome which took place during a 'well-wishing' pilgrimage.

AFTER THREE awkward days in Oxford, the king and his entourage left the city on the afternoon of 30 August 1605. Simultaneously, another party set out from a Catholic safe house in Essex, heading across the Midlands to the shrine of St Winefride in North Wales. At the head of the pilgrims' party was a short-sighted, overweight cleric with a delightful singing voice. Will Shakespeare described him thus in 'A Lover's Complaint':

> A reverend man that grazed his cattle nigh,
> Sometime a blusterer, that the ruffle knew
> Of court, of city, and had let go by
> The swiftest hours, observèd as they flew ...

Henry Garnet was born in Derbyshire in 1555. He earned himself a scholarship to Winchester College – one of the last schools in the country to accept the Protestant reforms – where he became a 'prepositor' or captain renowned for his 'modesty, urbanity, musical taste and quickness and solidity of parts'; he possessed the keen intellect and lively debating skills of the 'blusterer'.

After school, Garnet undertook an apprenticeship with Richard Tottel, a printer specialising in legal texts based at London's Temple Bar. As a proof-reader and 'corrector of the common law print', Garnet became familiar with the leading legal figures of the day: he knew the 'ruffle' of the City and the Inns of Court.

At the age of 25 he travelled to Rome to train for the priesthood. Received into the Society of Jesus in September 1577, Garnet was required to celebrate the Divine Office or Liturgy of the Hours, which entailed the daily observation of the eight canonical hours – Matins, Lauds, Prime, Terce, Sext, None, Vespers and Compline. He had let go by 'the swiftest hours observèd as they flew'.

Father Garnet returned to England as a missionary in 1586, the Jesuit General remarking that sending Garnet into Elizabeth's realm was 'exposing the meekest lamb to the cruellest butchery'. The lamb had not made the perilous journey on his own. Crossing the Channel with him was Will Shakespeare's distant kinsman, Father Robert Southwell.

It speaks volumes that Shakespeare had been able to summon Father Garnet at short notice to hear his lover's confession. Watching the reverend father talking softly with Jane on the bank of the Isis, the Great Tom bell tolling dissonantly behind him, his mind gambolled back to 1592, when Southwell was arrested and Will first bedded his 'breeding jennet'.

It says much, too, that Father Garnet had so suddenly chosen to launch a pilgrimage to St Winefride's Well. Winefride had been named by Shakespeare's father as his special patron in the 'Testament' he received from the Jesuits. 'Well-wishing' pilgrims prayed to St Winefride for healthy sons.

The words spoken by Father Garnet to assuage Jane's 'suffering ecstasy' are long forgotten. They were not printed with the rest of 'A Lover's Complaint' when Will's sonnets were dedicated to a 'well-wishing adventurer'. Presumably, the pilgrimage was part of Will's penance for having impregnated his married lover.

Jane was the door-keeper to Will's ruin – in Othello's words: 'You, mistress, / That have the office opposite to St Peter / And keeps the gate of hell.' He was reminded of the gates of hell every time he passed through Oxford, for the church tower of St Michael at the North Gate bore an ancient carving of a woman holding open her gaping vagina.

The pilgrims passed by this Sheela-na-Gig figure as they left the city, heading north to Stratford. There were several priests in the party, including the Jesuits Father Gerard, Father Tesimond and Father Oldcorne, as well as their servants and followers. They visited John Grant's house near Snitterfield and the Huddington home of Robert Wintour as they made their way to St Winefride's shrine at Holywell.

They did not know it, but their world was about to be blown to pieces.

13

The Way to Dusty Death

THEY CALLED it the Black Year.

It began with a performance of Ben Jonson's *Masque of Blackness* at Whitehall on Twelfth Night, 6 January. The pregnant Queen Anne and her ladies wore black make-up on their faces and forearms, their flimsy costumes considered 'too light and courtesan-like for such great ones'. Costing a staggering £3,000, the masque was the first of Jonson's collaborations with the brilliant designer Inigo Jones (the two men soon grew to hate each other). The evening ended with a banquet which was attacked with such gusto by the nobles that the tables collapsed.

The year ended with the timely discovery of a plot to massacre the king and his Parliament. At a few minutes past midnight on Tuesday 5 November 1605, a tall, brown-haired man was arrested. Some accounts state that he was lurking in a ground-floor room beneath the House of Lords; others, that he was apprehended in his lodgings, or in the street. The man was dragged into the king's bedchamber at Whitehall and questioned. He gave his name as John Johnson and declared that his intention had been to blast the Scottish courtiers back to Scotland.

His real name was Guy Fawkes – although in service with Sir William Stanley's regiment in the Netherlands he had changed his name to Guido.

The next day, Fawkes was committed to the Tower of London. King James insisted that 'the gentler tortures are to be first used unto him *et sic per gradus ad ima tenditur* [and so by degrees until the worst]'. The use of torture had been outlawed by Magna Carta in 1215. As Sir Edward Coke, Attorney-General since 1594, observed, 'there is no law to warrant tortures in this land'. The regimes of Elizabeth and James continually denied that they had tortured prisoners.

Already, on 5 November, a warrant had been issued for the arrest of Thomas Percy, Gentleman Pensioner to the King, who was 'discovered to have been privy to one of the most horrible Treasons that ever was contrived'. By the following evening, the Lord Chief Justice, Sir John Popham, could tell Cecil that he had 'pregnant suspicion' concerning 'Robert Catesby, Ambrose Rookwood, one Keyes, Thomas Wynter, John Wright and Christopher Wright and some suspicion of one Grant'.

Fawkes had not yet revealed his real name, let alone who his accomplices were.

The full scale of the atrocity, so narrowly averted, began to dawn. Londoners celebrated the king's miraculous escape by lighting huge bonfires. When Parliament finally reconvened it passed an Act 'for public thanksgiving to Almighty God every year on the Fifth day of November', thereby ensuring that the fires burn to this day in the annual festivities of Bonfire Night.

The same Parliament set up a committee to consider what new tortures might be used against 'Jesuits, seminaries and all other popish agents'.

THE GOVERNMENT had been aware that a plot was brewing as early as April 1604, when a spy named Henry Wright revealed its existence to Lord Chief Justice Popham and Sir Thomas Chaloner, governor to the king's eldest son. The plotters themselves were unclear as to which of them had devised the plan to blow up Parliament. Thomas Wintour claimed that it was Robert Catesby who hatched the plot; Guy Fawkes declared that it was he and Tom Wintour who planned it. Neither testimony is reliable.

Robert Catesby was related to Will Shakespeare. He was the son of Anne Throckmorton and Sir William Catesby, whose Lapworth home – part of the manor of Stratford – was possibly where John Shakespeare had received his 'Spiritual Testament' in 1580, when Robert would have been about 7 years old. He grew up to be over 6 feet tall, elegant and dangerously charming. In 1592 he married the daughter of Sir Thomas Leigh, a prominent Warwickshire Protestant, and had two sons. Only the younger survived.

Catesby's wife and father both died in 1598, triggering a personal crisis. He got caught up in the Essex rebellion of 1601 – a noted swordsman, he was wounded in the fray – and incurred a hefty fine. His father, a Catholic, had been impoverished by the State. Catesby ended up living with his mother at Ashby St Ledgers, close to the Warwickshire border.

Early in 1604, he summoned his cousin, Thomas Wintour, to join him at the house he had rented in Lambeth, across the river from the

Parliament building. When Wintour arrived he found Catesby in the company of John Wright, a clever, taciturn Yorkshireman who had also been imprisoned for his part in the Essex rebellion.

Catesby had a plan. The king had signalled his intention to penalise Catholics. So Catesby proposed to 'blow up the Parliament House with gunpowder', for it was there that 'they have done us all the mischief'.

Tom Wintour was a gifted linguist. He suggested that they should first broach the issue of religious toleration with the Constable of Castile, then in Brussels to negotiate the Anglo-Spanish treaty. But Spain, anxious for peace, was in no mood to quibble about human rights. Wintour's diplomatic mission came to nothing. He returned to England in late April, bringing with him a professional soldier named Guy Fawkes, who had been at school with John Wright.

A meeting was held on Sunday 20 May 1604 at the Duck and Drake on the Strand. Present were Catesby, Tom Wintour, John Wright, Guy Fawkes and Thomas Percy. The latter burst in demanding, 'Shall we always, gentlemen, talk and never do anything?'

PERCY WAS the oldest of the plotters – in his mid-forties, tall, red-faced, with a 'great broad beard' turning grey. He had been the 'gentleman bearer' chosen to carry letters between his kinsman, the Earl of Northumberland, and King James in Scotland, and had conferred with the king 'at great length' on his master's behalf.

A few days after the meeting at the Duck and Drake, Percy was appointed one of the king's special bodyguards by Northumberland, who commanded the guard.

It is often alleged that Percy joined the plot because he felt that King James had misled him over his attitude towards the English Catholics. In fact, Percy's conversion to Catholicism had come late in life, and though he advertised himself as the 'chief pillar of Papistry' in Yorkshire, he was described as 'no Papist but a Puritan' by someone who was interrogated after the plot had been exposed .

Percy's role in the plot is dubious. He was a confidante and 'most loyal and devoted servant' of the king. Geoffrey Goodman would later claim that a lawyer named Sir Francis Moore – knighted in 1616 – had seen his acquaintance Thomas Percy emerging from Sir Robert Cecil's house several times in the small hours. Goodman's testimony is not without its merits: he was chaplain to Queen Anne and rose to become Bishop of Gloucester, even though he was suspected of harbouring Catholic sympathies. Coming from a senior Anglican clergyman, Bishop Goodman's hint that Percy was Cecil's agent must be taken seriously.

Whenever the plot stalled, Percy found a convenient solution. His outburst at the meeting on 20 May 1604 got the plot moving. The five men present swore a solemn oath and then went into an adjoining room, where a priest administered the Holy Communion.

CATESBY DISCOVERED that Henry Ferrers of Baddesley Clinton – the moated grange in the heart of Shakespeare country – leased a 'house in Westminster belonging to the Parliament House' from the Keeper of the King's Wardrobe. Using his contacts, Thomas Percy promptly had the lease on this house transferred to him. Guy Fawkes was installed in the house, posing as Percy's servant. The plotters then settled down to await the outcome of the Anglo-Spanish peace talks that August.

On 7 July, the first Parliament of King James' reign was prorogued. There would be no need for a royal opening ceremony when Parliament reconvened on 7 February 1605, but the king wished to make a splash at the start of the next session, when his pet project, the unification of the kingdoms of England and Scotland, would be debated. One of the peers tasked with advancing the legislative union was William Parker, Lord Monteagle.

Parker was 30 years old and firmly entrenched in Catholic circles, having married the daughter of Sir Thomas Tresham and Muriel Throckmorton. He had been one of the delegates who paid Shakespeare's company to perform *The Tragedy of King Richard the Second* on the eve of the Essex rebellion, and was fined an eye-watering £8,000 for his involvement in the abortive uprising.

On the accession of James I in 1603, Parker had written to the king, professing that, though he was 'bred up in the Romish religion', he had now converted to Protestantism and had a 'desire to serve'. How Parker wished to serve His Majesty is unknown: the letter is mutilated at that point.

James clearly took him at his word. Parker forged a productive relationship with Cecil and was summoned to the king's first Parliament as the fourth Baron Monteagle.

When he wasn't engaged on the king's business, considering the proposed union of the British kingdoms, Monteagle was often to be found in the company of his 'dear Robin' Catesby, trying to get Father Henry Garnet to implicate himself in the Gunpowder Plot.

THE FAILURE of the Anglo-Spanish treaty to produce even a whisper of religious toleration should have given the plotters the impetus they needed. Parliament was to have reconvened in February, but on Christmas Eve it was prorogued again, until 3 October 1605.

The reason for the delay was simple – the plot had got nowhere.

More plotters had been recruited. Robert Keyes, a 'grave and sober man' of about 40, lived in Northamptonshire, where his wife was governess to the children of the Catholic Lord Mordaunt. Keyes was appointed to guard Catesby's house in Lambeth, where the conspirators stored their gunpowder.

John Wright's brother, Christopher, another veteran of the Essex debacle, was also inducted, as was Catesby's servant, Thomas Bates of Lapworth. Tom Wintour's elder brother, Robert, the master of Huddington, near Earl's Common in Worcestershire, was sworn into the plot at an Oxford inn in March 1605, as was his brother-in-law, the lionhearted John Grant of Snitterfield, whose father had conducted business with John Shakespeare.

Finally, on 25 March 1605, Thomas Percy got things moving again. He rented the large room underneath the Peers' Chamber, which had conveniently become available. This was the 'vault' with which Guy Fawkes would be forever associated, and here the plotters stockpiled their gunpowder, hiding the barrels under timber and firewood.

Gunpowder had been proclaimed a government monopoly in 1601 and was stored in the Tower of London. The amount acquired by the plotters is open to dispute. The government eventually settled on the figure of thirty-six barrels, although Cecil referred to 'two Hogsheads and some 32 small barrels'. A well-placed source remarked on 13 November 1605 that 'it is now confidently reported there was no such matter, nor anything near it more than a barrel of powder found near the court.' Guy Fawkes, in a statement dated 20 January 1606, confessed to having secreted 'twenty whole barrels of gunpowder' in the vault.

The nephew of Lord Monteagle later threatened legal action if the government refused to let him investigate the disappearance of so much gunpowder from the Tower of London. The government granted him leave to look into it, on the condition that his inquiry did not extend beyond the year 1604. Clearly, the authorities had something to hide.

Some gunpowder was indeed returned to 'His Majesty's Store' from the 'vault of the Parliament House' on 7 November 1605. Over 800kg of the stuff was received and officially registered as 'decayed'. Its constituent elements had separated, rendering it harmless.

Useless or not, the question arises: how had the plotters got their hands on close to a metric ton of explosive?

TENSIONS WERE rising during the summer of 1605. The Midlands were abuzz with talk of some imminent blow when Shakespeare bought his share of the tithes from the fields around Stratford that July.

The manor of Clopton lay a mile to the north of Stratford. It belonged to the original, and subsequent, owners of New Place.

Local tradition holds that Will married Agnes Whateley in the private oratory at Clopton House. He certainly knew the story of Charlotte Clopton, who suffered a miserable end in the year that he was born. She had been laid to rest in the family mausoleum, but when the crypt was reopened her body was discovered outside its coffin. Charlotte had been prematurely buried. The tale seems to have inspired the sepulchral atmosphere of Juliet's tomb in *Romeo and Juliet*.

In 1580, Joyce Clopton married Sir George Carew, cousin to Sir Walter Raleigh and a close friend of Robert Cecil's. On 4 June 1605, Sir George was raised to the peerage as Baron Carew of Clopton. His duties as a Member of Parliament and Lieutenant-General of Ordnance meant that he did not take up residence of Clopton House immediately, and so it was left in the care of an agent, Robert Wilson of Stratford, who let the house to a wealthy young horse-breeder from Suffolk.

Ambrose Rookwood was 26. He had been approached by Robert Catesby in the autumn of 1604 and asked to procure a quantity of gunpowder. The man responsible for the government's stockpile of gunpowder was Sir George Carew.

Carew inherited Clopton House in June 1605, shortly before Ambrose Rookwood moved into Clopton, where he had a large underground cellar dug out to conceal the Catholic paraphernalia – crucifixes, vestments, 'praying beads' – which Rookwood brought with him. It is possible that this cellar was the inspiration for the mine which, according to the government, the plotters attempted to dig beneath the Parliament building. The story was invented to account for the plotters' lack of progress in the winter of 1604.

Will Shakespeare's acquisition of the tithes in July 1605 gave him a reason to inspect the fields around Clopton and to witness the comings and goings of Rookwood and his fellow conspirators, Robert Wintour and John Grant.

The plotters' preparations alarmed the thirty-strong pilgrimage party which travelled up from Oxford in early September. Father Garnet was especially worried. Catesby and Lord Monteagle had been trying to trick him into condoning mass murder, asking him in July whether the Catholics were 'able to make their part good by arms against the King' (Monteagle had interjected: 'If ever they were, they are able now.

The King is so odious to all sorts.']. The Jesuit had refused to be drawn into a political discussion, and so Catesby had turned to Father Oswald Tesimond, confessing his plans to blow up the king and his Parliament. Horrified, Tesimond begged Catesby's permission to inform his superior.

Father Tesimond revealed the plot to Father Garnet while the two priests walked in a garden, since to have knelt throughout the confession would have been 'too tedious'.

On 24 July, Garnet wrote to his superiors in Rome, expressing his fears that some Catholics might be on the brink of committing an outrage. At the same time, he implored the conspirators to do nothing until he had sought the advice of the pope. Sir Edward Baynham was sent to apprise Pope Paul V of the emergency, Garnet confidently assuming that Baynham would not return with the papal verdict until after Parliament had reconvened on 3 October.

On 28 July, Parliament was again prorogued, this time until 5 November.

On 28 August, Father Garnet announced that he was undertaking a pilgrimage to St Winefride's Well. The party set out two days later. Father Tesimond was among them, as was Sir Everard Digby and his wife, and their chaplain, Father Edward Oldcorne. They could not help but notice that warhorses were being gathered at Catholic houses in the Midlands.

Whether or not Shakespeare travelled to Stratford with the pilgrims after Garnet had heard Jane's confession in Oxford, it is possible that he was in London for part of September. The King's Men produced *A Yorkshire Tragedy* at the Globe. This piece of tabloid theatre, based on the murder of two children by their father on 23 April, was improbably ascribed to 'W. Shakspeare' when it was published two years later.

Ben Jonson was back in prison. A royal favourite, Sir John Murray, had taken umbrage at his portrayal of Scottish courtiers in *Eastward Ho!* Ben and his collaborators, George Chapman and John Marston, were thrown into jail. It was reported that Jonson and Chapman were to have their ears and noses cut off in punishment.

From his cell, Jonson sent out a flurry of grovelling letters. Eventually, Robert Cecil (who had been created Earl of Salisbury in May) paid off Sir John Murray – and Jonson, suitably softened, was released. The burly playwright was next seen at a supper party hosted by Robert Catesby at his lodgings on the Strand on 9 October.

That same day, Shakespeare's company was performing in Oxford, the London theatres having closed, for no apparent reason, a few days earlier. If Will then made his way back to Stratford, he would probably have been at home in New Place when the gunpowder crisis broke.

THE NUMBER of plotters had reached an ominous thirteen.

On 14 October, Catesby recruited Francis Tresham, who had recently inherited his father's Northamptonshire estate. Tresham was Lord Monteagle's brother-in-law. His mother was a Throckmorton, so he too was distantly related to Shakespeare.

Uneasy about the plot, Tresham quickly sought a passport to leave the country.

The last of the recruits was similarly troubled. Aged 24, Sir Everard Digby was the darling of the Court; he had been knighted by King James in 1603. Digby had taken part in the pilgrimage to St Winefride's Well and was celebrating the Feast of St Luke with Father Garnet when Catesby introduced him to the conspiracy.

At last, Catesby had achieved what Cecil wanted. Ever since King James had confided that he wished to see England 'purged of such great flocks' of priests, the secretary had been plotting to destroy the Jesuits. He had twice postponed Parliament to give Catesby the time he needed.

The 'powder treason' was nothing without a link to the Jesuits, for this – as Cecil explained in a letter of 4 December 1605 – was the 'end whereto his Majesty shoots'.

Sir Everard Digby was recruited by Catesby under Father Garnet's nose. Cecil was happy. He wrote to a friend on 24 October, 'let his Majesty know that I dare boldly say no shower or storm shall mar our harvest, except it should come from the middle region.'

Once the London end of the conspiracy was exposed, all eyes would be turned towards the Midlands.

THE UNLIKELY hero of the hour was Lord Monteagle. He would be rewarded with a life pension of £500, plus an estate worth £200 a year. Cecil went to great lengths to cover up Monteagle's involvement with the plotters, and Ben Jonson wrote him a fawning epigram: 'My country's parents I have many known; / But saver of my country, THEE alone.'

On the evening of Saturday 26 October, Monteagle suddenly decided to dine at a little-used property he owned in Hoxton, north of London. As he sat down to supper he sent one of his servants out into the street. The servant was accosted by an 'unknown man of reasonable tall personage' who handed him a letter for Lord Monteagle.

Monteagle insisted that the letter be read out loud. The hints it contained – 'they shall receive a terrible blow this Parliament and yet they shall not see who hurts them' – were sufficient for Monteagle to make his way to Whitehall, 'notwithstanding the darkness of the night', where he presented the letter to Robert Cecil.

The letter was written 'in a hand disguised' on paper made in the Spanish Netherlands, where Cecil had stationed one of his best forgers, Thomas Barnes. Cecil chose to do nothing about the letter until the king had returned from a hunting trip a week later. Not for nothing was Cecil's motto *Sero sed serio* – 'Late, but in earnest'.

Word of the letter soon reached the plotters by way of Tom Wintour, who had been a secretary to Lord Monteagle. Catesby seems to have panicked. In a deathbed confession, one of his servants, George Bartlet, alleged that Catesby had visited Robert Cecil 'several nights before the discovery' of the plot and was 'brought privately in at the back door.' If true, this might suggest that Catesby was unnerved by the ploy of the Monteagle letter and fearful that he was about to be double-crossed. On 1 November, Catesby and Wintour accused Francis Tresham of trying to warn his brother-in-law to avoid the opening of Parliament, but this was just bluff and bravado.

Thomas Percy, meanwhile, had been in the north. Ostensibly, he was collecting rents from the Earl of Northumberland's estates, of which several thousand pounds went missing. On Friday 25 October, a pass was issued requiring local officials to let Percy 'make speedy repair to the Court about his Majesty's special service'.

The king returned to London on 1 November. Cecil showed him the Monteagle letter, professing himself unable to make head or tail of it. The idea was that the king – who had lost his father in a gunpowder explosion – would decipher the 'dark and doubtful letter' all by himself. To make doubly sure, another cryptic letter was found on a London street the next day: it warned that the 'actors' would soon see 'the tyrannous heretic confounded in his cruel pleasures'. The rumour mill was turning.

On 2 November, the Privy Council resolved to search the Parliament building two days later.

That Monday morning, Thomas Percy paid a visit to his kinsman, Northumberland, so that the Wizard Earl unwittingly became a suspect. At the same time, Cecil was preparing to give Lord Monteagle the credit for connecting Percy with the rented vault beneath the Peers' Chamber.

Early in the evening of 4 November, Percy assured Tom Wintour, John Wright and Robert Keyes that 'all was well'. An hour or two later, Robert Catesby left London, riding north with Wright and Thomas Bates. At ten o'clock, Keyes gave Guy Fawkes a watch, which Percy had provided. An hour later, Ambrose Rookwood took receipt of a fine sword engraved with scenes from the Passion of the Christ.

Shortly after midnight, Fawkes was arrested.

ROOKWOOD LEFT London, overtaking Keyes and then Thomas Percy and Christopher Wright before he caught up with Catesby. The plotters discarded their cloaks to increase their speed. At about six o'clock in the evening they came to Ashby St Ledgers, where Robert Wintour had just sat down to dinner with Catesby's mother.

Catesby sent a message summoning Wintour out into the fields and told him 'Mr Fawkes was taken and the whole plot discovered.'

The conspirators then rode on to Dunchurch, where Sir Everard Digby had gathered about 100 men on the pretext of forming a hunting party. When Catesby revealed the real purpose of the gathering – to seize the 9-year-old Princess Elizabeth from nearby Coombe Abbey – most of the hunters departed in horror. By ten o'clock, only forty remained. A servant at the Red Lion Inn overheard the words, 'I doubt not but that we are all betrayed.'

The fugitives sped westwards, breaking into the stables at Warwick Castle at about midnight and stealing several horses. They stopped briefly at John Grant's Snitterfield home, where weapons had been laid out in readiness. By the time the magistrates of Stratford-upon-Avon ordered a raid on Clopton House, early on 6 November, the plotters had slipped past the town.

Catesby wrote to Father Garnet. The Jesuit superior had accompanied Sir Everard and Lady Digby and their young children to Coughton Court, the seat of the Throckmortons, 8 miles from Stratford, where the household had celebrated All Saints and All Souls and, on 3 November, the feast day of St Winefride, before Digby left to join the hunting party at Dunchurch.

Thomas Bates was sent to Coughton with Catesby's letter. Garnet read it with a sinking heart, muttering to Father Tesimond, 'we are all utterly undone'. Mary Digby broke down as Garnet tried to comfort her. He sent Tesimond after Catesby and the others to persuade them to abandon their 'wicked actions'.

Father Tesimond caught up with the plotters at Alcester. They reached Robert Wintour's manor of Huddington at about two o'clock in the afternoon. Exhausted, the fugitives slept until three o'clock in the morning, when they were roused to hear Mass and make their confessions to the chaplain, Father Nicholas Hart. At about six o'clock, they took to the road again.

A windowpane in the main bedroom of Huddington Court bears an inscription, scratched in despair by Robert Wintour's wife, Gertrude. It simply reads 'past cark [hope], past care'.

THE FUGITIVES plodded northwards, breaking into Hewell Grange, near Bromsgrove, at about midday on 7 November and helping themselves to gunpowder, weapons and money.

Hewell Grange belonged to Thomas, Sixth Baron Windsor, whose father had maintained Father Hugh Hall before the priest's arrest in 1583. The 14-year-old Lord Windsor was in London, having expected to attend the opening of Parliament. His London residence was next door to Shakespeare's lodgings on Silver Street.

From Hewell Grange, the plotters made leaden progress through the drenching rain into Staffordshire. At ten o'clock they arrived at Holbeach House, the home of the Wintours' cousin, Stephen Littleton, where they prepared to make their last stand.

The High Sheriff of Worcestershire was closing in with a posse of 200 men.

Somehow or other, the plotters managed to blow up some of their damp gunpowder. John Grant was badly injured, his 'eyes burnt out'.

At about eleven o'clock in the morning of 8 November, the house was besieged.

Tom Wintour was crossing the courtyard when he was shot in the shoulder. The Wright brothers went down in the gunfire. Ambrose Rookwood was also hit.

Catesby called out to Wintour: 'Stand by me, Mr Tom, and we will die together.'

Thomas Percy was beside Catesby in the doorway when they were both struck by the same bullet. The lucky shot was fired by John Street of Worcester, who petitioned Cecil for the £1,000 reward offered by the king for the capture of Percy. King James had wanted to question – or maybe protect – his 'ancient Mercury', but Cecil had apparently issued a contradictory order regarding Catesby and Percy: 'Let me never see them alive.'

Two days later, the Earl of Northumberland wrote to one of his fellow Privy Councillors, 'I hear Mr Percy is taken, if that I hear be true, but withal shot through the shoulder with a musket.' By then, Northumberland was under house arrest and desperate that his kinsman be treated with care, since 'none but he can show me clear as the day'. But Percy's secrets went with him to the grave. He had perished the day after the siege.

Percy and Catesby were buried at Holbeach. Their bodies were later dug up and quartered, so that their heads could be displayed on the roof of the Parliament House.

ON 9 NOVEMBER, the king addressed Parliament, heaping credit on himself for having miraculously discovered 'this horrible form of blowing us all up by Powder'. He insisted that he had given the Catholics no legitimate cause for complaint, but added that no Catholic could be a loyal subject or a good Christian.

That same day, the Lieutenant of the Tower, Sir William Waad – a creature of Cecil's with a track record of forging evidence – wrote to advise Cecil that Guy Fawkes had finally promised 'to discover to your lordship only all the secrets of his heart, but not to be set down in writing'. Fawkes did in fact make a statement, dated 9 November, which he signed eight days later. Days of torture had reduced his signature – 'Guido' – to a pathetic scrawl.

The 'Declaration of Guy Fawkes' was published in the 'King's Book', which formed the official account of the treason, along with the 'Confession of Thomas Wintour', made on 23 November. Wintour's right arm had been put out of action at Holbeach. Nevertheless, by 21 November, Sir William Waad was pleased to inform Cecil that Wintour was able to 'settle himself to write that he verbally declared to you'. The confession was altered by Sir Edward Coke, the Attorney-General who was also Cecil's nephew by marriage, and all references to Lord Monteagle were removed.

The authorities stressed that Wintour had delivered the ten-page confession in his own neat handwriting. But the signature was not his own. His spelled his name 'Wintour', reflecting its Welsh origin. The name boldly written on the confession is 'Thomas Winter'.

Another confession was made on 29 November by Francis Tresham. The reluctant plotter had not attempted to leave London before his arrest on 12 November. Threatened with torture, Tresham implicated Father Garnet in the plot. The references to Lord Monteagle in Tresham's account were pasted over.

Tresham retracted his confession shortly before he died in the Tower of London at two o'clock in the morning of 23 December. His head was chopped off and his body buried within the confines of the Tower.

EIGHT OF the surviving plotters were brought to trial in Westminster Hall on 27 January 1606. Sir Everard Digby alone pleaded guilty. The others refused to do so because the arraignment named Henry Garnet, Oswald Tesimond and Father John Gerard as the prime movers in the plot, which the government was now calling the 'Jesuits' Conspiracy'.

Sir Edward Coke fiercely denounced the 'seducing Jesuits' who had yet to be caught. 'I never yet knew a treason without a Romish priest', he thundered. He also gave a grim rationale for the punishment for high treason.

The prisoners, being 'retrograde by nature', would be drawn to their place of execution backwards at a horse's tail.

They would be hanged by the neck 'between heaven and earth', being deemed worthy of neither.

They would be cut down alive. Their genitals would be hacked off and burned because they were 'unfit to leave any generation' after them.

Their innards would be taken out and burned, for they had 'inwardly' conceived and harboured the horrible treason in their hearts, which would also be cut out and thrown into the fire.

Lastly, their heads, 'which had imagined the mischief', would be struck off and their bodies quartered and 'set up in some high and eminent place, to the view and detestation of men'.

'And this is a reward due to traitors', concluded Coke.

Digby was tried separately. He was unable to prove his contention that King James had broken his promises to the Catholics. Those who might have provided the proof were now either dead (Percy, Tresham) or imprisoned (the Earl of Northumberland).

The first four executions took place on 30 January. Armed guards were stationed in every doorway between the Tower of London and the churchyard of St Paul's.

For having raised the subject of the king's broken promises, Sir Everard Digby was made to suffer. He lived to see his own heart ripped from his chest. When the hangman shouted, 'Here is the heart of a traitor!' Sir Everard reportedly gasped: 'Thou liest.'

After him, Robert Wintour was hanged, stripped and butchered, followed by the blind John Grant and Catesby's wretched servant, Thomas Bates.

The next morning, the other four were dragged from the Tower to the Old Palace Yard at Westminster. Ambrose Rookwood caught sight of his young wife watching from a window on the Strand. He called up to her, 'Pray for me, pray for me.'

She called back: 'I will and be of good courage and offer thyself wholly to God. I, for my part, do as freely restore thee to God as he gave thee to me.'

In his scaffold speech, Tom Wintour exonerated the Jesuits of any involvement in the plot and then mounted the ladder 'with a very dead and pale colour'. Rookwood prayed that God would make the king a Catholic, before he too was 'quickly despatched'. Robert Keyes leapt from the ladder with such defiance that the rope snapped. He was still alive when he was castrated and eviscerated.

The last to die was Fawkes. Weakened by sickness and torture, he could barely climb the ladder. But climb it he did, and so high that when he jumped the halter broke his neck.

BETWEEN THE Somerville Plot of 1583 and the Gunpowder Plot of 1605, nearly twenty treasonous conspiracies, all following much the same pattern, had been 'discovered' by the government. The first and the last had originated in Shakespeare's backyard, among his friends and kinsmen.

It is not known whether Will made the short walk from his Silver Street lodgings to St Paul's to witness the executions of John Grant, Robert Wintour and Sir Everard Digby – men he had known.

If he did, the unwholesome spectacle would have been overshadowed by the news that Father Garnet had been captured.

Striding the Blast

THE WORD 'godson' occurs only once in the known works of Shakespeare. It appears in Act Two of *King Lear*: 'What, did my father's godson seek your life? / He whom my father named, your Edgar?' Will had seen the statue of Edgar, reputedly the first King of All England, when he passed through the City of Bath with his company in 1604 and 1605. One of these visits is recalled in a pair of sonnets.

The last sonnets in the sequence, as published in 1609, described the hot springs at Bath as a 'cold valley-fountain' in which the little Roman 'Love-God' had steeped his 'heart inflaming brand'. The eyes of Will's mistress had newly fired 'love's brand' and Will had become 'sick withal', a 'sad distemper'd guest' who 'the help of bath desired'.

But there was no cure for Will in the warm waters of Bath: 'Love's fire heats water, water cools not love.' The only 'healthful remedy' was for Will to bathe in his 'mistress' eyes'.

The old gossip had resurfaced yet again in 1605. The scurrilous 'Willobie his Avisa' was published for the fourth time, in an edition which included 'The Victorie of English Chastitie, *Under the fained name of Avisa*'. English Chastity had, in fact, been far from victorious. By late August, Jane knew she was pregnant. Will hastily summoned Father Garnet to hear Jane's confession, indicating in 'A Lover's Complaint' where the riverside conversation had taken place: on Christ Church Meadow in Oxford.

The nod to the Carfax legend of King Lludd and the warring dragons in the opening line of 'A Lover's Complaint' revealed Will's current interest in ancient Britain. This was also manifested in *The True Chronicle History of the Life and death of King Lear*, which was very much on his mind when, on 3 March 1606, his own 'godson' was baptised at St Martin's Church, Carfax.

William, the second son of John and Jane Davenant, was born towards the end of February. John Aubrey, who knew the Oxford Davenants, would later remark of William's elder brother, born in 1603: 'I have heard parson Robert say that Mr W. Shakespeare haz given him a hundred kisses.' As for William Davenant, Aubrey reported that when he was 'pleasant over a glass of wine' he would declare that 'it seemed to him that he writt with the very spirit [of] Shakespeare, and was' – Aubrey changed this to 'seemd' – 'contendended [*sic*] enough to be thought his Son'. The uncertain paternity of William Davenant became a running joke in the seventeenth century.

Will's sole use of the word 'godson' occurred at around the very time that William Davenant was baptised. In his sonnets, Shakespeare quibbled with the name he shared with his godson: 'So will I pray that thou mayst have thy *Will*, / If thou turn back and my loud crying still.' The final pair of sonnets recalled Will's visit to Bath, when his theatre company toured the West Country, passing through the Primrose Valley on the road to Barnstaple, and Will's affair with Jane burst back into life. They were not the last sonnets he wrote, though. Quite possibly, the last was the curious Sonnet 126, which lacks a conclusion:

> O Thou my lovely Boy who in thy power,
> Dost hold time's fickle glass, his sickle, hour:
> Who hast by waning grown, and therein show'st,
> Thy lovers withering, as thy sweet self grow'st.
> If Nature (sovereign mistress over wrack)
> As thou goest onwards still will pluck thee back,
> She keeps thee to this purpose, that her skill
> May time disgrace, and wretched minute kill.
> Yet fear her O thou minion of her pleasure,
> She may detain, but still not keep her treasure!
> Her *Audit* (though delay'd) answer'd must be,
> And her *Quietus* is to render thee.
>
> [   ]
> [   ]

The empty brackets suggest that, like the missing portion of 'A Lover's Complaint', the last couplet was teasingly withheld when *Shake-speares Sonnets* were published in 1609.

THE BAPTISM of William Davenant on 3 March 1606 coincided with unhappy news.

At daybreak on Monday 20 January, armed men had surrounded Hindlip Hall on the outskirts of Worcester. The hall's owner, Thomas Habington, was Lord Monteagle's brother-in-law. He denied harbouring any priests in his house.

The hall was ransacked, and so many secret hiding places were discovered that the search continued for a week.

On the Thursday morning, two starving men emerged from behind the wainscot in the Long Gallery. They were lay brothers. Both had taken part in the St Winefride's pilgrimage back in September. One of them, Ralph Ashley, served Father Oswald Tesimond. The other was Father Garnet's devoted servant, Nicholas Owen.

Owen had been born in Oxford. Two of his brothers were Jesuit priests while a third ran a Catholic printing press. Nicholas Owen's particular skill lay in constructing hiding places. He was, in many ways, the mirror image of Robert Cecil: a tiny man with a 'crooked body' and a limp caused when a packhorse fell on him. Known in the Catholic community as Little John, he had saved many lives by means of his cunningly crafted 'priest-holes'.

The searchers' doggedness was finally rewarded when, on Monday 27 January, two priests staggered out of the cramped space they had occupied for nearly eight days. Edward Oldcorne was 45. He too had taken part in the pilgrimage to St Winefride's Well.

Oldcorne – alias Hall – was executed at Red Hill, near Worcester, on 7 April. He died with the name of St Winefride on his lips.

Henry Garnet was taken prisoner with Father Oldcorne. His legs had swollen during his days in the Hindlip hideaway, and he remained in pain throughout the long journey to the Tower of London.

Cecil resolved to treat Garnet with deceptive gentleness. It was a different story with Garnet's servant, Nicholas Owen. On 19 February, the Privy Council authorised the use of torture to get Owen to talk. Nobody knew the hiding places used by priests better than 'Little John'.

The craftsman already had a hernia. He was hung up by his wrists for hours on end. An iron plate, strapped to his abdomen to hold in his bowels, cut into his flesh. His belly ruptured. Owen died in agony in the early morning of 2 March 1606. The government pretended that he had ripped open his own stomach with a blunt knife.

Just hours after 'Little John' was tortured to death, another child of Oxford was baptised – Shakespeare's godson, William Davenant.

THE NATIONAL mood was frantic in the wake of the Gunpowder Plot. On 7 November 1605, Ben Jonson was instructed to 'let a certain priest know (that offered to do good service to the state)' that the Privy Council wanted to see him. Jonson wrote a long letter to Cecil the next day. He had failed to get hold of any priests at all. Even his contact with the Venetian ambassador's chaplain had availed him nothing. Unless Cecil expressly desired it, Ben was unwilling to make any extra effort.

Jonson paid for his disobedience; accused in January 1606 of being 'by fame a seducer of youth to the popish religion', he was let off with a small fine. Cecil had made his point.

Shakespeare, meanwhile, had produced his initial response to the plot.

Work on *King Lear* had been suspended. Will was already giving thought to a play based on the love of Mark Antony for Cleopatra. In Plutarch's *Life of Antony* he came across an anecdote concerning Timon of Athens, a rich benefactor who turned misanthrope when he lost his money and his friends turned their backs on him.

This inspired Shakespeare's *Life of Timon of Athens*, which reflected the government's treatment of Henry Percy, Ninth Earl of Northumberland. The Wizard Earl had been on Cecil's hit list. It was now alleged that Northumberland was the intended ruler of Britain after the king and Parliament had been blown up. The earl was placed in the custody of the Archbishop of Canterbury on 7 November 1605 and questioned a week later by the Privy Council.

Northumberland's wife Dorothy – sister to the late Earl of Essex – petitioned King James, praying that the king 'would not allow the ill will of a certain great one to ruin [Northumberland] in fame, fortune and life'. She meant, of course, Cecil, who had previously ruined her brother. Northumberland, meanwhile, was demanding a fair trial. He was committed to the Tower of London on 27 November, along with three Catholic grandees who were also suspected of complicity in the powder treason.

In *Timon of Athens*, Will portrayed the Wizard Earl as a wealthy and indulgent patron. A Poet observes that when Fortune 'in her shift and change of mood / Spurns down her late beloved', all who have benefitted from Timon's largesse will 'let him fall down'. Timon is unaware that his money has run out. Like Northumberland, who was rather deaf, he ignores the pleadings of his faithful steward, Flavius, and then queries the steward's accounting. Flavius defends himself: 'If you suspect my husbandry of falsehood, / Call me before th'exactest auditors / And set me on the proof.' Northumberland's steward, Thomas Percy, was said to have embezzled thousands of pounds from the earl's northern estates. No one knows what happened to this money.

Abandoned by those who had enjoyed his hospitality, Timon rages against his fair-weather friends:

> Live loathed and long,
> Most smiling, smooth, detested parasites,
> Courteous destroyers, affable wolves, meek bears,
> You fools of fortune, trencher-friends, time's flies …

Only his steward laments his downfall: 'Poor honest lord … Rich only to be wretched, thy great fortunes / Are made thy chief afflictions.'

Timon retreats to a woodland cave, where, digging for roots, he uncovers a cache:

> What is here?
> Gold? Yellow, glittering, precious gold? …
> This yellow slave
> Will knit and break religions, bless th'accursed,
> … place thieves,
> And give them title, knee, and approbation …

Word spreads. The false friends seek Timon out, eager for a share in his 'mass of treasure'. But Timon has realised that he knows just one honest man, 'and he's a steward'.

Either Shakespeare was being naive, suggesting that the one person who had not betrayed the Wizard Earl was his steward, Thomas Percy, or he was simply challenging the official version of events. Some of his original text is lost. The material was so problematic, so likely to land the King's Men in trouble, that *Timon of Athens* was passed to Thomas Middleton for revision.

TWO OTHER characters stand out in *Timon*. The war-like Alcibiades was modelled on Sir Walter Raleigh, who also became a suspect in the Gunpowder Plot, even though he had been a prisoner in the Tower of London since 1603.

Raleigh was yet another victim of Cecil's machinations. His alleged involvement in the 'Main Plot' to dethrone King James led to an infamous travesty of justice, which is replicated in *Timon*: the Athenian captain pleads on behalf of a friend and is banished, commenting acidly of his enemies, 'I have kept back their foes / While they have told their money and let out / Their coin upon large interest'.

Northumberland and Raleigh renewed their friendship when they both found themselves incarcerated in the Tower. In Shakespeare's play, Alcibiades encounters Timon in the woods as the former is about to attack the 'coward and lascivious town'. The civic authorities appeal in due course to Timon to save them from ruin, but Timon no longer cares if Alcibiades takes his revenge on the people who conspired to destroy him.

The second character of note is Apemantus, who reads like a portrait of Ben Jonson. The 'churlish philosopher' shares Jonson's habit of railing against society: he has 'a humour there / Does not become a man'.

Apemantus seeks out Timon in the wilderness. He protests that Timon's misanthropy, unlike his own, is a 'nature but infected, / A poor unmanly melancholy, sprung / From change of fortune.' During their acerbic exchange, Timon cites a range of animals to illustrate the behaviour of men. 'If thou wert the lion, the fox would beguile thee', he spits.

The lion was the emblem of the English Crown, which in the days of Elizabeth had been beguiled by the 'old fox', Lord Burghley.

Venturing onto more dangerous ground, Shakespeare had Timon proclaim, 'Wert thou the unicorn, pride and wrath would confound thee, and make thine own self the conquest of thy fury.'

The unicorn symbolised the Crown of Scotland, now joined with the English lion. It was King James who had been confounded by his own fury and pride.

The cynical Apemantus answers Timon's outburst: 'The commonwealth ... is become a forest of beasts.'

BEN JONSON struck back with his own beast fable, *Volpone*. Its subtitle, *The Fox*, hints at its Gunpowder Plot connections – the words 'Fox' and 'Fawkes' had the same pronunciation.

Volpone was written and staged in just five weeks. Ben insisted that it gave the lie to those '(whose throats their envy failing) / Cry hoarsely, "All he writes is railing"', happily boasting that, unlike Will's *Timon*, revised by Thomas Middleton, Ben's play came from 'his own hand, without a coadjutor, / Novice, journeyman, or tutor.'

Jonson inverted the patron-steward relationship depicted by Shakespeare in *Timon of Athens*. Volpone collaborates with his steward Mosca (a 'fly') to defraud a host of parasites. The play opens with a homage to gold which parodied Timon's speeches:

> O, thou son of Sol,
> But brighter than thy father, let me kiss,

With adoration, thee, and every relic
Of sacred treasure, in this blessèd room.

The Earl of Northumberland had claimed to be too exhausted to attend
the opening of Parliament on 5 November 1605. He was in bed when Lord
Monteagle called on him to inform him of Fawkes' arrest. Accordingly,
Volpone spends much of Jonson's play in bed, feigning illness, where he
is visited by various crow-like people who hope to inherit his fortune; the
implication being that Northumberland and his steward had inveigled
the Jesuits ('massing Crows') into supporting his attempt, by way of the
Gunpowder Plot, to become the de facto King of England.

The plot is referenced by Sir Politic Would-be, a twittering parrot
who sees 'plots' everywhere. He is symptomatic of the obsession with
foreign spies and traitors which had been nurtured by Lord Burghley
and his son, Robert Cecil. But when faced with a genuine conspirator –
Volpone, masquerading as a snake-oil salesman – Sir Pol merely extols
the brilliance of the Wizard Earl and his intellectual circle:

They are the only knowing men of Europe!
Great general scholars, excellent physicians,
Most admired statesmen, professed favourites,
And cabinet counsellors, to the greatest princes!

Jonson couldn't resist having a dig at his main rival. It comes early
on in the play, when three deformed bastards to whom Volpone is
patron perform an entertainment detailing the 'metempsychosis' or
transmigration of the soul of Pythagoras through many generations,
until it ends up in the body of a fool called Androgyno.

As far back as 1598, Francis Meres had written, 'As the soul of
Euphorbus was thought to live in *Pythagoras*: so the sweet and witty
soul of *Ovid* lives in mellifluous and honey-tongued *Shakespeare.*'

The exotic Androgyno, servant to Volpone, is a hermaphrodite. Jonson
had previously alluded to Shakespeare's alleged bisexual tendencies in
Every Man Out of his Humour – it was a standard charge levelled at
the followers of Raleigh and Northumberland (witness the smearing
of Christopher Marlowe). In addition to his homosexual tastes, which
he apparently shares with his master, Androgyno possesses the soul
of Pythagoras.

The soul had adopted the 'coat' of a Puritan 'in these times of
reformation'. Its 'dogmatical silence' had been forced out of it by an
'obstreperous lawyer', and it passed into:

> a very strange beast, by some writers called an ass;
> By others, a precise, pure, illuminate brother,
> Of those who devour flesh, and sometimes one another;
> And will drop forth a libel, or a sanctified lie,
> Betwixt every spoonful of a nativity-pie.

But the Puritan mask has slipped. Androgyno now prefers to be a 'fool', the 'only creature that I can call blessed': 'Your Fool, he is your great man's dearling, / And your ladies' sport and pleasure; / Tongue and bable are his treasure.' Lest there be any doubt as to which lady had enjoyed the fool's tongue and 'bauble', Jonson left some clues. Sir Politic Would-be is accused by his wife of being 'the patron, or St George / To a lewd harlot', and an innocent woman, maligned by her jealous husband, neighs 'like a jennet'.

Volpone was a nasty piece of propaganda, designed to prepare the public for the Earl of Northumberland's trial. Like Volpone, Northumberland was betrayed by his steward – 'the chief minister, if not plotter, / In all these lewd impostures'. Sentence is passed on Volpone:

> And, since the most was gotten by imposture,
> By feigning lame, gout, palsy, and such diseases,
> Thou art to lie in prison, cramped with irons,
> Till thou be'st sick, and lame indeed.

Northumberland was eventually condemned on false charges and fined the enormous sum of £30,000. A later portrait by Anthony Van Dyck shows him resting his head on one hand, eyes blank, face expressionless – a disenchanted Timon. He remained a prisoner in the Tower of London until 1621.

First performed by the King's Men in March 1606, *Volpone* is Jonson's most popular comedy.

There is no record of any performance of *Timon of Athens* in Shakespeare's lifetime.

CECIL WAS determined to portray Father Garnet as the 'principal conspirator' of the Gunpowder Plot. No effort was spared in trying to make him confess. He was deprived of sleep and threatened with torture ('I have heard / The rack had cured the gout,' joked Ben Jonson in *Volpone*). Spies listened in on his conversations.

The government already had all the evidence it would ever have against the Jesuit. In December 1605, Cecil's ageing nephew, Sir Edward

Coke, decided to search a chamber belonging to the late Sir Thomas Tresham. There, the Attorney-General discovered two copies of a document. Originally called *A Treatise on Equivocation*, the title had been altered to *A Treatise Against Lying and Fraudulent Dissimulation* by its author, Father Henry Garnet.

The doctrine of equivocation had evolved after Garnet and his fellow priests narrowly escaped capture at Baddesley Clinton in 1591. It was the art of answering a question in a way that was truthful but open to misinterpretation. Equivocation avoided the sin of outright denial – as Garnet had written, 'Judas sinned by betraying Christ, but [St] Peter sinned also by denying him' – and allowed Catholics to be both honest and misleading at the same time.

The issue had been central to the trial of Father Southwell in 1595. Forced to betray Southwell to the authorities, Anne Bellamy testified that the Jesuit had taught her to equivocate so as not to incriminate herself and others. In the case of Southwell's colleague, Father Garnet, Cecil and his ministers – who frequently indulged in fraudulent dissimulation – were hell-bent on proving that the Jesuits were inherently deceitful. The matter of equivocation was therefore allowed to dominate Garnet's trial, which took place on Friday 28 March 1606 at the Guildhall. The result was a foregone conclusion.

Garnet was charged with having conspired with Robert Catesby to 'alter and subvert the government of the kingdom and the true worship of God established in England' and of plotting with 'false traitors' to blow up the king, the prince, the Lords and the Commons. He pleaded 'Not Guilty'.

The jury of wealthy London businessmen took fifteen minutes to reach their verdict. The Jesuit would be 'hanged without equivocation', noted an observer.

The next day, hurricane-force winds blasted the country, 'causing great shipwreck'.

GARNET'S EXECUTION was scheduled for 1 May, traditionally a festival of misrule. Fearing disorder, the authorities put the execution back to 3 May, which for Catholics was also the Feast of the Invention of the Holy Cross.

The scaffold was erected on the west side of St Paul's Churchyard. Huge crowds gathered to watch the superior of the Jesuits in England dragged on a hurdle to the place of his death. They were restive, expectant. The government had spread the rumour that Garnet would make a last-minute conversion to Protestantism.

He did no such thing. His final prayer was, 'Mary, Mother of Grace, Mother of mercy, protect us from the enemy, and receive us at the hour of our death.'

Then he climbed the ladder, crossed his arms over his chest and was pushed until he dangled from the noose.

The atmosphere changed. Many surged forwards, pulling at Garnet's legs 'to put him out of his pain, and that he might not be cut down alive'. There was no response to the words 'Behold the heart of a traitor', no cries of 'God save the King!'

For some reason, Garnet's head did not decompose in the normal way. It 'appeared in that lively colour as it seemed to retain the same hue and show of life which it had before it was cut off'. Even after it was parboiled and stuck on a pole over London Bridge, it refused to turn black, 'as usually heads cut from bodies do'.

THE POET John Masefield imagined Shakespeare writing the first two acts of *Macbeth* in one sustained sitting. That might be an overstatement, and yet it is conceivable that Will did pen most of the first two acts in a single burst, and that he did so immediately after the gruesome execution of the 'reverend man' whom Jane Davenant had called 'Father'.

Macbeth opens with thunder and lightning. Three witches gather on a blasted heath. They were played by male actors, and we soon discover that they have beards.

The 'weird sisters' were, in effect, Robert Cecil, First Earl of Salisbury; Cecil's ally, Thomas Howard, First Earl of Suffolk; and Suffolk's uncle, Henry Howard, First Earl of Northampton. King James described them as his 'trinity of knaves'.

Though the Howards were Catholics, they had colluded with Cecil for personal gain. Henry Howard had acted as Cecil's emissary to King James in Scotland, and so instrumental had the Howards been in smoothing James' path to the English throne that the king admitted to loving 'the whole tribe of them'.

The opening scene of *Macbeth* lasts a mere eleven lines. The witches agree to meet with Macbeth and are summoned away by their familiars: Paddock – a 'toad', one of the popular nicknames for Cecil – and Grimalkin or 'Grey Mary' (Northampton's first wife had been his stepsister Mary Dacre, the daughter of Lord Greystock). They scurry off, clearing the stage for the entrance of King Duncan.

Shakespeare now reminded the audience that the Jesuits had supported the accession of King James and had even uncovered a plot to kidnap the king. The Bye Plot – also known as the 'Treason of the Priests' – had been hatched by a secular priest who was then under the protection of the Bishop of London and was seemingly intended to force James to adopt a more tolerant religious policy. The plot had been exposed by Father Garnet and his fellow Jesuit, John Gerard, who received no credit for this loyal act, but in the course of its investigations the government discovered a parallel conspiracy, the Main Plot, which led to the trial and imprisonment of Sir Walter Raleigh.

King Duncan is the Garnet figure in *Macbeth*. He hears reports of an attempted rebellion and of Macbeth's valour in crushing his enemies.

The witches return, gloating over the mischief they have been causing. One of them has been plaguing a sailor's wife whose husband is the 'master o'th' Tiger'. The ship was back in the news, having been hijacked by pirates off the coast of Java. But as Shakespeare knew, the *Tiger* had been the flagship loaned by Queen Elizabeth to Sir Walter Raleigh for his 1585 expedition to Virginia; its Portuguese pilot, Simon Fernandez, had been known to the crew as 'the swine'. The seaman persecuted by the witches was therefore Raleigh, then a prisoner in the Tower of London, whose wife Bess was fighting to keep possession of Raleigh's Sherborne estate in the face of Cecil's malice.

Another witch produces a grisly relic – a 'pilot's thumb', cut from the hand of a priest who was '[W]racked as homeward he did come'. Then Macbeth enters with Banquo.

Will had watched the re-creation of the legendary scene in which Macbeth and Banquo – the reputed ancestor of King James – were hailed by three witches when it was staged for the king on the outskirts of Oxford on 27 August 1605. This had been shortly before Father Garnet heard Jane's confession on the riverbank, a moment which, for Will, was frozen in time. There was a direct link between the witches' prophecy and the slaughter of Garnet and his fellows. The one had led to the other, as if the promise of the throne and the wave of executions were separated by little more than three days and the length of an Oxford street.

The witches are later seen consorting with their goddess, Hecate, who describes Macbeth as a 'wayward son, / Spiteful and wrathful'. King James had commissioned a stately monument for his mother, Mary, Queen of Scots, to partner the one being made for her cousin, Elizabeth I, in Westminster Abbey. Shakespeare presented James in *Macbeth* as the 'wayward' offspring of the English Jezebel – a veritable 'Son of [Eliza]beth'.

Just as the 'trinity of knaves' had secured the throne for James, so the 'weird sisters' assure Macbeth that he will be king.

The Main and Bye Plots of 1603 – 'treasons capital, confessed and proved' – had been dealt with. King James had the support of the Jesuits. But a ghastly plan was already occurring to him.

KING DUNCAN greets Macbeth, 'I have begun to plant thee, and will labour / To make thee full of growing,' recalling the Jesuit image of England as a 'vineyard'. Duncan then names his own son as his successor and Prince of Cumberland. Malcolm's elevated status mirrors the perilous position of that other northern prince, Northumberland, who had championed the cause of the Catholics.

Macbeth realises that Malcolm stands in his way. Meanwhile, the Lady – Macbeth's wife – grasps the potential in the witches' promises.

James could not achieve unconditional sovereignty while the Jesuits had a foothold in the kingdom. The Lady offers to suckle the 'murdering ministers' of the land in return for the death of King Duncan. She also starts the litany of references to 'night' which toll like a funeral bell through the play: 'Come, thick night, / And pall thee in the dunnest smoke of hell ...' The Latin for 'night', *Nox*, echoed the name of John Knox, the dour architect of the Scottish Reformation. He is repeatedly invoked in *Macbeth*: his 'black agents' harry their prey while his 'bloody and invisible hand' tears up the social bonds.

The saintly Duncan arrives at Macbeth's castle. Macbeth rehearses the Gunpowder Plot in his mind – 'that but this blow / Might be the be-all and the end-all here'. He knows that Duncan:

Hath borne his faculties so meek, hath been
So clear in his great office, that his virtues
Will plead like angels, trumpet-tongued against
The deep damnation of his taking off,
And pity, like a naked new-born babe,
Striding the blast ...
Shall blow the horrid deed in every eye
That tears shall drown the wind.

A newborn had indeed appeared between the discovery of the plot and its bloody conclusion. Will's godson, William Davenant, was a living symbol of pity, a cherubic reminder of Father Garnet.

Macbeth's wife steels him to the task. He becomes a ravishing Tarquin, his deed as dark as the rape of Lucrece. The Lady would have done it herself, had Duncan 'not resembled / My father'. Queen Anne, the wife of King James, was a closet Catholic whose Danish father had vaguely resembled Henry Garnet.

The murder committed, Macbeth finds that he cannot say 'Amen'. Duncan's blood will be forever on his hands. He will never sleep soundly again.

Then, Macbeth is startled by a pounding at the gate.

BETWEEN THE passing of his sentence and his execution, Sir Everard Digby wrote a poem in the Tower of London: 'Who's that which knocks? O, stay, my Lord, I come ...' The banging at the gate of Macbeth's castle is also the knocking of a Christ-like figure. The image came from the medieval Mystery plays, which Shakespeare remembered from his childhood. In the Mystery cycles, the Crucifixion was followed by the Harrowing of Hell, when Christ descended to free the souls of the dead. This presented an opportunity for some crude comedy in the old pageants. As Christ stood knocking at the gate of hell, he was taunted and mocked from within by a devilish Vice.

In *Macbeth*, the Vice is played by a drunken porter.

Father Garnet died on the day which commemorated the Finding of the Holy Cross. If Shakespeare walked back to his lodgings on Silver Street, fresh from the scene of Garnet's execution, and sat down to write his *Tragedy of Macbeth*, he had now reached the point where he could no longer hold his feelings in.

The porter reveals that it is Garnet who is pounding on the gates of hell:

> PORTER: Here's a knocking indeed! If a man were porter
> of hell-gate he should have old turning the key.
> *Knock within*
> Knock, knock, knock! Who's there, i'th' name of
> Beelzebub? Here's a farmer that hanged himself
> on th'expectation of plenty.

'Farmer' was an alias used by Father Garnet. The knocking continues:

> Knock, knock. Who's there, in th'other devil's
> name? Faith, here's an equivocator that could
> swear in both scales against either scale,
> who committed treason enough for God's sake,
> yet could not equivocate to heaven. O, come in,
> equivocator.

Knock within
Knock, knock, knock. Who's there? Faith, here's
an English tailor come hither for stealing out
of a French hose.

French hose were notoriously tight. Garnet – a Jesuit 'tailor' who measured up converts for their heavenly garb – was caught as he stole out of a hiding place so cramped that his legs had swollen up.

Knock within
Knock, knock. Never at quiet. What are you? –
But this place is too cold for hell. I'll devil-porter
it no further. I had thought to have let in some
of all professions that go the primrose way
to th'everlasting bonfire.

Will had followed his own 'primrose way' when he seduced Jane at Banwell in Somerset's Primrose Valley. It was Father Garnet who came to Jane's spiritual assistance when their affair was rekindled and Jane was pregnant with the 'naked new-born babe' whose birth would straddle the blast. Justice was reversed; Garnet had gone to the 'everlasting bonfire' ahead of the philandering Will.

The porter opens the gate, turning to the audience: 'I pray you remember the porter.'

It was a cry from the heart. In the dialect of the time, 'porter' sounded like *Pater* – 'I pray you, remember the Father.'

15

There is a World Elsewhere

AS WAS noted at the time, the Gunpowder Plot shared certain similarities with a previous attempt on the life of the king.

On Tuesday 5 August 1600, King James of Scotland was hunting near his palace of Falkland. He was repeatedly approached by Alexander Ruthven, a brother of the Earl of Gowrie, who claimed to have encountered a 'base like fellow' hiding a 'great wide pot' of gold under his cloak. After a hard day's hunting, James was finally persuaded to accompany Ruthven back to Saint Johnstoun – now Perth – some 15 miles away.

The king arrived with Ruthven and a few followers at Gowrie House, where James was lured into a small turret room. A man 'with a very abased countenance' held a dagger to his breast and accused him of having murdered Ruthven's father, the first Earl of Gowrie, who had been executed in 1584.

The king's attendants were told that James had left and was riding back to Falkland. They quickly mounted their horses, but the porter insisted that nobody had passed through the gate. The Earl of Gowrie called his porter a liar.

At that moment, James appeared at a window, crying out that he was being murdered. The king's followers slew Alexander Ruthven on the stairs. His brother, the earl, raced up to the turret room, armed with two swords. There was a desperate struggle. Gowrie was stabbed through the heart. The king searched his pockets and found a small bag 'full of magical characters, and words of enchantment'. Gowrie's wounds, it was claimed, only bled when these talismans were removed from his body.

King James left Perth at about eight o'clock that evening, riding through the rain and crowds of onlookers. Bells rang and bonfires burned in celebration of the king's deliverance. Gowrie was maligned as a papist and a dabbler in witchcraft.

James returned to his palace at Falkland and wrote up a detailed account of the events. This was sent to the Privy Council in Edinburgh at nine o'clock the next morning. As with the Gunpowder Plot, five years later, it was the king's personal 'Narrative' which became the official 'Account published by Authority'. In London, meanwhile, Robert Cecil received his own report on the Scottish king's miraculous escape.

THE GOWRIE conspiracy has mystified commentators ever since that August evening in 1600. The King's 'Narrative', written up after a long day of exhausting activity, does not quite ring true. There were suspicions that the Earl of Gowrie had been rather too intimate with James' queen, the pretty Anne of Denmark, and there is little doubt that Henry, James' eldest son, born in 1594, was not much like his father. Also, by seizing Gowrie's estates, the king was able to pay off his colossal debts. As James would soon admit in a letter to the Earl of Northumberland, 'princes make sometimes use of treason'.

The Gowrie incident occurred on a Tuesday, the fifth day of the month. James considered this his 'lucky' day. So, after being twice postponed, the opening of the English Parliament was scheduled for Tuesday, 5 November 1605 – and James was again preserved by a combination of good fortune and divine intervention.

Shakespeare knew about the Gowrie Plot. The King's Men had been censured for performing *The Tragedy of Gowrie* in December 1604, it being forbidden to represent living persons on the stage.

Two of Gowrie's younger brothers fled to England the day after the events at Perth. They were protected by Queen Elizabeth. In Will's *Tragedy of Macbeth*, two sons of the murdered Duncan take flight, seeking refuge at the English Court. Malcolm, Duncan's chosen successor, is followed there by Macduff, whose knocking at the gate had so pestered the drunken porter, and who discovered the bleeding body of King Duncan ('Confusion now hath made his masterpiece'). It may be no coincidence that among the dependants of the Earl of Gowrie who were hanged after the conspiracy was one John McDuff, the 'baron bailie' of the Gowrie estate in Strathbraan.

Macduff implores Malcolm to come to Scotland's rescue and then receives word that his wife and children have been slaughtered by Macbeth's goons.

'He has no children,' groans Macduff. Even though his wife has 'given suck', Macbeth, it seems, is childless. Was Shakespeare hinting at the questionable paternity of Henry, Prince of Wales, and James' secret motive for wanting the Earl of Gowrie dead?

MACBETH WAS first performed on or around 7 August 1606, two days after King James celebrated the annual thanksgiving for his escape from Gowrie and his kinsmen. Two women were hanged for witchcraft on that same day.

It was also the day on which James' brother-in-law, Christian IV of Denmark, became a Knight of the Garter, an honour which had already been granted to Robert Cecil in May as a reward for his sure handling of the Gunpowder Plot.

King Christian had arrived on 17 July. A week later, the royal parties were welcomed to Cecil's mansion of Theobalds in Hertfordshire. The kings were greeted with a short presentation penned, at Cecil's behest, by Ben Jonson. Three performers, representing Law, Justice and Peace, perched on 'clouds' at the entrance to the Inner Court: 'Enter, O longed-for princes, bless these bowers, / And us, the three, by you made happy, Hours ...' The contrast between Jonson's sycophantic 'Hours' and Shakespeare's equivocating witches, who would soon appear before the two kings, could not have been much sharper.

While they were at Theobalds, the kings took part in an evening of revelry involving an 'entertainment made of Solomon and his Temple and the Queen of Sheba'. The lady playing the Queen of Sheba was so tipsy, she tripped and dropped her load of cream, jellies and wine over King Christian, who promptly decided to dance with her but then fell down dead drunk and had to be carried from the chamber. Three ladies representing Faith, Hope and Charity were too inebriated to speak and ended up vomiting in the lower hall. Victory presented a sword to King James, who refused to accept it, and was led away and laid down to sleep on the stairs. Peace attacked those in her path with an olive branch.

Sir John Harington, who witnessed the chaos of that evening, remarked that 'the gunpowder fright is got out of all our heads'. It was 'as if the devil was contriving every man should blow himself up, by wild riot, excess, and devastation of time and temperance'.

Against such a background, Will's dose of strong medicine must have had a sobering effect. King James 'liked not' the play of *Macbeth*. Shakespeare had gone too far, portraying the execution of Father Garnet as a treacherous murder committed by a bloody tyrant and his 'fiend-like' queen.

This could explain *Macbeth*'s unlucky reputation – except that, as Garry Wills pointed out in *Witches and Jesuits*, the theatrical superstitions attached to 'the Scottish play' are a recent invention. The 'curse' of the play only arose after producers started omitting the Hecate scenes. As the lingering influence of Elizabeth I, Queen Hecate was integral to Shakespeare's strategy.

Hecate first appears after Macbeth has begun to fear imaginary phantasms. The witch-goddess declares that she will 'raise such artificial sprites / As by the strength of their illusion / Shall draw him unto confusion.' The principal illusion descends as a *'Spirit like a Cat'*. This would have put the audience in mind of Robert Catesby, a descendant of 'the Cat', William Catesby, who had served as a councillor to the hunchbacked King Richard III. The manner in which Hecate and her witches invoke the Cat and other spirits suggests that, as far as Will was concerned, the entire Gunpowder Plot was an illusion, conjured up by Cecil and his confederates in order to beguile the paranoid king.

The spirits remain onstage while Macbeth consults the witches about his future. They whip up a spectacle: 'Show his eyes and grieve his heart'. Eight kings appear in succession. Some carry 'twofold balls and triple sceptres' – a reminder that James had united the thrones of England and Scotland and his brother-in-law had arrived from Denmark on a ship called *The Three Crowns*.

Last comes a kingly spectre 'who bears a glass … Horrible sight!'

The mirror was held up to King James, seated in the front row, who saw his own guilty reflection staring back at him.

'Let this pernicious hour / Stand aye accursed in the calendar,' snarled Macbeth.

WILL'S DAUGHTER, Susanna, fell foul of the laws introduced by Cecil in the wake of the Gunpowder Plot. She was charged with having failed to receive the sacrament at Easter, 20 April 1606. Under the new legislation she was liable for a punitive fine.

The case was eventually dismissed, probably because her father had taken decisive action. He arranged for her to marry a prominent Protestant of Stratford-upon-Avon.

Will had known Dr John Hall for some time. In an age when the medical profession was as likely to kill as to cure, some of Hall's remedies must have raised the odd eyebrow. He would one day treat his wife Susanna for the colic by pumping a pint of warm sherry into her rectum. Will almost certainly used Dr Hall as his model for the ineffectual Doctor of Physic who fails to cure Lady Macbeth's telltale sleepwalking.

Susanna, then aged 24, married Dr Hall on 5 June 1607. Shakespeare's new son-in-law was open-minded enough to treat papists – his clients included a 'Romish priest' and one 'Mr Winter' and his Catholic 'Widow' – but he was nevertheless a notable Protestant. The marriage cleansed Susanna of the taint of Catholicism, and maybe Shakespeare allowed himself a wry smile, for he, who had posed as 'Will Hall', was now the father of Mrs Susanna Hall.

Trouble with daughters had been a theme of *King Lear*, which Will completed in 1606; it was performed before the king at Whitehall on 26 December. The opening scene recalled the king's initial pretence of religious tolerance. At first, James had allowed three forms of faith – Catholicism, Protestantism and Puritanism – to co-exist. Thus, King Lear vows to divide his kingdom equally between his three daughters, but subjects them first to a test: 'Which of you shall we say doth love us most?'

Two of the daughters express their devotion in wildly extravagant terms. The third resolves to 'Love and be silent.' Her name, Cordelia, derives from the Latin for 'heart'. She symbolised those Catholics who felt unable to swear the new Oath of Allegiance imposed by Cecil in May 1606.

For refusing to make a false show of love to her royal father, Cordelia is banished.

Shakespeare himself had three daughters: Susanna, Judith and his 'silent' child by Agnes Whateley. It is interesting to note that Dr John Hall treated a 'Mrs Sheldon of Grafton' soon after she had given birth at the age of 24. Mrs Sheldon was afflicted with 'Fits of the Mother', an old term for hysteria which Shakespeare would use in *King Lear*: 'O, how this mother swells up toward my heart! / *Hysterico passio*, down, thy climbing sorrow; / Thy element's below.'

King Lear discovers that the love professed by his first two daughters was unreal. The king has handed his kingdom over to the two factions which had no real love for him at all. The third daughter has been exiled to France, where her virtues are appreciated.

The king becomes a homeless beggar, caught in a ferocious storm. Those who remained true to him are likewise reduced to the status of beggars and madmen or are horribly tortured by their opponents. Help, in the form of a French invasion, comes too late.

Shakespeare radically altered the traditional happy ending of the tale. In the first version of his play, Cordelia's doctor cures Lear's madness, but the tragic catastrophe cannot be averted. Lear's fool is hanged. So is Cordelia, who was probably played by the same actor. Lear dies of a broken heart.

Like King James, he had wrought havoc by trusting the wrong people.

WILL HAD become obsessed with adultery and bastards. In *Lear*, the Earl of Gloucester has a legitimate son, Edgar, who at the end of the play stands poised to be King of All England. Gloucester's other son, Edmund, is a 'whoreson'. He betrays his brother and conspires with the cruel daughters of King Lear.

As if to stress his relationship with an illegitimate boy, Shakespeare gave the bastard in *King Lear* the name of his youngest brother. Edmund Shakespeare, born when Will was 16, had become an actor and, potentially, a conduit for damaging gossip; he died in London in 1607.

In a play dominated by family strife, Edmund soliloquises on his illegitimacy – 'Why "bastard"? Wherefore "base"?' – and uses it to justify his wickedness: 'Now gods, stand up for bastards!' These meditations were concurrent with the infancy of Will's illegitimate son by Jane Davenant. Edmund reveals that 'My father compounded with my mother under the Dragon's tail and my nativity was under Ursa Major, so that it follows I am rough and lecherous.'

Will Shakespeare had passed through Bath, with its statue of King Edgar, and the Primrose Valley in Somerset when his company took to the road in 1605. If Jane had been staying with her family at the George Inn, Banwell, then Will might have copulated with her under the sign of St George and the Dragon, unleashing his self-disgust after the act in his angriest sonnet: 'Th'expense of Spirit [semen] in a waste [waist] of shame / Is lust in action, and till action, lust / Is perjured, murderous, bloody full of blame ...' His colleague, Augustine Philips, had recently died; perhaps Will was instinctively replenishing the human stock. Nine months later, William Davenant was born 'under Ursa Major', the Great Bear. Around the corner from the Davenants' Taverne stood The Bear, one of the oldest inns in Oxford, where medical procedures were carried out.

The brazen sexuality of Will's sonnets to his 'Dark Lady' echoes in the rage of King Lear, who has sex on the brain:

> I pardon that man's life. What was thy cause?
> Adultery? Thou shalt not die for adultery.
> No, the wren goes to't, and the small gilded fly
> Does lecher in my sight.
> Let copulation thrive ...

A woman's body is the seat of iniquity:

> Down from the waist
> They're centaurs, though women all above.
> But to the girdle do the gods inherit;

Beneath is all the fiend's. There's hell, there's darkness,
There's the sulphury pit ...

The motif of sexual infatuation and adultery was carried through into another of Will's tragedies written in 1606. The story of Antony and Cleopatra had been on his mind when he wrote *Timon of Athens*. Macbeth also refers in passing to Mark Antony. More than anything, Will had been inspired by the sight of Jane making her confession to Father Garnet on the bank of the Isis in Oxford. His poem of the occasion, 'A Lover's Complaint', drew on Samuel Daniel's 'Complaint of Rosamond', which had been reissued with Daniel's tragedy of *Cleopatra* in 1594.

Will seems to have had a certain fondness for the pleasure-loving Mark Antony, whom he had portrayed as the eloquent and sybaritic avenger of *Julius Caesar*. Jane naturally became his Cleopatra, the tawny, capricious queen with whom Antony fell adulterously and tragically in love.

From his reading of Plutarch, Will knew that Cleopatra was 38 when she died – the same age as Jane Davenant when Will's *Tragedy of Antony and Cleopatra* was premiered. At the start of the play, Antony is 42, the same age as Shakespeare in 1606.

Plutarch wrote of Mark Antony, 'some say that he lived three-and-fifty years'. By a strange quirk of fate, Will Shakespeare would die at the start of his fifty-third year.

ON 30 JANUARY 1607 a violent storm surge destroyed part of the sea defences at Burnham, near Banwell. The Primrose Valley was inundated to a depth of 3 metres. 'In this civil Wars between the Land and the Sea,' noted a chapbook of the time, 'many Men, Women and Children lost their lives.'

Fortunately, Jane was not there when Banwell was flooded. But the disaster affected Will imaginatively and formed a springboard for his *Pericles, Prince of Tyre*.

Ben Jonson hated *Pericles*, dismissing it as 'some mouldy tale' and making sure that it was left out of the First Folio in 1623. Even so, *Pericles* became one of the most popular plays of the Jacobean period, and nowhere was it better appreciated than amongst the recusant community. In 1609, a troupe of actors embarked on a tour, taking *Pericles* and *King Lear* to the great Catholic households of northern England. It is possible that Shakespeare went with them, taking the part of the ancient poet John Gower, who narrates the play – 'Only I carry winged Time / Post on the lame feet of my rhyme'.

The sea is never far away in *Pericles*. The tale encompasses fishermen, pirates, two shipwrecks, and a birth and a burial at sea. To woo the daughter of the King of Antioch, Pericles must answer a riddle. A row of severed heads serves as a reminder that failure to give the right answer will result in death. The riddle therefore has something in common with the 'Bloody Question' devised to entrap Catholics.

Pericles divines the awful truth: the king and his daughter have committed incest. He has glimpsed the terrible reality behind the 'Bloody Question'. By solving the riddle, he has put his life at risk.

He flees, but is shipwrecked on the coast of Pentapolis. His dead father's armour is dredged up in a fisherman's net, and we hear the authentic voice of Will Shakespeare, forever grateful to have inherited his father's 'coat of worth': 'My shipwreck now's no ill, / Since I have here my father gave's in's will.'

Wearing his father's rusty armour, Pericles wins the hand of the lovely Thaisa. They are married and a 'babe is moulded'. Thaisa dies giving birth onboard ship in the midst of a tempest, and Pericles is compelled to cast his wife's body overboard inside a chest. In an image drawn from the sea-flood around Banwell – 'I never saw so huge a billow, sir, / Or a more eager' – the coffin washes up on the shore. A lord who has 'studied physic' opens it up (shades of Jane Clifford, or Fair Rosamund: 'Soft, it smells / Most sweetly in my sense') and revives Thaisa, who then becomes a nun-like votaress of Diana.

By this point, Will had blended the contemporary flooding of the Primrose Valley with the history of his relationship with his 'sacred nun' and the birth of their illegitimate daughter. The child is named Marina, 'for she was born at sea'. She grows up to be so beautiful and accomplished that the jealous queen sends a man to murder her, but the girl is kidnapped by pirates and sold to a brothel-keeper. Even at 14, Marina is so virtuous that she converts her would-be clients to piety.

Pericles arrives by ship. Believing that his wife and daughter are dead, he is unable to speak. Marina is touchingly reunited with her father, and then Pericles is visited in a dream by the goddess Diana, who instructs him to make a sacrifice at her temple. There, he discovers that his beloved Thaisa, 'supposèd dead and drowned', is still alive.

The play ends on a note of reconciliation:

In Pericles, his queen, and daughter seen,
Although assailed with fortune fierce and keen,
Virtue preserved from fell destruction's blast,
Led on by heav'n, and crowned with joy at last.

Whether it was the apocalyptic flooding of Banwell, which raised the image of drowned lovers and children, or the marriage of Susanna Shakespeare, Will's thoughts had returned to his long-lost daughter by Agnes Whateley. His first child had been conceived during a 'storm' of sectarian conflict; she was now 24, having grown up under the protection of the Sheldon masters of Temple Grafton, and if she was the 'Mrs Sheldon of Grafton' who was treated by Dr John Hall for hysterical fits after childbirth, then Will had become a grandfather.

Pericles sent out a message of hope to the long-suffering Catholics; of recovery after many tribulations. Will's next play, the last of his Roman tragedies, would be his final word on the Gunpowder Plot.

UNREST HAD broken out across the Arden region in the summer of 1607. Beginning on the eve of May Day, the Midlands Rising saw 'many of the meanest sort' assembling 'riotously in multitudes' to protest against acquisitive landlords. Though Will was a Warwickshire landowner, it is unlikely that he approved of the extreme violence used to quell the revolt.

There was widespread hardship the following summer. On 2 June 1608, King James issued an ineffectual 'Proclamation for the preventing and remedying of the dearth of Grain, and other Victuals'. Shakespeare was back in Stratford that August, pursuing a local man over a £6 debt, and so he was probably present when his mother was buried at Holy Trinity Church on 9 September.

The Tragedy of Coriolanus opens with a mutinous crowd hungry for bread. They are addressed by the 'worthy' Menenius, 'one that hath always loved the people', who introduces one of the themes of the play – that of bodily dismemberment.

The mob is then accused by Martius Caius of being fickle: 'With every minute you do change a mind, / And call him noble that was now your hate, / Him vile that was your garland.'

Much has been made of Shakespeare's supposed distaste for the common herd, but this is misleading. In *Coriolanus*, it is the ease with which public opinion is manipulated by devious politicians that causes the crisis.

Martius Caius, a proud, disdainful warrior, owed much to Robert Catesby, and the character's relationship with the conciliatory Menenius drew on the contacts between Catesby and Father Garnet. Menenius considers himself a 'father' to Martius, and his remark to the tribunes who are scheming against Martius – 'I am known to be a humorous patrician, and one that loves a drop of hot wine' – reflected Garnet's nature and his fondness for wine, which had allowed the authorities to portray him as a drunkard.

The first act of *Coriolanus* restages the Essex rebellion of 1601. An attack is launched against Rome's traditional enemies, the Volscians. Martius distinguishes himself by his swordsmanship and is wounded in the arm, as was Catesby when he fought for Essex at the entrance to the City of London. For his brave actions at the city of Corioles, Martius is given the honorary title 'Coriolanus'.

So far, so Catesby. Coriolanus is expected to stand for consul. The tribunes persuade the citizens that Coriolanus 'ever spake against / Your liberties and the charters that you bear'. Their tone is that of the Reformation propagandist, insisting that the people would lose their wealth and freedoms if the Catholics were given free rein.

Coriolanus makes his contempt for the senate plain when he hears that the people have not elected him. Driven to fury, much as Catesby and his ilk were enraged by the parliamentary Acts against Catholics passed at the start of James' reign, he lambastes the parliamentarians and the divisions they promote. For this, he is condemned as a traitor and banished.

'There is a world elsewhere,' observes Coriolanus. He goes over to Rome's enemies, visiting the house of his eternal rival, Tullus Aufidius, who is clearly a portrait of Robert Cecil, right down to his splayed foot. Coriolanus had most recently confronted Aufidius in the action at Corioles – a reconstruction of the Essex rebellion, which Cecil had thwarted. He now becomes Aufidius' weapon against Rome.

Like Father Garnet, Menenius worries. When he first hears that Coriolanus is plotting with Aufidius to 'burn us all into one coal' he can hardly believe it, though he knows of 'three examples of the like': it was not the first time Cecil had turned a Roman Catholic against his own. Repeating Garnet's words – 'We are all undone' – Menenius hopes that Coriolanus can be dissuaded from attacking Rome.

He speaks with Coriolanus as his 'old father' – 'O, my son, my son, thou art preparing fire for us' – but Coriolanus refuses to listen. It is only when his mother approaches him, with his wife and young son and a 'noble sister', the 'moon of Rome', that Coriolanus wavers. His mother begs him not to 'tear with thunder the wide cheek o'th' air' and 'charge thy sulphur with a bolt / That should but rive an oak.'

There were rumours at the time of the Gunpowder Plot that the wives, mothers and sisters of the plotters had persuaded them to abandon their crazy mission. Catesby pointedly avoided meeting his mother at Ashby St Ledgers on the evening of the plot's discovery, so perhaps there was some substance to the rumours. Shakespeare certainly implied in *Coriolanus* that, where Father Garnet's imprecations had failed, the blandishments of the women had done the trick.

Word reaches Rome that the 'ladies have prevailed'. Menenius is mightily relieved: 'You have prayed well today.'

This leaves Tullus Aufidius with a problem – how to prevent Coriolanus from appearing 'before the people, hoping / To purge himself with words.' Aufidius acknowledges that he 'raised' Coriolanus:

Made him joint-servant with me, gave him way
In all his own desires; nay, let him choose
Out of my files, his project to accomplish,
My best and freshest men ...

Coriolanus must therefore be stopped, 'Ere he express himself or move the people / With what he would say'. His assassination will ensure that 'his tale pronounced shall bury / His reasons with his body.' And so, like Catesby and Percy at Holbeach House, Coriolanus is treacherously slain by Rome's enemies, with whom he had conspired.

Will Shakespeare had known the plotters, their houses, their families, their priests. He knew Robert Cecil, too. It was clear to him that Cecil had used Catesby, and that the powder treason was simply one more action in Cecil's obsessive war against the Church of Rome.

As with his *Timon of Athens*, there is no evidence that *Coriolanus* was performed in Will's lifetime.

BEN JONSON took three years to come up with a riposte to Will's last Roman tragedy. By then, Ben had abandoned his pretence of Catholicism. His 'true reconciliation' in 1610 was as dramatic as his original 'conversion'. Jonson marked his return to the Anglican Church by downing a full cup of communion wine.

In *Coriolanus*, Will had given a cynical insider's view of the Gunpowder Plot. Ben's *Catiline His Conspiracy* stuck slavishly to the government's line. Lucius Sergius Catilina, an ambitious young nobleman, plots to destroy the State by means of fire and a 'violent blow'. His conspiracy is foiled by the petty 'upstart', Marcus Tullius Cicero, whom Catiline and his conspirators had originally planned to assassinate early on the morning of 7 November.

Catiline presented Robert Cecil – 'Cicero' – as the saviour of his country. As in *Coriolanus*, the title character stands for consulship. Unlike Coriolanus, Catiline achieves this. He is then roundly condemned in a painfully long speech by the Cecil character (who admits to having spies everywhere). Catiline leaves the city, as did Catesby, and the play ends with the joyful news of his death in a violent standoff.

Ben's play was jeered and heckled when it was presented by the King's Men in 1611. The audience at the Globe could see what Jonson was up to – flattering the egregious Cecil by shamelessly rewriting his role in the Gunpowder Plot – and they made their feelings known. They might also have been appalled by Jonson's subplot, in which the details of Catiline's conspiracy are leaked by a loose-living womaniser named Quintus Curius.

Curius is intimate with the conspirators. He takes their oath to bring down the government and drinks from their cup of wine and blood, just as Catesby's plotters received the Eucharist after they had sworn their oaths.

Quintus Curius also has a mistress: a vain, married woman who has grown tired of him. Her name is Fulvia, a name she shared with the wife of Mark Antony.

At first, Fulvia rejects his advances, even when Curius threatens her with rape (he invokes the memory of Lucrece; Fulvia calls him 'sweet Tarquin'). When Curius drops heavy hints about the Catiline conspiracy, however, Fulvia leads him on, trading sexual favours for information, which she passes on to Marcus Tullius Cicero.

Cicero praises Fulvia for doing the right thing and invites Curius, with the utmost courtesy, to become his informant among the conspirators. Curius and Fulvia collude in divulging the secrets of the plot to Cicero, who agrees that the adulterous pair 'must receive reward, though it be not known'.

Jonson was being anything but subtle. The relationship between Curius and Fulvia is an old one, reignited at the time of the Gunpowder Plot. Curius lives among the 'suburb-brothels, bawds, and brokers' of Southwark, where the Globe theatre stood. He compares Fulvia's beauty to a 'fool's treasure' – echoing the androgynous fool in *Volpone* – and refers to himself as a 'well-taught waiter'; in other words, a 'well-wishing' penitent. He also accuses his mistress of overacting (something that Shakespeare despised) and cites the 'universal flood' of Banwell.

Ben Jonson was eager to tell the world that Catesby and his fellow conspirators were betrayed to Cecil by one who moved freely amongst them, but whose lust for his married lover prompted him to turn informer. For this, Ben suggested, Shakespeare had been amply, if tardily, rewarded – enough, perhaps, to pay for his share of the tithes around Stratford.

This, of course, sheds an interesting light on *Macbeth*, for there are clear similarities between the Lady, Macbeth's wife, and Shakespeare's 'Dark Lady' – a connection forged partly by the insistent juxtapositions, in both *The Tragedy of Macbeth* and the later sonnets, of 'foul' and 'fair'. In 'A Lover's Complaint', Jane addressed Henry Garnet as 'Father', while the Lady in *Macbeth* remarks of the Garnet-figure, King Duncan, that he resembled her 'father', which is why she could not murder him herself. If, as Ben Jonson implied, Shakespeare had been persuaded to betray Father Garnet and the gunpowder plotters by his married lover, the 'Dark Lady' of his sonnets, then she would have been both 'fair' and 'foul' in Will's eyes: his beloved 'partner in greatness' – 'Bring forth men-children only' – and the 'fiend-like' gatekeeper to his private hell. And he, Will, was as much a hangman and a 'butcher' as his fictional Macbeth.

THE AUDIENCE at the Globe was unimpressed with Jonson's Roman play. But Shakespeare's reputation was already in tatters. In 1609, two years before Ben's *Catiline His Conspiracy* provoked angry catcalls, 'Willobie his Avisa' had been published yet again. This reminder of the love-triangle involving the mistress of the George Inn, the young gentleman 'H.W.' and the old player 'W.S.' coincided with the unauthorised release of Will's sonnets by Ben Jonson's publisher, Thomas Thorpe.

The 154 sonnets, 'Never before Imprinted', had been acquired, presumably, from their original recipients – Henry Wriothesley, Third Earl of Southampton, who had embraced Protestantism and prospered under King James, and Jane Davenant, née Sheppard, whose 'grave and sober' husband must have realised, at last, that his second son was not his own.

The 1609 Quarto of *Shake-speares Sonnets* came with a cryptic dedication:

TO.THE.ONLIE.BEGETTER.OF.
THESE.INSVING.SONNETS.
Mr.W.H. ALL.HAPPINESSE.
AND.THAT.ETERNITIE.
PROMISED.
BY.
OVR.EVER-LIVING.POET.
WISHETH.
THE.WELL-WISHING.
ADVENTVRER.IN.
SETTING.
FORTH.

T.T.

10 London, 1616, by Claes Van Visscher.

The 'only begetter' of the sonnets was Will Shakespeare, a 'well-wishing adventurer' who had instigated the notorious pilgrimage to St Winefride's Well. Also published with the sonnets was the first part of 'A Lover's Complaint', which anticipated that pilgrimage.

It is possible that the 'well-wishing' Shakespeare was indeed 'setting forth' on a tour of Catholic households in the north of England when his sonnets were published without his consent.

That they were advertised as *Shake-speares Sonnets* – and not 'Sonnets: By W. Shakespeare, gent' – indicates that Will had nothing to do with their publication. They exposed his deepest secrets, and it is somehow comforting to know that the first edition sold badly.

Jonson begrudged Will his success, as he proved by his attempts at improving on Shakespeare's Roman tragedies. He also resented the fact that, whereas he – Ben – had been imprisoned more than once, Will had stayed out of jail, even though both playwrights had been employed in the fraught occupation of the spy or 'intelligencer'. With Shakespeare challenging Cecil's account of the Gunpowder Plot in *Coriolanus*, Ben Jonson – Cecil's creature – was empowered to reveal Will's undercover pseudonym.

The sonnets were printed by George Eld, who also printed Jonson's works. The year before, Eld had issued a pamphlet written by Thomas Hariot, which included a description of a message sent by Galileo to Johannes Kepler concerning the planet Venus. This message had made use of a simple cipher, in which dots were used to indicate a space. Where a space appeared between words, those words were meant to be joined together.

The same cipher was used in the dedication to *Shake-speares Sonnets*, which were properly dedicated to:

THE ONLY BEGETTER OF
THESE ENSUING SONNETS
Mr W HALL

Part Three

Opportunity

So when thou hast, as I
Commanded thee, done blabbing, –
Although to give the lie
Deserves no less than stabbing, –
Stab at thee, he that will,
No stab the soul can kill.

Sir Walter Raleigh
The Lie

16

Our Revels Now Are Ended

SHAKESPEARE PREDICTED the manner of his death five years before it happened. What he did not, and could not, foresee was that his death would occur in the midst of a national scandal.

The roots of that scandal can be traced back to the dark days of the Gunpowder Plot.

On 5 January 1606, precisely two months after Guy Fawkes was arrested, a wedding took place in the Chapel Royal at Whitehall. The bride, a beautiful girl of 14, was given away by the king; she was Frances Howard, the youngest daughter of Thomas Howard, Earl of Suffolk. The groom was not yet 15, though in his solemnity he seemed much older. He was Robert Devereux, Third Earl of Essex.

In the evening, the guests were entertained with an elaborate masque penned by Ben Jonson. The playwright flattered his monarch as the 'Prince of Peace' and called upon the gods of old to favour the young couple:

And *Juno*, whose great *powers* protect
The *Marriage-bed*, with good effect
    The labour of this *night*
    Bless thou …

In fact, the bride and groom had no intention of sharing a bed that night, or for many nights to come. The marriage was a political fix. The bride's father was a close associate of Robert Cecil, who was believed to have caused the downfall of the groom's father, the Second Earl of Essex. Cecil feared that the younger earl would seek to avenge his father's death, and so a marriage to the attractive daughter of Cecil's ally was arranged to bring Essex into the fold.

The couple would live apart until they had both reached the age of 18. The flaw in this plan was hinted at in Ben's *Hymenaei* masque: 'Then, know to end, as to begin; / A minute's loss, in Love, is sin.' When Essex and Lady Frances were finally reunited in 1609, they quickly discovered that they had nothing in common. And before long, Frances' eye had fallen on another.

IN *MACBETH*, Shakespeare portrayed King James as a murderous tyrant, plagued by bloody thoughts and imaginary fears. From then on, Will's public career was drawing to its end. The final phase began with *Pericles*, the first of his fantastical 'tragi-comedies'.

The King's Men had moved into a new theatre. James Burbage bought the Blackfriars building in 1596, intending to use it as a base for his company; the site had been a Dominican priory before the Reformation and was technically outside the jurisdiction of the City authorities. But local residents opposed the idea of a playhouse in their backyard. Shakespeare and his fellows were left with no option but to tear down Burbage's original Theatre and rebuild it on the south bank of the Thames.

The Blackfriars became home to a theatrical company of children. Ben Jonson's *Eastward Ho!* was performed there in 1605, with the result that Jonson was sent to prison and King James vowed that the child actors 'should never play more, but should first beg their bread'. The playhouse went dark.

Shakespeare and his colleagues at last became housekeepers of the Blackfriars in August 1608, using the indoor theatre as their winter venue while the roofless Globe was reserved for the summer season. The Blackfriars was in a fashionable part of town – Ben Jonson lodged nearby with the king's cousin, Esmé Stuart. The Catholic underground was also entrenched in the Blackfriars district. In March 1613, Will Shakespeare would make his only purchase of a London property there.

The more sophisticated clientele at the Blackfriars cannot alone explain the peculiar atmosphere of Shakespeare's late romances. His plays of the early 1600s had been direct appeals to the king to show clemency to his Catholic subjects, an approach which culminated with the savage tragedies of *Macbeth* and *King Lear*. With *Pericles*, Will began to shift his attention away from the king, towards the Catholic gentry.

The tone of the tragi-comedies is bittersweet, mingling optimism and resignation, the personal and the political. Their mood suggests that Shakespeare was looking back over his life and the terrible times his country had been through.

CYMBELINE IS set in an ancient Britain akin to that of *King Lear*. The first words of the play – 'You do not meet a man but frowns. Our bloods / No more obey the heavens than our courtiers / Still seem as does the King' – attest to the spiritual crisis which has gripped the realm.

Britain has been conquered by Julius Caesar on behalf of Rome, which now demands tribute. But Cymbeline, King of Britain, is refusing to honour his obligations to Rome. He is encouraged in his defiance by the (unnamed) Queen and her son, Cloten, whose homage to gold sums up the Elizabethan era:

> 'Tis gold
> Which buys admittance – oft it doth – yea, and makes
> Diana's rangers false themselves, yield up
> Their deer to th'stand o'th' stealer; and 'tis gold
> Which makes the true man killed and saves the thief ...

Rome sends an ambassador to collect what is owed. Rebuffed, Caius Lucius declares war on Britain.

If Caius Lucius represents the Counter-Reformation and the Jesuits, as his 'Luke' name suggests, then the Catholic soul of Britain resides in Cymbeline's daughter, Innogen. She incurs her father's wrath by marrying a poor gentleman, Posthumus Leonatus. Like many an impoverished Catholic, Posthumus is banished. The Queen then resolves to poison Innogen while the reckless Cloten sets out to woo her.

Posthumus goes into exile in Rome, where he is hoodwinked by a swindler named Iachimo into believing that Innogen has been unfaithful. Iachimo typifies those English spies who spread despair among the Catholic exiles by pretending that their loved ones at home had abandoned their faith. Posthumus summons his innocent wife to Wales, where he plans to have her murdered.

Innogen discovers that Posthumus has been tricked into doubting her. She disguises herself as a boy named Fidele ('Faithful') and hides out with a banished lord who has taken the name 'Morgan'. This lord kidnapped the sons of King Cymbeline when they were children, implying that the true heirs to the kingdom had been brought up in secret. The Queen's son, Cloten, disguises himself as Innogen's husband and is decapitated by one of the king's sons – rather as the wayward Earl of Essex lost his head when he tried to pose as England's saviour. Innogen wakes up beside his headless corpse and assumes that her husband, Posthumus, has been slain. Shakespeare was hinting that Essex was never the true 'husband' of England; the natural successors to the throne were to be found among the disenfranchised Catholics.

Posthumus lands with the Roman forces, but elects to fight against Rome. The invading army is held back by the displaced Catholic gentry.

The nameless Queen dies in the manner of Elizabeth, 'With horror, madly dying, like her life, / Which being cruel to the world, concluded / Most cruel to herself.'

Caius Lucius, the Roman general, is taken prisoner. He pleads for the life of Innogen, whom he believes to be a man: 'He hath done no Briton wrong, / Though he hath served a Roman.' Innogen is reunited with her husband, and the banished Lord Belarius, alias Morgan, introduces King Cymbeline to his natural sons, missing for so many years.

Cymbeline acknowledges Rome's authority:

> Although the victor, we submit to Caesar
> And to the Roman empire, promising
> To pay our wonted tribute, from the which
> We were dissuaded by our wicked queen,
> Whom heaven in justice both on her and hers
> Have laid most heavy hand.

Thus, under a newly enlightened, magnanimous king, the toxic legacy of the Tudors is overturned. The name of the game is reconciliation – of fathers with daughters, servants with masters, and England with the Church of Rome.

NO CHURCHES were built under Elizabeth and James, and those which stood were stripped of their 'cost' or splendour. What did get built were palatial mansions for the nouveaux riches and the first shopping malls.

The New Exchange, otherwise known as Britain's Burse, opened on the Strand in 1609. This grand venture was funded by Robert Cecil, who had been appointed Lord Treasurer the previous May – an occasion for which Cecil commissioned a celebratory entertainment from his pet poet, Ben Jonson. Jonson was hired again in 1609 to write an entertainment for the opening of the New Exchange.

Ben's *Entertainment at Britain's Burse* listed the sort of luxury goods that were on sale in Cecil's mall:

> What do you lack? What is't you buy? Very fine China stuffs of all kinds
> and qualities? China chains, China bracelets, China scarves, China fans
> … caskets, umbrellas, sundials, hourglasses, looking-glasses, burning-

glasses, concave glasses, triangular glasses, convex glasses, crystal globes ... Very fine cages for birds, billiard balls, purses, pipes, rattles, basins, ewers, cups, cans, voiders, toothpicks, targets, falchions, beards of all ages, vizards, spectacles? See what you lack?

The transformation of England, from a communal culture to a consumer society, was almost complete. It had been driven by two ruthless and rapacious statesmen: William Cecil, Lord Burghley, and his stunted son Robert, Earl of Salisbury.

Shakespeare lampooned Ben's efforts in *The Entertainment at Britain's Burse* in his companion piece to *Cymbeline*. Jonson appears in *The Winter's Tale* as Autolycus, a ballad-monger and 'snapper up of unconsidered trifles', who steals from those to whom he hawks his wares:

Lawn as white as driven snow,
Cypress black as e'er was crow,
Gloves as sweet as damask roses,
Masks for faces, and for noses ...
Pins and poking-sticks of steel,
What maids lack from head to heel
Come buy of me, come, come buy, come buy,
Buy, lads, or else your lasses cry. Come buy!

The action of *The Winter's Tale* dramatises the division between an island nation ('Sicily') and mainland Europe ('Bohemia'). But whereas *Cymbeline* presented that division as having been caused by a wicked queen, *The Winter's Tale* identifies the cause as the insane jealousy of a king.

Polixenes, King of Bohemia, is visiting his childhood friend Leontes. Leontes tries to persuade Polixenes to stay for a few more days and turns to his pregnant wife, Hermione, to prevail upon his friend. When Polixenes agrees to stay, Leontes is suddenly seized with an Othello-like suspicion that his wife is having an affair with Polixenes. He even doubts that his son, Mamillius, is his own.

Leontes is a portrait of King James, whose wife was a Catholic convert, and who had reacted with rage to the fact that Catholicism was widespread in England. The paranoid king exclaims, 'There is a plot against my life, my crown. / All's true that is mistrusted', and demands that his wife be imprisoned.

Hermione gives birth to a daughter in prison. Leontes – now suffering the sleeplessness to which King James was prone – disowns the child.

He wants the baby to be burned (contemporary audiences would have recognised the allusion to Father Robert Southwell's poem, 'The Burning Babe'), but then instructs one of his lords to abandon the infant in 'some remote and desert place'.

Too late, Leontes' messengers return from the Temple of Apollo with the pronouncement of the oracle: Hermione is guiltless, Leontes is a jealous tyrant, and 'the King shall live without an heir if that which is lost be not found'.

Leontes ignores the evidence of the oracle, until the news is brought to him that his son, Mamillius, has died. Hermione faints dead away. Belatedly, Leontes realises that 'I have too much believed my own suspicion.'

His wife and son dead, his daughter abandoned on a foreign shore, Leontes gives himself over to perpetual repentance.

IN CONVERSATION with William Drummond, Ben Jonson remarked: 'Shakespeare, in a play, brought in a number of men saying they had suffered Shipwrack in Bohemia, where there is no sea near by some 100 miles.' Jonson was surely aware that the character of Autolycus in *The Winter's Tale* was modelled on him and was therefore keen to ridicule the play. He might also have known that Shakespeare had visited Prague as 'Will Hall', and so there was no excuse for the geographical error. All the same, it is clear that the 'Bohemia' of *The Winter's Tale* was really the Catholic heartland of England: a place not unlike the Forest of Arden.

The baby girl – Perdita, the 'Lost One' – is abandoned on the Bohemian coast, along with a box and a scroll revealing her identity. The ship which brought her is then smashed up in a sea-storm and the lord who left her is savaged by a bear.

An Old Shepherd finds the child. This Old Shepherd appears to have been based on John Shakespeare. He bemoans the proclivities of young men – 'getting wenches with child, wronging the ancientry' – much as Alderman Shakespeare might have done when Will was in his teens. The Old Shepherd's son, simply designated 'Clown', is a self-effacing portrait of Will Shakespeare himself, deriving, in part, from Ben Jonson's portrayal of Will as the 'essential Clown', Sogliardo, in *Every Man Out of his Humour*.

The Clown describes the breaking up of the ship, as if Will was recalling the storm which had battered the *Tiger* off the coast of Virginia when Sir Walter Raleigh's colonists were deposited there. He also describes the bear attack. Mentally, Shakespeare was revisiting his youth – the arrest of John Somerville and the execution of Edward Arden, all for the benefit of the Earl of Leicester, whose emblem was Warwickshire's Bear and Ragged Staff, and possibly his own near-shipwreck onboard the *Tiger* in 1585.

The Old Shepherd and his son open the box which was left with Perdita and find that it is full of gold. 'This is fairy gold,' says the father; 'It was told me I should be rich by the fairies' – an admission, perhaps, that John Shakespeare and his son had earned a bounty from the Fairy Queen, Elizabeth, for informing on their fellow Catholics.

Sixteen years pass by. The traditional sheep-shearing feast approaches. The Clown ventures out to buy party foods and encounters Autolycus, who pretends to have been attacked and picks the Clown's pockets as the latter helps him to his feet. Will had, of course, helped Ben Jonson after his trial for the murder of Gabriel Spenser, only to be abused by Jonson in return.

Autolycus dons a false beard and turns up at the sheep-shearing feast, selling ballads. Shakespeare jokes about 'Two Maids Wooing a Man' as the Clown – Will's juvenile persona – purchases trinkets for two amorous wenches. Prince Florizel is also there, wooing Perdita, the Queen of the Feast, as is Florizel's father, King Polixenes, in disguise.

When Florizel announces his intention of marrying Perdita, Polixenes throws off his disguise and denounces them all – his son, for seeking to marry a 'low-born lass'; the Old Shepherd ('old traitor') for encouraging the match; and Perdita, for being 'a fresh piece / Of excellent witchcraft'. All seems lost.

Prince Florizel decides to sail to Sicily and present himself at the Court of King Leontes. In a steal from Ben Jonson's *Volpone*, Autolycus swaps clothes with his former master, Florizel.

After years of 'saint-like sorrow', Leontes is joyfully reunited with his long-lost daughter, Perdita, and his old friend, Polixenes. The Old Shepherd is thanked by Leontes, and his son forces Autolycus to admit that he, the Clown, is a 'gentleman born'. Autolycus begs pardon for 'all the faults I have committed to your worship' and Will, coming to the end of his career, was prepared to forgive.

The Winter's Tale ends with one of the most audacious scenes in all of Will's work. Leontes, Perdita, Florizel and Polixenes visit a chapel to see a statue of Hermione. The statue is astonishingly lifelike. The mistress of the chapel – one of the most overtly Catholic characters in Shakespeare – tells the onlookers, 'It is required / You do awake your faith. Then, all stand still.'

The statue comes to life. Hermione descends, like one of the gods in Ben Jonson's *Hymenaei* masque, and embraces her husband.

The old religion, which had seemed dead, as if frozen in stone, breathes again.

THREE THINGS conspired to ensure that Will bade farewell to the public stage in 1611.

Jonson's *Catiline* was performed by the King's Men (Shakespeare was not in the cast) and published with commendatory verses by Francis Beaumont, John Fletcher and Nathan Field. Though neither *Shakespeares Sonnets*, published in 1609, nor *Catiline His Conspiracy* proved instantly popular, both damaged Will's reputation.

More harm was done by the Puritan historian, John Speed. In his *Theatre of the Empire of Great Britaine*, published in 1611, Speed branded Robert Persons, Jesuit rector of the English College in Rome, and Will Shakespeare as 'this Papist and his Poet, of like conscience for lies, the one ever feigning, and the other ever falsifying the truth.'

Speed's statement was unfortunately timed. King Henri of France had been assassinated by a deranged Catholic in May 1610. King James took fright and banned Catholics from his court, his alarmist reaction reflected in *The Winter's Tale*. More priests were executed, and Jonson made a public show of returning to the Protestant faith.

When the position of Archbishop of Canterbury fell vacant in November 1610, it was expected that the king would appoint the moderate Lancelot Andrewes. Instead, in March 1611, James raised the puritanical George Abbott – the 'bitterest persecutor' of the Catholics – to the most senior post in the Church of England.

The years that followed represented a low period in the history of the stage. One by one, the better writers went quiet, and it was not until Abbott aimed a crossbow at a deer in 1621 and missed, killing a man, that the archbishop's mental imbalance and physical infirmity allowed the literary arts to blossom again.

But by then, Shakespeare was dead.

THE TEMPEST took pride of place in the First Folio of 1623. It wound up the sequence of romances which Shakespeare had begun with *Pericles* and completed the circle of his career: *The Two Gentlemen of Verona*, probably his first play, featured two young friends setting out for Milan; *The Tempest* concerned an old man's attempts to get back to Milan.

Robert Persons and Edmund Campion had travelled from Milan to England in 1580, bringing copies of Cardinal Borromeo's 'Testament of the Soul', one of which would be signed by John Shakespeare. Imaginatively, Will had spent much of his career trying to reach Milan, the epicentre of the Counter-Reformation, and with his last play for the public stage it looked as though the end of the road was in sight.

The play opens onboard a ship in a storm, like the tempest which lashed the *Tiger* when she grounded on a sandbar in 1585. The memory of that journey had been awoken when a fresh crop of colonists was shipped to Virginia in 1609. Their flagship, the *Sea Venture*, was wrecked in Bermuda, although the survivors eventually arrived at Jamestown, where Captain John Smith had suffered a serious accident; he was replaced as president of the Jamestown settlement by George Percy, whose brother, the 'Wizard Earl' of Northumberland, was, like Sir Walter Raleigh, still a prisoner in the Tower of London.

The sea-storm with which *The Tempest* starts has been created by magic. The ship is wrecked on an island that is home to Prospero, the rightful Duke of Milan, and his daughter Miranda.

The name Prospero harked back to *Every Man in his Humour*, in which Shakespeare had acted in 1598. Ben Jonson revised his play for publication in 1616, changing the name of Signor Prospero to Master Wellbred. It is possible that Shakespeare played Prospero in the original production, having recommended Ben's script to the players, and that Jonson later altered his text simply in order to distance it from *The Tempest*.

Prospero explains to his daughter how they came to be marooned on a desert isle. As Duke of Milan, he had been so 'rapt in secret studies' that he was easily overthrown by his brother, Antonio. Prospero was placed in a 'rotten carcase' of a boat, along with his books and his 3-year-old daughter, and set adrift.

They were washed up on the island 'twelve years since' – that is, in 1599, when the Globe theatre opened. The isle is 'almost inaccessible' and 'as 'twere perfumed by a fen', much like the Globe, which was 'flanked by a ditch and forced out of a marsh', in the words of Ben Jonson. The desert isle is, in effect, the 'great globe itself'. We discover that it is 'full of noises, / Sounds, and sweet airs, that give delight and hurt not'. It is here that Prospero controls his 'meaner ministers', just as Shakespeare directed his actors on the stage.

The isle was not entirely deserted when Prospero arrived. A 'foul witch', Sycorax, had given birth to a 'freckled whelp' on the island. The witch had also kept a sprite named Ariel, a 'spirit too delicate / To act her earthly and abhorred commands'. In her 'unmitigable rage', the witch had imprisoned this spirit in a cloven pine, where he languished for twelve years before Prospero appeared.

Ariel now serves Prospero. Symbolically, he was Shakespeare's muse, his poetic genius, which had been shackled by the hag-like Queen

Elizabeth and her 'most potent ministers', until Will had felt able to set it free on the stage of the Globe.

Prospero also enslaved the filthy son of Sycorax. At first, he pitied Caliban:

> When thou didst not, savage,
> Know thine own meaning, but wouldst gabble like
> A thing most brutish, I endowed thy purposes
> With words that made them known.

But all for nothing. Caliban sought to 'violate the honour' of Prospero's daughter. They have been enemies ever since.

Caliban – a loose anagram of 'cannibal' – was Ben Jonson, or 'Down, Ben!' (from the Italian *calare*). Shakespeare had helped Ben, teaching him how to write for the stage, to which Jonson responded by mocking Will's coat of arms and his love for Jane Davenant. He became Will's 'most lying slave'. As Caliban sneers, 'You taught me language, and my profit on't / Is I know how to curse.'

PROSPERO CREATED the sea-storm in order to deposit his adversaries on the enchanted isle. The first to appear is Ferdinand, the son of the King of Naples, who falls in love with Miranda.

Ferdinand's father, Alonso, is wandering the island with Gonzalo, the wise old councillor who made sure that Prospero and Miranda had enough to live on when they were abandoned to the waves twelve years earlier.

Like Miranda, the names Alonso and Gonzalo point to the noble Zúñiga dynasty of Spain. Juan de Zúñiga, Count of Miranda, had been Viceroy of Naples when he oversaw the signing of the Anglo-Spanish treaty at Valladolid in 1605; his kinsman, Don Pedro de Zúñiga, had served as Spanish ambassador to England. Caricatured by Ben Jonson in *The Alchemist* (1610), Don Pedro had taken a keen interest in the English colonisation of the New World – on 10 September 1608, he sent King Philip of Spain a crude map of Virginia together with a report 'given me by a person who has been there'. Zúñiga advised the Spanish king to 'put an end to those things done in Virginia' before the English established a firm foothold in America.

Also with Alonso and Gonzalo are Antonio, the brother who usurped Prospero's dukedom of Milan, and Sebastian, Alonso's brother. Together, Alonso, Antonio and Sebastian are the 'three men of sin', comparable with the 'trinity of knaves' that served King James: Robert Cecil, Thomas Howard and Henry Howard – all three had been receiving

Spanish pensions since the peace talks of 1604. Their presence in the play suggests that Prospero is seeking recompense for the betrayal of the Catholics during those talks. King James was hoping to marry his son and heir, Prince Henry, to the Spanish Infanta when *The Tempest* was written. Such an alliance might have improved the lot of the English Catholics immeasurably.

The remaining castaways on the isle are a drunken butler, Stephano (another name drawn from *Every Man in his Humour*), and a Thomas Nashe-like jester named Trinculo. Shakespeare replayed a scene from Jonson's *Volpone* when the 'tortoise' Caliban hides under a gabardine and is mistaken for a 'strange fish' by Trinculo, who imagines how much money could be made from this creature in London: 'Any strange beast there makes a man. When they will not give a dolt to relieve a lame beggar, they will lay out ten to see a dead Indian.' Trinculo also shelters under the gabardine when the drunken Stephano enters. Stephano plies Caliban with alcohol – a fateful decision, for Ben Jonson and drink were a dangerous combination. Caliban volunteers to 'swear upon that bottle to be thy true subject' and becomes a 'most perfidious and drunken monster' willing to kiss his new master's boot.

Inebriated, the 'poor, credulous monster' offers to make Stephano the king of the isle, much as Jonson had so eagerly served the drunkard King James. But Caliban must first destroy Prospero, who 'by his cunning hath cheated me of the island'. He tells Stephano, 'I'll yield him thee asleep / Where thou mayst knock a nail into his head.'

'There thou mayst brain him, / Having first seized his books', said the 'most lying slave' to his drunken lord and king, a full five years before Shakespeare's skull was pierced by the point of a dagger.

Prospero later exclaims, 'I had forgot that foul conspiracy / Of the beast Caliban and his confederates / Against my life.'

Will had sensed that there was, or would be, a plot to silence him. The culprits were identified: a drunkard who would be the King of the Island and his 'Servant monster', who first put the idea into his master's head.

PROSPERO UTILISES his magic to torment his enemies and to conjure up a wedding masque for his daughter and her beloved Ferdinand.

The pairing of Ferdinand and Miranda symbolised the marriage of England's soul to the guardians of the Holy Mother Church. Prospero strips Ferdinand of his pride, as if making Catholic Spain subservient to England's interests. He then produces an ethereal entertainment which both echoed and surpassed Ben Jonson's *Hymenaei*, written for the marriage of Frances Howard and the Earl of Essex. But Prospero interrupts his own masque when he suddenly remembers the 'foul conspiracy' of Caliban and Stephano against his life.

He distracts them with 'trumpery' – fine garments – which 'King' Stephano distributes to his new favourites: 'Wit shall not go unrewarded while I am king of this country.' The wardrobe belonging to Queen Elizabeth had been broken into, shortly after King James came to power, for the Christmas season and the theatrical performances which began on St Stephen's Day, hence the identification of King James as 'Stephano'.

The boozy 'king' and his confederates are then chased from the stage by *'spirits in shape of dogs and hounds'* – a fitting punishment for a king obsessed with hunting.

All the castaways are finally brought into Prospero's presence. Old enemies are reconciled. Their ship, it is discovered, is 'tight and yare and bravely rigged', like the storm-damaged *Tiger* which, after its battering on the Outer Banks, was hauled onto the beach at Wococon and repaired, ready for its homeward voyage.

Prospero faces the prospect of his long-awaited return to Milan, where 'Every third thought shall be of my grave.' He acknowledges the 'thing of darkness', Caliban, as his own – Shakespeare ruefully accepting responsibility for Ben Jonson's career. Caliban promises to be 'wise hereafter': 'What a thrice-double ass / Was I to take this drunkard [King James] for a god, / And worship this dull fool.'

Shakespeare released his creative muse, bidding Ariel, 'Be free, and fare thou well.' Then, in a brief Epilogue, he addressed his audience directly and begged to be liberated from 'this bare island', the Globe:

> Now I want
> Spirits to enforce, art to enchant;
> And my ending is despair
> Unless I be relieved by prayer ...

'As you from crimes would pardoned be, / Let your indulgence set me free,' he said, as if he knew he was dying, and thus he appealed to the spectators to perform the time-honoured, though now forbidden, Catholic rites for a soul in Purgatory.

And with that, Will Shakespeare took his bow.

17

All Is True

'HE FREQUENTED the plays all his younger time,' wrote Rev. John Ward of Shakespeare in 1662, 'but in his elder years lived at Stratford'. Even in retirement, though, Will's spirit stalked the London stage.

On 31 October 1614, Ben Jonson's *Bartholomew Fair* was performed by a company formed under the patronage of the king's daughter, Princess Elizabeth. Ben was still obsessed with Shakespeare: *The Tempest* and *The Winter's Tale* had made an impression. 'If there be never a servant-monster in the fair, who can help it,' wrote Ben in *Bartholomew Fair*, being 'loath to make nature afraid in his plays, like those that beget tales, tempests, and such-like drolleries.'

Jonson cautioned his audience not to behave like a 'state-decipherer, or politic pick-lock' determined to tease out hidden meanings in his play, such as 'who was meant by the gingerbread-woman ... what great lady by the pig-woman, what concealed statesman by the seller of mousetraps'. The 'pig-woman' glanced at Sycorax, the 'swine-crow' of *The Tempest*; *The Mousetrap* was *Hamlet*'s revealing play-within-a-play. Ben was highlighting the coded messages in Shakespeare's works, the cryptic hints at real people and events, while insisting that his own play contained nothing so subversive.

There were some, Ben warned, who out of a 'virtuous and staid ignorance' had not altered their opinions. 'He that will swear, *Jeronimo* or *Andronicus*, are the best plays yet' was one whose 'judgement shews it is constant, and hath stood still these five and twenty or thirty years.'

On the face of it, Jonson was criticising those playgoers who scorned anything new. More pertinently, he was pointing a finger at those who had not changed their religion when it was expedient to do so, as Jonson had done. Theirs was a 'confirmed error', he claimed, and 'such a one the author knows where to find him.'

Bartholomew Fair was presented before the king and his courtiers at Whitehall on 1 November 1614. Jonson reminded His Majesty of the dangerous subtexts in Shakespeare's plays and the fact that Shakespeare had stayed stubbornly true to his faith 'these five and twenty or thirty years'.

Should the need ever arise, Ben assured the king, he knew where to find him.

WILL WAS not spending all his time at Stratford. On Monday 11 May 1612, he was in Westminster, giving evidence at the Court of Requests.

The case involved his former landlord. Will had been lodging with Christopher Mountjoy, a maker of headdresses, and his wife Marie in their house on Silver Street when, in November 1604, the Mountjoys' apprentice, Stephen Belott, married their 'sole child and daughter', Mary. Six months later, the young couple moved into a house belonging to George Wilkins, a Cripplegate tavern-keeper.

No sooner had the Belotts arrived than George Wilkins took up a new career as a playwright. His first known effort, *The Miseries of Enforced Marriage*, was performed at the Globe in early 1606. The play was based on the true story of Walter Calverley, a Yorkshire squire who murdered two of his children in April 1605. Calverley had been forced into marriage with the granddaughter of William Brooke, Tenth Baron Cobham, bringing him into the extended family of the man who, in 1596, became the patron of Will's theatre company.

Calverley's murderous frenzy had included an assault on his wife, who was sympathetically treated in another play about the incident: *A Yorkshire Tragedy* was also performed by the King's Men and attributed to Shakespeare. Two plays about the same crime seems like overkill, but what makes George Wilkins' version interesting is that he named his Calverley character 'William Scarborrow'. Wilkins had an associate with the same initials who had been forced into marriage with a woman not of his choosing.

Wilkins' play proved to be a hit. It was published in 1607, by which time Wilkins was collaborating with Shakespeare on *Pericles*. He might have been one of Will's protégés, like Ben Jonson, but his interest in writing for the theatre soon dissipated. He published a novel, *The Painful Adventures of Pericles Prince of Tyre (Being the True History of the Play of Pericles)*, and thereafter appeared repeatedly before the Clerkenwell magistrates, charged with violent behaviour.

Shakespeare was called to testify in May 1612 in the matter of a disputed dowry. Marie Mountjoy – who made headgear for Queen Anne and was possibly a go-between for Will Shakespeare and Jane Davenant's brothers, who provided the royals with perfumes and gloves – had since died. Her husband denied ever having promised his son-in-law a legacy.

Will's testimony under oath was noncommittal. There had been talk of a marriage portion, he recalled, but he could not remember how much.

He did disclose that Marie Mountjoy had entreated him to 'move and persuade' Stephen Belott to 'effect the said marriage' to the Mountjoys' daughter. This Will had done. He signed his deposition 'Willm Shaks' and failed to turn up at the second session held to examine the case on 19 June.

The Belott-Mountjoy case informs us that, not for the first time, Will had been called upon to promote the idea of marriage. He had done so with his sonnets to Henry Wriothesley, Earl of Southampton, in 1592, and again, in 1604, at the behest of his landlady. On both occasions, he had ended up in the arms of his lover, Jane, no doubt wondering at the irony of his being considered a worthy advocate for marriage.

There is, after all, a dearth of happily married couples in his works.

ANOTHER MARRIAGE was in trouble in 1612.

After their lavish wedding in 1606, Lady Frances Howard and Robert Devereux, Third Earl of Essex, had lived apart for three years. Essex returned from a European tour in 1609 to find that his wife had flowered into the beauty of the Court, her heart-shaped face framed by fashionably frizzled hair. But Essex was no ladies man. He seemed unable to penetrate his lovely partner during the three years that they shared a bed.

The marriage had been arranged partly to protect Robert Cecil from a potential adversary. Cecil had been widely blamed for the spectacular downfall of Essex's father and, by pairing him off with the daughter of his ally, Thomas Howard, Cecil hoped to nullify any thoughts of revenge the earl might have harboured.

Years of overwork had taken their toll on the king's 'little beagle'. Cecil fell ill in February 1612 and travelled to Bath to recuperate. His absence from Court delighted his enemies. He made another five-day journey to Bath but felt the urgent need to return to London and confront his 'underminers'. Cecil got as far as Marlborough in Wiltshire where, on 24 May 1612, he collapsed and died.

'I never knew so great a man so soon and generally censured,' wrote a contemporary. Like his father before him, Cecil had pushed through vicious anti-Catholic legislation, enriching himself enormously in the process. As a jingle of the time put it: 'And through his false worship such power did he gain / As kept him o' the mountain and us on the plain.'

Now that the 'Toad', *Robertus Diabolus*, was dead, the very rationale behind the Essex marriage – which was already in crisis – had been removed.

Rumours were circulating that Frances Howard was having an affair with Prince Henry, a 'most religious and Christian youth' who was the hope of the Puritan faction. By August, King James and Queen Anne were anxious to find a suitable match for the prince, who had 'begun to show a leaning to a certain lady of the court'. In fact, Lady Frances was in love with another man altogether. It was an infatuation she shared with the king himself.

Robert Carr was in his mid-twenties and extremely attractive, 'equally sharing the beauty of both sexes'. On 24 March 1607, he had taken part in the annual tournament to celebrate the king's accession to the throne. As he dismounted in front of King James, his horse reared. Carr fell, breaking his leg. The king was smitten.

By the end of the year, Carr had been knighted and made a Gentleman of the Bedchamber, requiring him to sleep in the same room as King James. Before long, he was recognised as the king's special favourite. He received many gifts, including the sequestered property of a wealthy Catholic and the Sherborne estate in Dorset, which the king confiscated from Sir Walter Raleigh.

Carr was an assiduous favourite, never minding when James slobbered over him or pawed at him; rather, he was said to have encouraged James with 'whorish looks and wanton gestures'.

Consequently, his influence grew. Created Viscount Rochester on 25 March 1611, he became the first Scot to take a seat in the English House of Lords. The following month he was admitted to the Order of the Garter, and on 22 April 1612 he was made a Privy Councillor at the age of 25.

The death of Robert Cecil in May 1612 created a vacancy, which James resolved not to fill, choosing to take on the burden of administration himself. This meant that ambassadors would send their despatches to Robert Carr, Viscount Rochester, who read them out to the king and answered them as James desired. Realistically, neither Carr nor the king was up to the task, but at least Carr had an intellectually gifted companion who could cope with the mountain of correspondence. His name was Thomas Overbury.

Five years older than Carr, Overbury was well educated and good-looking. He was also insufferably arrogant. Ben Jonson befriended him and wrote him an epigram:

> So PHOEBUS make me worthy of his bays,
>> As but to speak thee, OVERBURY, is praise:
> So where thou liv'st, thou mak'st life understood!
>> Where, what makes others great, doth keep thee good!

Inevitably, though, Jonson and Overbury fell out. Ben later told William Drummond that 'Overbury was first his friend, then turned his mortal enemy'.

Robert Carr relied on Overbury as 'a kind of oracle'. It was probably at Carr's request that Overbury was knighted by the king in 1608. The bond between the two friends seemed unbreakable. When Carr fell in love with the beautiful Frances Howard, it was Overbury who wrote her love letters on Carr's behalf. But what began as a bit of a joke – Overbury later protested that Carr 'would speak ill of her yourself' – soon became more serious. Trapped in a loveless marriage, Frances was besotted with the handsome favourite and even procured love philtres from the quack Simon Forman in order to keep Carr interested in her.

Forman's clients had included Shakespeare's landlady, Marie Mountjoy, and Jane Davenant – hopefully, neither resorted to the sort of witchcraft that Lady Frances was alleged to have practised with the aim of maintaining her husband's impotence.

By the spring of 1612, Carr and Lady Frances were lovers. Just before Christmas that year, Lady Frances and the Earl of Essex shared a bed for the last time. Overbury, meanwhile, was horrified that his bosom friend and meal ticket was so utterly bewitched by that 'filthy base woman'.

The influential Howards were quick to see the potential in a match between Lady Frances and the royal favourite. Even King James smiled on the relationship. A special commission was appointed to determine that the marriage of the Earl and Countess of Essex should be annulled.

But there were obstacles. One was the Earl of Essex and his supporters, including Shakespeare's erstwhile patron, the Earl of Southampton. Another was the commission of nullity itself, which was headed by the 'stiffly principled' Archbishop of Canterbury. A third was Sir Thomas Overbury, who refused to believe that Carr would 'dare to leave him'.

At first, Overbury appeared to be the least of the problems. He was offered the post of ambassador to Russia or the Spanish Netherlands. This was done in the knowledge that Overbury would decline such a posting. When word was brought to him of Overbury's contemptuous response, King James ordered that Sir Thomas be imprisoned.

On the evening of 21 April 1613, Overbury was taken by armed guards to the Tower of London, where he was held incommunicado, unable to influence the commission of nullity which convened on 15 May.

IN MARCH 1613, Shakespeare bought the upper floor of the Blackfriars Gatehouse for 'one hundred and fortie pound of lawfull money'. The transaction was a complicated one: the title of the property was sold to Shakespeare and his three trustees, who then leased it back to the vendor.

In his will of 1616, Shakespeare would bequeath to his daughter Susanna his rights to the Blackfriars Gatehouse 'wherein one John Robinson dwelleth'. This was presumably the same John Robinson who signed Shakespeare's will as one of its five witnesses.

Robinson's association with the Gatehouse predated Shakespeare's purchase. In the 1580s he had served as a steward to John Fortescue, a previous owner of the Gatehouse, whose uncle, Sir John Fortescue, was the Master of the Royal Wardrobe; both Fortescues used the Blackfriars Gatehouse as a Catholic hideout. Relatives of the martyred Edmund Campion had lodged there, as had the sister of Father Robert Southwell, and a kinswoman of the Hoghtons of Lancashire had died there 'in all her pride and popery'. In 1591, two priests filled the house with 'stuff … brought from Rome'.

The Gatehouse had been raided in 1598 by the maniacal Richard Topcliffe and his henchmen, who were bewildered by its labyrinth of 'back-doors and byways, and many secret vaults and corners'. Father John Gerard had approached Ellen Fortescue in 1605, seeking to use the Gatehouse as a meeting place. When asked which 'excellent men of noble birth, and Catholics' would be meeting there, Gerard named 'Catesby, Percy, Winter, Digby, and several more'. After these men had been captured or killed in the wake of the Gunpowder Plot, Father Gerard sought refuge at the Gatehouse, 'disguised by a false beard and hair'.

As recently as 1610 it had been remarked in Naples that the Blackfriars Gatehouse was a Jesuit base.

John and Ellen Fortescue retired to St Omer in France. Their steward, John Robinson, had been seized in connection with the arrest of Edward Arden in 1583. He was reported for sheltering a Catholic priest in 1599, and in 1605 he sent his son, Edward, to the college at St Omer, founded by Father Robert Persons, where the only non-religious text on the curriculum would be Shakespeare's *Pericles*. Edward Robinson later presented himself at the English College in Rome, intent on training for the priesthood – this in 1613, when Shakespeare bought the Blackfriars Gatehouse and installed John Robinson as his tenant.

Meanwhile, across the river at the Globe, a new Shakespeare play was about to be performed.

THE TWO *Noble Kinsmen* was not included in the First Folio of Shakespeare's plays. When it was finally printed in 1634, the title page advertised that it had been 'Written by the memorable Worthies of their time: Mr John Fletcher, and Mr William Shakespeare. Gent.'

John Fletcher was in his early thirties when Shakespeare retired. His father, Richard Fletcher, a churchman of extreme Protestant views, had made his mark at the execution of Mary, Queen of Scots, by praying loudly and shouting out 'So perish all the Queen's enemies!' Richard Fletcher became chaplain to Queen Elizabeth and, successively, Bishop of Bristol, Worcester and London, before dying, disgraced and indebted, in 1596.

By 1606, his son John was writing for the Children of the Queen's Revels at the Blackfriars. John Fletcher usually wrote in collaboration – most successfully with Francis Beaumont – and had the rare distinction of being 'loved' by Ben Jonson. Fletcher commended Jonson's *Catiline His Conspiracy* in 1611 and, that same year, produced *The Woman's Prize, or the Tamer Tamed*, which was both a sequel and a Puritan response to Shakespeare's *Taming of the Shrew*.

Will's retirement allowed Fletcher to become the principal playwright for the King's Men. He quickly set about undermining Will's reputation by rewriting two plays to which Shakespeare's name was attached.

It is not difficult to imagine what Will might have intended with his play of *The Two Noble Kinsmen*. War breaks out between Athens and Thebes. Two young gentlemen fight for Thebes and are taken prisoner. From their prison cell, they spy the lovely Emilia.

One of the noble kinsmen, Arcite, is released from prison and banished; however, he does not leave the country but adopts a disguise in order to serve Emilia. The other, Palamon, remains in prison, where the Jailer's Daughter falls in love with him and helps him to escape. Palamon finds Arcite and challenges him to a duel for the hand of Emilia. They are interrupted by the arrival of Theseus, Duke of Athens, who decrees that the two must return in one month and that Emilia will marry the winner of their contest.

In the end, Arcite narrowly beats Palamon, thereby winning Emilia's hand, but he then suffers a fatal riding accident. With his dying breath, he bequeaths Emilia to Palamon.

In Shakespeare's original, Palamon would have represented those English Catholics who, consigned to jail, inspired a kind of foolishness or divine madness in others. Arcite would have been his Protestant counterpart, and though Arcite's victory implied the triumph of Protestantism, it was destined to be short-lived. Unable to govern, the extreme Protestants would be overthrown, clearing the way for the Catholics to lay claim to the soul of England.

Little of that subtext survived Fletcher's revisions. The Prologue owes much to Ben Jonson, and what follows is simply a pastiche of Shakespeare's works (the Jailer's Daughter, for example, is a silly caricature of *Hamlet*'s Ophelia, with a touch of Perdita from *The Winter's Tale*) shorn of subtlety and rendered superficial. The checklist of Shakespearean touches has been ticked – the shipwreck and the stag hunt are referenced – but all trace of deeper meaning has been erased.

Worse, though, is what happened to *Henry VIII* – or, as it was then known, *All is True*. Loosely based on the middle period of King Henry's reign, the play is about the origins of the English Reformation, although it barely mentions the Reformation at all.

Again, it is possible to discern what Shakespeare had in mind. The character of Cardinal Wolsey, Lord Chancellor and Archbishop of York, has features in common with the Cecils, father and son: 'No man's pie is freed / From his ambitious finger'. Wolsey 'dives into the King's soul and there scatters / Dangers, doubts, wringing of the conscience' – as Robert Cecil had been wont to do with King James.

Like the Cecils, Wolsey came from 'humble stock'. After his death in the play, Queen Katherine describes him thus:

> He was a man
> Of unbounded stomach, ever ranking
> Himself with princes; one that by suggestion
> Tied all the kingdom. Simony was fair play.
> His own opinion was the law.

Wolsey's death on the road back to London compares with Cecil's collapse at Marlborough. The death of Robert Cecil had altered the political complexion of the State, encouraging Shakespeare, perhaps, to submit a new play to the King's Men – one that reflected on the role of the Cecils in the ongoing Reformation of England.

The problem with *Henry VIII* is that it takes all sides at once. No one is to blame for the terrors unleashed by the king's divorce and the subsequent assaults on the Church. While Shakespeare took pity on the Catholic characters (notably the 'saint-like' Queen Katherine), John Fletcher took pains to exculpate the Protestants. All voices which bemoan the rise of the radical reformers are swiftly silenced.

The manifestly un-Shakespearean title *All is True* is misleading. The play succeeds on its pageantry, but it is far from true in historical terms. Refashioned by Fletcher, the action builds towards one slanted end.

The hints are carefully planted. First, we hear of the 'spleeny Lutheran', Anne Boleyn:

Beauty and honour in her are so mingled
That they have caught the King, and who knows yet
But from this lady may proceed a gem
To lighten all this isle.

The play claims that the people of England were delighted with Henry's divorce from Katherine of Aragon and his marriage to Anne Boleyn – which was not true – and that Henry revelled in his daughter by Anne, when in fact he disowned her. No mention is made of the beheading of Anne Boleyn for her failure to produce a son. Rather, the baby Elizabeth is portrayed as the son of King Henry, as like her father as 'cherry is to cherry'.

It is inconceivable that Shakespeare would have approved the words spoken by Archbishop Cranmer at the baptism of Elizabeth in the play:

Good grows with her.
In her days every man shall eat in safety
Under his own vine what he plants, and sing
The merry songs of peace to all his neighbours.
God shall be truly known, and those about her
From her shall read the perfect ways of honour,
And by those claim their greatness, not by blood.

This was pure Fletcher. From such nonsense as this was the myth of the Elizabethan 'Golden Age' born.

Having rewritten history to serve his own ends, John Fletcher then extolled the reign of James I: 'Her ashes new create another heir / As great in admiration as herself.'

It is disturbing to realise that, in his retirement, Shakespeare's work was altered by another hand to present the polar opposite of his beliefs. In *As You Like It*, Will had reflected on the murder of Christopher Marlowe: 'When a man's verses cannot be understood, nor a man's good wit seconded with the forward child, understanding, it strikes a man more dead than a great reckoning in a little room.'

Now his own verses were being adjusted, his own good wit misrepresented, in order to turn him into a standard-bearer for the Protestant regime.

'Remember', whispered Caliban to the would-be 'King' Stephano in *The Tempest*: 'First to possess his books, for without them / He's but a sot as I am, nor hath not / One spirit to command ...'

'There thou mayst brain him, / Having first seized his books ...'

'Burn but his books.'

THE TRAVESTY that was *All is True* was performed just three or four times by the King's Men at the Globe. The production had powerful backers: fabulous costumes had been donated, and real cannons were used.

The cannons were fired at a crucial moment. Cardinal Wolsey hosts a banquet. The stage directions called for 'chambers' to be discharged as King Henry is about to enter. There, he will meet Anne Boleyn – 'O beauty, / Till now I never knew thee' – and the course of history will be changed forever.

The afternoon of St Peter's Day, Tuesday 29 June 1613, was warm and sunny. The chambers were discharged on cue.

Sir Henry Wotton – who found the pageantry of the play 'ridiculous' – described what was 'thought at first but idle smoke'. The audience was 'more attentive to the show'. But the fire 'kindled inwardly, and ran round like a train, consuming within less than an hour the whole house to the very ground'.

There were no casualties, other than a man whose breeches caught fire, 'that would perhaps have broiled him, if he had not by the benefit of a provident wit, put it out with a bottle of ale'.

Ben Jonson, after his own disastrous fire in 1623, recalled the playhouse inferno as a 'cruel Stratagem' of the 'lame Lord of Fire', '(Which, some are pleas'd to style but thy mad Prank) / Against the *Globe*.'

The belief that the conflagration was started by the firing of two small cannons smacks of guesswork; the fire was out of control before anybody took much notice of it. In his 'Execration Upon Vulcan', Jonson disclosed that another cause had been suspected at the time:

Nay, sigh'd, ah Sister 'twas the Nun, *Kate Arden*
Kindled the Fire! But, then one did return,
No Fool would his own harvest spoil, or burn!

If that were so, thou rather would'st advance
The Place, that was thy Wives Inheritance.

Who was this 'Nun', Kate Arden, who was rumoured to have 'Kindled the Fire'?

In underworld slang, a 'kate' was a picklock (a 'cate' was something delicate, a dainty morsel). In his *Batholomew Fair* of 1614, Ben Jonson dismissed one who trawled his works for hidden meanings as a 'state-decipherer, or politic pick-lock'.

Also destroyed with the Globe was an adjoining house, once 'in the occupation of William Shakespeare and others'. Will's share in the Globe would have been part of his wife's inheritance, and the reference to Arden surely located the suspect in Will's world, for was he not a lame 'Fool' of Arden who had secretly married a 'sacred nun', and who had opened his *Life of Henry the Fifth* at the Globe by calling for a 'muse of fire'?

Ten years after the event, Ben Jonson reminded Londoners of what had been muttered – that the Globe was destroyed on St Peter's Day by Shakespeare, or someone in his circle, who had broken into the adjoining house in order to kindle the fire.

Had the King's Men not staged *All is True*, John Fletcher's flagrantly propagandist revision of Will's work, the theatre might have remained standing.

THE DESTRUCTION of the Globe coincided with a hiccup in the Essex divorce. In an attempt to prove that Lady Frances was still a virgin after seven years of marriage, the Howards insisted on a gynaecological examination. The midwives declared that Frances was *virgo intacta*, but in early July the Earl of Essex tried to get that verdict quashed. Though Archbishop Abbott ruled against this, it was becoming clear that he was unhappy about the proceedings.

The archbishop could find no precedent in English law of a case in which a husband had been impotent with his wife but not with other women. Even Henry VIII's divorce from Anne of Cleves on similar grounds was deemed inadmissible by Abbott, since King Henry had been 'a strange prince in that kind'.

By mid-July, King James was in no doubt that the archbishop was entirely on the side of Essex and thoroughly hostile towards Lady Frances and her Howard clan. The commission of nullity had reached deadlock.

The king decreed that the commission would reconvene on 18 September. He was openly interfering by this stage, padding the commission with bishops whose opinions he could rely on and forbidding the commissioners to state their reasons for supporting or opposing the nullity. The vote, on 25 September 1613, went seven to five in favour of annulling the marriage.

Public opinion was divided, but the Howards had got their way. The lovely Lady Frances was free to marry the king's favourite, Robert Carr.

Nobody seemed troubled by the fact that, just eleven days earlier, on 15 September, Carr's friend Thomas Overbury had died in the Tower of London.

18

Double Falsehood

SUPREME CONTROL of the performance and publication of plays lay in the hands of the Lord Chamberlain, a post that, between 1602 and 1614, was held by Thomas Howard, First Earl of Suffolk and father to the beautiful Lady Frances.

As Lord Chamberlain, Suffolk would have approved the performance, before the Duke of Savoy's ambassador at Whitehall on 8 June 1613, of a play called *Cardenna*. This was not the first performance of the play: Shakespeare's old colleague John Heminges had received payment for 'six several plays' presented at Whitehall before 20 May 1613, one of which was known as *Cardenno*.

It was not until 1653 that a publisher entered 'The History of Cardenio. By Mr. Fletcher. & Shakespeare' in the Stationers' Register. The play then seems to have disappeared, eventually to resurface in the form of an adaptation entitled *Double Falshood; Or, The Distrest Lovers*.

This new version of the play, 'Written Originally by *W. SHAKESPEARE*', was staged at the Theatre Royal, Drury Lane, on 13 December 1727. It had been 'Revived and Adapted' by Lewis Theobald, a trained lawyer turned professional writer, who claimed to have acquired three manuscripts of the original. One had been copied out by the prompter who served Sir William Davenant's theatre company in the 1660s. Another had reached Theobald via a 'Noble Person', who intimated that the play had been written by Will Shakespeare during his retirement as a present for his 'Natural Daughter'.

The original *History of Cardenio* would appear to have been commissioned for performance at Court during the Christmas season of 1612. The story was drawn from the first part of Cervantes' *Don Quixote*, which had been translated by Thomas Shelton and published in 1612 with a dedication to Theophilus Howard, son of the Earl of Suffolk and brother to Lady Frances. Shakespeare's 'lost' play of *Cardenio* was almost certainly procured by none other than the Lord Chamberlain himself.

The timing was critical.

The death of Robert Cecil in May 1612 had removed an obstacle to the advancement of Catholic interests and the pro-Spanish policies favoured by the Howards. By that August, it was evident that Frances Howard was enamoured of Robert Carr, the king's favourite. After Lady Frances and the Earl of Essex shared a bed for the last time, shortly before Christmas, all the efforts of the Howard faction were devoted to securing the annulment of their marriage, so that Frances could wed Carr.

There were concerns that Prince Henry had fallen for Frances. King James hastily sought to finalise a marriage agreement between his eldest son and the daughter of the Duke of Savoy. This came to nothing, however, because on 6 November 1612, Henry Stuart, Prince of Wales, died of fever at the age of 18.

Protestant commentators strove to create the impression that the entire nation was in 'utter desolation' over the death of the prince. In fact, Henry's priggishness had driven a wedge between him and his father, who had effectively cut him off from the Court at Whitehall. King James did not attend the funeral for his eldest son, held on 7 December.

A wax model of Prince Henry, 'decked with robes, collar, crown and golden rod, as he went when he was alive', lay in state in Westminster Abbey until the end of the year. Meanwhile, the king insisted on pressing ahead with the wedding of his daughter Elizabeth to Prince Frederick of the Rhine. As if the heir to the throne had not died, Christmas 'was kept as usual at Whitehall'.

Disastrous as it seemed to the Puritans, the death of Prince Henry was a boon to the crypto-Catholic Howards. Even Shakespeare was showing signs of optimism: his investment in the Blackfriars Gatehouse in March 1613 suggests that he could feel the pendulum swinging. His arch-rival, Ben Jonson, was out of the country, chaperoning the son of Sir Walter Raleigh on a debauched tour of Europe. Cecil was dead, as was the prurient Prince of Wales, and the Archbishop of Canterbury was at odds with the king over the Essex divorce.

The fiery destruction of the Globe in June must be seen in the context of a furious Protestant propaganda campaign and a newfound confidence amongst the Catholics.

Shakespeare had written *Cardenio* at the behest of the Lord Chamberlain, Thomas Howard. A study of the play – or what survived in Lewis Theobald's adaptation – reveals why it led to the murder of Will Shakespeare.

THE HENRY Wallis painting of *A Sculptor's Workshop* was described earlier (in Chapter 2). It shows Ben Jonson supervising the completion of the limestone bust of Shakespeare for the funerary monument in Holy Trinity Church. Jonson holds a death mask, pointing to a spot above the right eyebrow.

Two young children are playing with figurines. A miniature mule lies sideways on the floor tiles, beside a fallen shield. Close by is another figurine reminiscent of the images inspired by *Don Quixote* which were drawn by Wallis' contemporary, Honoré Daumier. The toy mule recalls the precise moment in *Don Quixote* when the Cardenio story begins, with the discovery, in the mountains of the Sierra Morena, of a dead mule.

The fallen shield reflects the fact that, in March 1613, Shakespeare was paid for devising a motto for the *impresa* or decorative shield borne by the Earl of Rutland in the annual Accession Day tournament; the same earl had also carried the royal shield at Prince Henry's funeral. Robert Carr had been carrying a similar *impresa* at the Accession Day tournament of 1607, when he fell from his horse and won the heart of the king.

Elsewhere in his painting, Henry Wallis hinted at the epic struggle between the thuggish Hercules and the shape-shifting Achelous, which resulted in the mutilation of the river god's brow. Ben Jonson appears to be indicating the very spot on the death mask where Shakespeare's brow was damaged. The two children on the floor mirror the attitudes of *The Chess Players* – supposedly Shakespeare and Jonson – in a painting of 1603, with additional imagery taken from the start of the Cardenio episode in *Don Quixote*. A third child stands apart, like Shakespeare's 'Natural Daughter'.

The message of *A Sculptor's Workshop* seems to have been this: Shakespeare died after a violent struggle with Ben Jonson, the cause of which had something to do with the 'lost' play of *Cardenio*.

DOUBLE FALSEHOOD is a much adulterated version of *Cardenio*. Shakespeare's play was revised by John Fletcher after the death of Prince Henry. Most likely, the text was further altered during Sir William Davenant's lifetime, and again in Lewis Theobald's adaptation. Even so, it is possible to catch a glimpse of Will Shakespeare at work.

The play opens with Duke Angelo in conversation with his son, Roderick, whose 'irregular' brother, Henriquez, is causing concern. The duke resolves to summon 'Julio, good Camillo's son' to be an 'honest spy' on Henriquez' riotous behaviour. In the original tale, Julio was named Cardenio.

Camillo receives a letter demanding his son's attendance at Court. Camillo is perplexed: 'Horsemanship? What horsemanship has Julio? I think he can no more but gallop a hackney, unless he practis'd riding in France.'

Cardenio – the original form of Julio – was surely based on Robert Carr, whose horse-riding accident had been the making of him; as Carr's prospective father-in-law, Thomas Howard, quipped, 'If any mischance be to be wished, 'tis breaking a leg in the King's presence, for this fellow owes all his favour to that bout'.

Carr once reminded King James that, 'I was even the son of a father whose services are registered in the first honours and impressions I took of your Majesty's favour.' The loyal services performed by Carr's father for King James in Scotland are referenced in the play – the duke remarks:

> Your good old father
> Once ... preserv'd my life.
> For that good deed, and for your virtue's sake,
> Though your descent be low, call me your father.

Julio is dismayed to have been summoned to Court. He had hoped to marry his beloved Leonora. 'Which is better, to serve a mistress, or a duke?' he wonders, neatly summarising Carr's position as the lover of both Frances Howard and the king; 'I am sued to be his slave, and I sue to be Leonora's.'

His father remarks, 'You shall find your horsemanship much prais'd there. Are you so good a horseman?'

The quibbles on horsemanship do more than point to Carr's happy accident. The possibility that he has 'practis'd riding in France' hints at his love affair with Lady Frances, which had blossomed in 1612, leading the Howards to seek an annulment of her marriage to the Earl of Essex.

Almost certainly, *Cardenio* was commissioned by Frances' father to advance their cause. Will was keen to oblige because the proposed marriage of Frances Howard to Robert Carr would benefit the pro-Spanish faction. Consequently, the play dwells on the plight of the 'Distrest Lovers'. Leonora is dragged to the altar to marry a man she does not love; she then vanishes into a convent, just as Frances Howard had disappeared into virginal seclusion after her arranged marriage to Essex.

The villain of the piece was named Fernando in the source, although he appears in *Double Falsehood* as 'false Henriquez', the troublesome son of the duke. Logically, this would make him – in real life – a son of King James, the obvious contender being Prince Henry, who, it was feared in 1612, had an eye for Frances Howard.

The rift which had opened up between King James and his eldest son would account for the duke's anxiety about Henriquez. We soon learn that Henriquez arranged for Julio to be summoned to Court simply to get him out of the way.

Henriquez claims to be in love with a maid named Violante. He rapes her, and then writes to her, '*Our prudence should now teach us to forget what our indiscretion has committed.*' Henriquez next proceeds to woo Leonora, knowing that her lover, Julio, is otherwise occupied with the duke. The 'double falsehood' of the play is entirely Henriquez' – he is a false friend, a deceitful lover and a cold-hearted rapist who thinks like a Puritan.

The death of Prince Henry in November 1612 brought forth an outpouring of Puritan grief and required urgent alterations to *Cardenio*. Henry's younger brother, Charles, became heir to the throne, and so it is Roderick, the duke's steadier son, who helps to put everything right at the end of the play. At first, though, he has no idea of the depths to which his brother has sunk. He even helps Henriquez to spirit Leonora away from the nunnery in which she has been hiding. The means they contrive to accomplish this had a chilling contemporary relevance:

> To feign a corpse – by th' mass, it shall be so!
> We must pretend we do transport a body
> As 'twere to's funeral; and coming late by,
> Crave a night's leave to rest the hearse i'th' convent.

When *Cardenio* was first performed, the memory of a fake body, made of wax, transported in a hearse and left to rest in Westminster Abbey, would still have been sharp. This strange re-enactment of Prince Henry's funeral occupied the fourth act of the play, which scholars attribute to John Fletcher, brought in at a late stage to rework Will's script in the light of recent events.

It was Fletcher who furnished the neat resolutions of the play. Julio, who had run mad into the mountains when he thought Leonora had betrayed him, is reconciled with his beloved. Violante also escaped into the mountains where, disguised as a shepherd, she is saved from a second violation by the timely appearance of Roderick. She reveals Henriquez' treachery by producing the letter he sent her.

Leonora, in what might be a relic of Shakespeare's original, speaks out on behalf of England's Catholics:

> Think, Julio, from the storm that's now o'erblown,
> Though sour affliction combat hope awhile,

When lovers swear true faith the list'ning angels
Stand on the golden battlements of heav'n
And waft their vows to the eternal throne.

Cardenio – the play written for the Lord Chamberlain to reflect the love of his daughter for Robert Carr – was later alleged to have been a 'present of value' for Will's 'Natural Daughter'. The real gift was perhaps the Blackfriars Gatehouse, which Will purchased after writing *Cardenio*, thereby providing his daughter by the 'sacred nun', Agnes Whateley, with a Catholic refuge in London.

ON 26 DECEMBER 1613, Frances Howard married Robert Carr. The king, who had elevated his favourite to the earldom of Somerset, visited the couple in bed the next morning, for which intrusion he gave the new Countess of Somerset a jewel worth £3,000.

Her husband received a gift from Ben Jonson – a poem, 'To the most noble, and above his Titles, Robert (Carr), Earl of Somerset' – which was delivered to the earl on his wedding day:

They are not those, are present with their face,
 And clothes, and gifts, that only do thee grace
At these thy Nuptials; but, whose heart, and thought,
 Do wait upon thee: and their Love not bought ...

Ben was not present with his face and clothes at Carr's wedding, and he did not include this poem in his published works. It was a temporary gesture.

Another of Ben's epigrams shows what he really thought of Carr:

On Some-thing, That Walks Some-where
At Court I met it, in clothes brave enough,
 To be a Courtier; and looks grave enough,
To seem a statesman: as I near it came,
 It made me a great face, I ask'd the name.
A Lord, it cried, buried in flesh, and blood,
 And such from whom let no man hope least good,
For I will do none: and as little ill,
 For I will dare none. Good Lord, walk dead still.

Some-thing and *Some-where* alluded to Carr's new title, Earl of Somerset. Typically, Ben was capable of grovelling for favour while masking his true feelings. It had become habitual for Jonson to hide his ambivalence beneath a studied poetic veneer.

Somerset was now one of the most powerful individuals in the land. On 10 July 1614, six months after his marriage, he was appointed Lord Chamberlain, his father-in-law Thomas Howard being promoted to Lord Treasurer. The 'house of Suffolk', it was noted, 'was at the highest pitch'.

But King James was about to fall in love again.

GEORGE VILLIERS was 'the handsomest bodied man in England' when the king clapped eyes on him on 3 August 1614. Twenty-one years old, long-legged and graceful, 'there was no blemish in him'. Soon, James would describe Villiers as his 'sweet child and wife'.

The anti-Howard faction quickly took Villiers under its wing. The Puritan cabal, led by William Herbert, Earl of Pembroke, and his brother Philip, a onetime favourite of the king, along with George Abbott, Archbishop of Canterbury, plotted to undermine the Earl of Somerset by grooming the new favourite. By November, King James was planning to make Villiers a Groom of the Bedchamber.

Somerset fiercely opposed this. He grew jealous of Villiers and argued furiously with James.

Early in 1615, the king wrote an extraordinary letter to Somerset, warning his former favourite that 'all the violence of my love will in that instant be changed in as violent a hatred' if the earl did not curb his 'fury and insolent pride'. 'It lies in your hand to make of me what you please,' insisted the king, 'either the best master and truest friend or, if you force me once to call you ingrate, which the God of Heaven forbid, no so great earthly plague can light upon you.'

Somerset's opponents were ruthless. They recruited Queen Anne who, though sickened by the king's fondness for male favourites, was willing to favour Villiers, such was her loathing of Robert Carr. On 23 April 1615 she arranged for Villiers to appear in her bedchamber when the king was present. Anne then took a sword from Prince Charles and begged her husband to knight the young favourite 'whose name was George, for the honour of St George', whose day it was. The king did so, and Sir George Villiers promptly became a Gentleman of the Bedchamber.

Desperate to impress the king, Somerset intervened in the delicate negotiations then underway to marry Prince Charles to a Spanish princess. The Spanish ambassador had confidently predicted that within a few years of the marriage of the heir apparent to a daughter of the King of Spain, the Catholics in England would outnumber the Protestants. Naturally, the Puritan faction at Court was doing everything in its power to block the arrangement. When it became clear that Somerset was actively promoting the Spanish match, his enemies began to present themselves as the 'aggregation of good patriots'.

SHAKESPEARE WAS in London in late 1614. His cousin, Thomas Greene, travelled down to Westminster to plead on behalf of the Stratford Corporation against a scheme to enclose farmland in Old Stratford. In mid-November, Greene visited Shakespeare to 'see him how he did'. He found Will in the company of his son-in-law from Stratford, Dr John Hall.

The significance of this meeting is that it places Shakespeare within easy reach of Somerset when the earl was serving as Lord Chamberlain. If Carr had wanted to hire a sympathetic playwright – the author of *Cardenio* – then Will was close at hand.

Will's rival, meanwhile, was ensconced with the opposing party. The Puritan faction was spearheaded by Jonson's patron, the Earl of Pembroke.

Ben became active in championing the king's new favourite. He provided a masque, entitled *Mercury Vindicated From the Alchemists at Court*, for a performance on 6 January 1615. According to an eye-witness, the 'principal motive' for Jonson's masque was 'thought to be the gracing of young Villiers and to bring him on the stage'. Ben vindicated the king's right to promote his cupbearer, who had been created by the '*Alchymists*' of the Court to be their 'instrument': 'their Male and their Female; sometimes their *Hermaphrodite*: what they list to style me.'

By the late spring of 1615, the Court was divided into two hostile groups: the pro-Spanish Somerset and his Howard in-laws, and the Puritan supporters of the rising star, George Villiers. 'The new seems to grow daily,' wrote an observer, 'and, from the old, a general defection.'

THE CRISIS broke in the summer of 1615, when, in the words of Sir Gervase Elwes, Lieutenant of the Tower of London, 'It should seem there was lately some whispering that Sir Thomas Overbury's death would be called in question.'

Overbury had been locked up ostensibly because he had declined a diplomatic posting overseas. The order to remove him to the Tower of London had come from the king, as had the instruction that Overbury was to be held 'close prisoner', with no contact with the outside world.

In reality, Overbury was punished for his antagonism towards the relationship between his intimate friend, Robert Carr, and Frances Howard, and for having insulted Frances' honour. Soon after Overbury was interned, Sir William Waad was dismissed from his post as

Lieutenant of the Tower. Lady Frances' great-uncle, Henry Howard, Earl of Northampton, then placed the inexperienced Sir George Elwes in charge of the prisoners in the Tower.

Overbury had not been in perfect health when he was imprisoned. He had also asked Carr to provide him with an emetic so that he could feign illness, hoping that way to appeal to the king's mercy. As the weeks wore on, Overbury developed full-blown hypochondria. He was treated for a range of symptoms by various doctors (a list of the prescriptions issued to him during his five-month stay in the Tower covered twenty-eight sheets of paper). Overbury consumed a host of quack remedies and was repeatedly bled.

It was probably the incompetence of the physicians and the recourse to so many questionable cures that resulted in his death on the morning of 15 September 1613.

An inquest was held. Overbury's body was found to be 'consumed away'. There was a large plaster on his back, beneath which the coroner discovered a 'black ulcer' between the shoulder blades, and 'in the brawn of the left arm he had an issue [a medical wound], kept open with a little pellet of gold'. The inquest returned a verdict of death by natural causes. The foul-smelling corpse was hastily buried.

'He was a very unfortunate man,' wrote John Chamberlain, 'for nobody, almost, pities him and his friends speak very indifferently of him.' For the next two years, Sir Thomas Overbury was largely forgotten. But by the summer of 1615, with the Puritan faction gaining ground, dark rumours were circulating.

King James almost certainly slept with his 'dog', Sir George Villiers, during his progress that summer through the southern counties. At the same time, the Secretary of State, Sir Ralph Winwood, took it upon himself to investigate the rumours surrounding Overbury's death.

By refusing to delegate to the Secretary of State, Somerset had made an enemy of him. Winwood's revenge was to question Sir Gervase Elwes in August 1615 about the circumstances leading up to Overbury's death in the Tower of London. Elwes claimed to have foiled a plan to poison Overbury, but that other attempts had been made on the prisoner's life.

The Puritan faction scented blood.

In September, Richard Weston was arrested. He had been appointed Overbury's jailer in May 1613, having previously helped to arrange clandestine meetings between Robert Carr and Lady Frances. Weston was interrogated by four Privy Councillors, including the Chancellor of the Exchequer, Sir Fulke Greville, a man of extreme Protestant views. Under pressure, Weston confessed that Lady Frances had promised him a reward in return for administering a phial of yellow-green liquid to Overbury.

The inquiry now had Frances, Countess of Somerset, in its sights. Feverish attempts were made to gather damning evidence, with the likes of Archbishop Abbott gleefully pitching in. The Earl of Somerset pleaded with the king for protection from his enemies. James hugged and kissed his former favourite – but as soon as Somerset had gone, the king smiled grimly and said, 'I shall never see his face again.'

Somerset was put under house arrest on 17 October, the same day as his wife, then seven months pregnant, was placed in the custody of her brother-in-law, Lord Knollys.

Two days later, Richard Weston's trial began. He was charged with having poisoned Overbury's broth on 9 May 1613, having supplied Overbury with poisoned tarts and jellies, and with having aided and abetted the murder of Sir Thomas Overbury by means of a mercury sublimate enema.

Weston was hanged at Tyburn on 25 October 1615. That same day, Sir Gervase Elwes was deprived of his post of Lieutenant of the Tower.

On 2 November, the Earl of Somerset was stripped of his seals of office and confined to the Tower of London.

THE SECOND person to stand trial for the alleged murder of Overbury was Anne Turner. She was a long-standing servant and confidante of Lady Frances; both women had consulted the astrologer-physician Simon Forman, and so accusations of witchcraft were added to the sensational mix. Charged with 'comforting, aiding and assisting' Richard Weston, Mrs Turner was pronounced guilty and executed on 14 November.

Sir Gervase Elwes was tried on 16 November. He defended himself well in the face of the abuse hurled at him by the Lord Chief Justice, but he met his fate just outside the Tower of London, where he was hanged on 20 November.

Imprisoned in the Tower, the Earl of Somerset was not allowed to see his wife, who gave birth to a baby girl on 9 December. Two weeks later, the post of Lord Chamberlain was awarded to Somerset's main enemy – and Ben Jonson's patron – William Herbert, Third Earl of Pembroke.

It was Pembroke, therefore, who oversaw the entertainments at Court that Christmas. These included a new masque by Ben Jonson.

The Golden Age Restored was performed by the King's Men at the Banqueting House on 1 January 1616. Ben's masque opened with the goddess Pallas Athene descending in a chariot:

Jove can endure no longer
>Your great ones, should your less invade;
>Or that your weak, though bad, be made
A prey unto the stronger.

Pallas is resolved to reinstate Astraea, goddess of innocence, purity and justice, and to re-establish the Golden Age on Earth. The world, as Jonson presented it, was currently in the grip of the Iron Age and the enemies of peace and justice.

The Iron Age summons its forces – Ambition, Pride, Scorn, Treachery, Folly and Ignorance – to overthrow Jove (one of Jonson's favourite designations for King James), much as the Earl and Countess of Somerset, along with their Howard relations, had been intent on poisoning the royal family, if the Lord Chief Justice was to be believed.

Pallas transforms the lowly people of the Iron Age: 'Die all, that can remain of you, but stone / And that be seen awhile, and then be none!'

The goddess then proclaims the end of the debased Iron Age and the rebirth of the Golden Age. Old poets are called forth – 'You far-fam'd spirits of this happy isle ... CHAUCER, GOWER, LIDGATE, SPENSER' – to celebrate the new era:

Now Peace.
>And Love.
>>Faith.
>>>Joys.
>>>>All, all increase.
And Strife,
>And Hate,
>>And Fear,
>>>And Pain,
>>>>All cease.

At best, this was wildly unrealistic. The country was on a slippery slope, heading towards the Civil War which would erupt within five years of Jonson's death. But Ben was acting as the mouthpiece of the Puritan faction – the 'justice' he proclaimed was nothing if not partisan.

With the 'Iron Age' of the Howards collapsing, Jonson conjured up an earthly paradise, in which men and women would be free to love without lust, all thanks to the peace-loving king:

> Of all there seems a second birth,
> It is become a heaven on earth,
>   And Jove is present here,
> I feel the god-head; nor will doubt
> But he can fill the place throughout
>   Whose power is every where.

The conceits were absurd, but the triumphalism of *The Golden Age Restored* was not misplaced. The trials and deaths of some of the lesser persons suspected of conspiring to murder Overbury had already signalled a radical power shift in the State.

Robert Carr, with his Catholic sympathies, was no longer Lord Chamberlain. Jonson's patron was. And though the Earl and Countess of Somerset had yet to stand trial, the Earl of Pembroke and his Protestant hardliners felt assured of victory.

Thus, the year 1616 had begun with a landmark performance – Ben Jonson's celebration of the downfall of the Howards, the rise of the Puritan clique, and a return to the callous injustice of the 'Golden Age' of Elizabeth I.

19

Blest be the Man

BETWEEN THE death of Robert Cecil in May 1612 and the detention of Robert Carr in November 1615, there had been hope for the Catholics. But *The Golden Age Restored* sent out a strident message: the crypto-Catholic Howards and their followers were done for.

Within days of Jonson's masque being performed, Shakespeare took the precaution of preparing his will. He approached Francis Collins, the Warwick-based lawyer who had recently drafted a will for his friend, John Combe, to draw up the document.

There was no mention of Shakespeare's wife in the original draft. Will declared himself to be 'in perfect health & memory' and signed his name with a firm hand on 18 January 1616.

The will was revised ten weeks later. New provisions were inserted, including the notorious bequest: 'ITEM I give unto my wife my second best bed with the furniture [bedlinen]'. The amended will was dated 25 March 1616. The signature, 'By me William Shakspeare', is a shaky scrawl.

The difference in the signatures tells its own story. When Shakespeare signed the first draft in January, he was preparing for the end. When he signed the revised draft in March, he knew it was coming.

SIR EDWARD Coke was one of England's foremost jurists. He presided over the trials of the Earl of Essex, Sir Walter Raleigh and the gunpowder plotters, but he was easily carried away by his own fanaticism and, blinded by his hatred of Catholics, liable to conjure up conspiracies.

While investigating the death of Overbury, Lord Chief Justice Coke came across a letter from King James to his former favourite which shocked him profoundly. Coke's discovery of this letter alarmed the king, who decided that he could no longer entrust the prosecutions of the Earl and Countess of Somerset to the Lord Chief Justice. The case was handed over to the Attorney-General, Sir Francis Bacon, an associate of Ben Jonson's. Bacon had an audience with the king on 19 January 1616 – the day after Shakespeare first signed his will.

King James was in two minds over whether or not to proceed against his former favourite and the daughter of his Lord Treasurer. If the Somersets were prosecuted, it was vital that they be found guilty. It was also imperative that Somerset be prevented from revealing too many intimate details of his relationship with the king. At least Sir Francis Bacon, himself a pederast, could be expected to handle these matters with sensitivity.

Meanwhile, the Pembroke faction was in disarray. They were losing patience with their protégé, Sir George Villiers, becoming 'disgusted with the new favourite because he doesn't appreciate the fact that his power is due to them'. On 22 February, the Tuscan ambassador observed that 'The Queen is now said to favour the Earl and Countess [of Somerset], though previously she was bitterly opposed to them.'

While the Puritans quarrelled among themselves, the pressure on the Somersets seemed to ease. 'The wind begins to tack about,' wrote Sir John Holles on 23 February, 'and the new faction, though from private interests falling asunder into parts, yet all parts seem to wish well to the afflicted.'

Having hastily drafted his will in January, Shakespeare was now waiting to see what would happen.

11 George Vertue's 1737 sketch of New Place, Shakespeare's home in Stratford.

ON 10 FEBRUARY 1616, Will's youngest daughter married Thomas Quiney. At 31, Judith was rather old to be marrying for the first time, and the wedding took place during the season of Lent. The couple had failed to get a special licence from the Bishop of Worcester; they then ignored a summons to appear before the consistory court, with the result that Shakespeare's new son-in-law was briefly excommunicated on 12 March.

Thomas Quiney had in fact got another woman pregnant. He was found guilty of 'carnal copulation', although his penance was for some reason reduced to a modest fine. Quiney's behaviour is often cited as the reason why Shakespeare altered his will. This would have been remarkably uncharitable, given that Will Shakespeare had also got another woman pregnant at the time of his own marriage to Anne Hathaway.

More likely, Shakespeare struck the words 'sonne in L[aw]' out of his will because Quiney was a Catholic. Anything that was bequeathed to him was at risk of sequestration. Will left 'One Hundred & ffyftie pounds' to Judith, plus another £150 if 'shee or Anie issue of her bodie' was still alive three years after Will's death. The bulk of Will's estate was left to Susanna, whose marriage to Dr John Hall rendered her possessions safe.

The sole mention of Will's wife of thirty-three years was a reminder that she had only ever been his 'second best bed'. As for the '2 or 300 pounds per annum' which, according to John Aubrey, Shakespeare left to a 'sister' nearby, that provision – if it was ever made – was arranged in secret.

SHAKESPEARE'S NEED to finalise his will was precipitated by events in London. Sir John Digby, the English ambassador to Spain, returned on 20 March. He was immediately closeted with the king and then questioned by the Lord Chief Justice.

For the past year, Sir John Digby had been negotiating a Spanish match for Prince Charles, the heir apparent. The Puritans were opposed to such a marriage, but what really got Digby's friends – the Earl of Pembroke and the Archbishop of Canterbury – excited was that the Earl of Somerset had intervened to speed the negotiations along.

Digby also revealed that members of the Howard circle had been receiving Spanish pensions. The Earl of Somerset had merely solicited a pension from Spain, but in the twisted mind of the Lord Chief Justice, this became a conspiracy of epic proportions. 'Somerset,' he declared, 'did falsely and traitorously compass and imagine the death of the King and Queen.'

Only the day before Digby presented his evidence to the king, the Earl and Countess of Somerset had been formally indicted as 'accessories to murder' – the supposed murder of Sir Thomas Overbury – 'before the fact done'.

There was now little doubt that the Somersets would stand trial (the date of 15 April was already being mooted) and that the pro-Spanish faction at Court was as good as finished. News of these developments was probably brought to Will Shakespeare by John Robinson, his tenant of the Blackfriars Gatehouse, who then witnessed Shakespeare's will.

As the poet most strongly identified with the pro-Spanish faction – the author of *Cardenio* who had repeatedly criticised King James for giving the Protestants too much rein – Shakespeare was uniquely vulnerable. The resurgent Puritans were in vengeful mood. Will's hand shook when he signed his will for the last time on 25 March.

In the event, the trials of Frances, Countess of Somerset, and her husband, Robert Carr, were held on 24 and 25 May 1616. Summonses were sent out to the twenty-five peers of the realm chosen to act as jurors on 24 April. The day before, in Stratford-upon-Avon, Will Shakespeare breathed his last.

IT WAS the feast day of St George, the patron saint of England – a day associated with dragon-slaying.

It was the first anniversary of the moment when, ambushed by the queen, King James had knighted George Villiers, the pretty boy set up by the Puritan faction to take Carr's place in the king's affections.

It was Shakespeare's birthday. Believing, like Cassius in *Julius Caesar*, that his friend had been overwhelmed by his enemies, Will would die, like Cassius, on his birthday, and in the town where he was born, stabbed by his own 'servant' – the 'Servant monster' who, as Will had predicted in *The Tempest*, would conspire to brain him.

As recently as 1 February, Ben Jonson had been granted a royal pension by King James 'in consideration of the good and acceptable service done and to be done'.

The king's reputation was at stake. James had ordered the imprisonment of Overbury, who then died in custody. There was talk that James had arranged to have his own son and heir, Prince Henry, poisoned. And then there was the nature of the king's relationship with his former favourite. Sodomy was a hanging offence. The playwright who had effectively denounced James as a 'tyrant' and a 'butcher' could not be allowed to present the case for Somerset or expose the king's duplicity. As Ben Jonson observed, 'it sometime was necessary he should be stopped'.

The Roman poet Virgil claimed that the mythical Golden Age had been restored under the Emperor Augustus, whose victory at the Battle of Actium in 31 BC led to the suicides of Mark Antony and Cleopatra.

Jonson would illustrate his remark about Shakespeare by quoting Augustus: *Sufflaminandus erat* – 'The brake had to be applied.'

SOMETIME AFTER 4 April 1616, when the Countess of Somerset was removed to the Tower of London in preparation for her trial, Ben Jonson left London. He made his way to Clifford Chambers, 2 miles south of Stratford, where Michael Drayton was staying at his favourite 'place of health and sport'. Ben needed Drayton to accompany him to the 'merry meeting' because Shakespeare would not have agreed to meet Jonson alone.

The three poets sat down together, possibly at the tavern run by Thomas Quiney on the High Street. Drayton later recalled that Jonson offered to make 'Rhymes' with his fellows. Ben commenced his own epitaph, which Will completed with a pungent insult. This was enough to make Jonson angry, but he controlled himself.

More drink flowed. Shakespeare became 'merry'. Perhaps he invited Jonson and Drayton back to New Place.

The poets left the tavern. Will's home was a few yards away. Through the main entrance on Chapel Street lay a private courtyard. The full Moon was starting to wane.

The tale that was told was that Shakespeare had died of a 'fever'.

THE SEVENTEENTH-century clergyman Richard Davies, chaplain of Corpus Christi College, Oxford, and later the rector of Sapperton in Gloucestershire, recorded that Shakespeare 'died a papist'. This rather open secret posed a problem. The law stated that Catholics should not be buried in consecrated ground. Body parts might also be retrieved by Catholics to be preserved as relics. The grave that was dug for Shakespeare in the chancel of Holy Trinity Church was therefore deep – 'deep enough to secure him'.

It was perhaps Dr John Hall who made the first death mask of his father-in-law. Will's face was lathered with soap before soft wax was spread over it. The result was unsatisfactory: Will's face looked swollen; the lump on the upper left eyelid was too pronounced.

A second death mask was made when burial was imminent. Less care was taken this time – the crystalline fluid which had seeped out from under Will's eyelids was not washed away. The flying mould pulled small hairs from the face as it was peeled off. A knife was used to emphasise the moustache and the narrow goatee beard.

Will's body was then carried to Holy Trinity Church for burial on Thursday 25 April 1616. A simple stone, engraved with a four-line inscription, was placed over the grave:

GOOD FREND FOR IESVS SAKE FORBEARE,
TO DIGG THE DVST ENCLOASED HEARE.
BLESTE BE Y^E MAN Y^T SPARES THES STONES,
AND CVRST BE HE Y^T MOVES MY BONES.

The likelihood that Jonson composed this epitaph is suggested by the gravestone itself. The poetic 'Bleste' precedes the words 'Be Y^e Man'. Jonson's first name was properly pronounced 'Binyamin', with 'Be ye man' being a close enough approximation.

Ben had his reasons for not wanting Will's remains to be exhumed, and so it was 'Blest Benjamin [that] Spares These Stones'.

The contraction y^t was a familiar shorthand for 'that', just as ye was an old form of 'the'. On the gravestone, each y^t is formed by placing the T above the Y, so that the letter T appears to dominate. Ben Jonson had, of course, been branded on his thumb with a T for 'Tyburn' as a reminder that he had escaped hanging for the killing of Gabriel Spenser.

If it was 'Blest Benjamin (T_y)' who spared Shakespeare's grave, the ^TY of the last line indicates from whom, precisely, he was sparing it.

To the left of the final ^TY are the words 'BE HE'. This is the fourth appearance of the letter H in the inscription, and the only occasion on which the H stands on its own. Elsewhere – in 'THE', 'HEARE' and 'THES' – the H is conjoined with its adjacent letter. Only in the 'HE' of the last line is the H rendered independently. The slightest adjustment to the angle of the crossbar would turn the H into an N: 'AND CVRST BE NE ^TY MOVES MY BONES.'

Robert Bennet, Dean of Windsor, had been appointed Bishop of Hereford on the accession of King James I in 1603. Within two years, he had been the cause of riots in Herefordshire when he refused to allow the churchyard burial of an elderly Catholic on the grounds that she was 'excommunicate'. The unrest, coming immediately before the discovery of the Gunpowder Plot, provoked an angry response from the king, who declared that it was 'needless any longer to spare' the blood of Catholics who, 'contemning his clemency', had dared to rebel.

In March 1609, Bishop Bennet wrote to Cecil, complaining that his diocese was overrun with recusants and 'lawless ladies'. The bishop sought a commission to 'subdue their proud spirits'. The next year, he petitioned Cecil for a change of diocese. The climate of Hereford was affecting his health; the neighbouring diocese of Worcester would, he felt, suit him better. As a nudge, Bennet reminded Cecil of the years he had spent as chaplain to his father, Lord Burghley.

Had Robert Bennet been granted the bishopric of Worcester, he would have become responsible for the church in which Shakespeare was buried.

However, Bennet's appeals to Cecil had fallen on deaf ears. He remained Bishop of Hereford until 1617 – a year after Shakespeare was buried. Nevertheless, the possibility that the dogmatically anti-Catholic bishop would seek to have Will's remains disinterred and reburied at a crossroads needed to be addressed.

The orientation of Shakespeare's gravestone shows that its 'curse' was designed to be read, not by the laity, but by the clergy. 'Blest Benjamin' spared the stones, 'AND CURSED BENET [v] MOVES MY BONES.'

'Thou art a monument without a tomb,' wrote Ben in the First Folio. By then, Shakespeare's funerary monument was in place, overlooking his grave.

Beneath the effigy of Shakespeare is a Latin inscription followed by six lines of verse:

STAY PASSENGER, WHY GOEST THOV BY SO FAST,
READ IF THOV CANST, WHOM ENVIOVS DEATH HATH PLAST
WITH IN THIS MONVMENT SHAKESPEARE: WITH WHOME,
QVICK NATVRE DIDE WHOSE NAME, DOTH DECK Y^s TOMBE,
FAR MORE, THEN COST: SIEH ALL, Y^T HE HATH WRITT,
LEAVES LIVING ART, BVT PAGE, TO SERVE HIS WITT.

This, too, has Jonson's fingerprints all over it.

Ben followed a tried and trusted formula when composing epitaphs. His 'Epitaph on Henry, Lord La-Ware', for example, begins: 'If, passenger, thou canst but read, / Stay, drop a tear for him that's dead'. Similar openings can be found in his epitaphs on 'Elizabeth, L.H.' – 'Wouldst thou hear what man can say / In little? Reader, stay'; on 'Master Philip Grey' – 'Reader, stay!'; and on 'Cecilia Bulstrode' – 'Stay, view this stone; and if thou beest not such, / Read here a little, that thou mayst know much'.

The epitaph on the Shakespeare monument, though, is baffling. Apart from the jumbled phrases and erratic punctuation, it includes a word – 'SIEH' – with no obvious meaning. Most commentators render it 'SITH', as in 'since', but it is clearly spelt *sieh*. 'SIEH' is immediately preceded by a colon, one of two which break up the inscription, thus:

Stay Passenger, why goest thou by so fast, / Read if thou canst, whom envious Death hath plast / With in this monument Shakespeare:
With whome, / Quick nature dide whose name, doth deck y^s Tombe, /

Far more, then cost:
Sieh all, y^t he hath writt, / Leaves living art, but page, to serve his witt.

The first section implies that someone has been placed ('plast') with Shakespeare in his monument. The second part suggests that, whoever it was, they had been *dyed* ('dide') by 'quick' nature, far more than by 'cost' or outward show. The name which living nature had dyed was the name which 'doth deck this Tomb' – that of Shakespeare. So, somehow or other, Shakespeare had been placed by 'envious Death' in the monument with himself.

Two colons break up the inscription. They also indicate that abbreviations are to follow. The first comes after 'SHAKESPEARE' and before 'WITH', the second falling between 'COST' and 'SIEH'. The word that follows the first colon is an elision. The letters of 'WITH' have been crushed together to hint that the person placed in the monument with Shakespeare was 'Wl.H'. The second colon anticipates the peculiar 'SIEH', signalling that it should be read 'S.i.e.H'. The next word is 'ALL', hence: 'S.$_{.I.E.}$H ALL.' This should recall the cunning dedication of *Shakespeares Sonnets* to a 'M^r.W.H. ALL'. The person who had been 'plast' in the monument with 'SHAKESPEARE' was 'Wl.H' or 'S i.e. H ALL'. Jonson was inviting any 'Passenger' who could 'read' the monument to realise that Will Shakespeare was also 'Will Hall'.

Some years earlier, in *Pierce Penniless his Supplication to the Devil*, Ben's colleague Thomas Nashe had noted that murder was 'the Companion of Envy':

> But were Envy nought but words, it might seem to be only women's sin; but it hath a lewd mate hanging on his sleeve, called Murder, a stern fellow, that, like a Spaniard in a fight, aimeth all at the heart. He hath more shapes than Proteus, and will shift himself upon any occasion of revengement into a man's dish, his drink, his apparel, his rings, his stirrups, his nosegay.

Jonson had accepted the role of 'envious Death' because it allowed him to dispose of a protean shape-shifter with more than one identity: Will Shakespeare, the poet, and Will Hall, the informer. Shakespeare, he observed, was 'dyed' by nature. He was born to be the betrayer of his kinsmen, and his alternative name, 'Wl. H', decked his monument far more than any ornament or decoration.

The murder of 'gentle' Shakespeare could therefore be justified, because into the tomb with him went the slippery 'Will Hall'.

BUT WAS all of Shakespeare buried in Stratford?

In 1879, a 'Warwickshire Man' described how the theft of Shakespeare's skull from its Stratford grave was inspired by Horace Walpole's offer of 300 guineas to anyone who could bring him the skull (see Chapter 3).

Five years later, the same author – Rev. Charles Jones Langston, a native of Alcester – followed up his account of the theft with a description of the skull's discovery. As if by accident, Langston had found the skull in a vault beneath the Sheldon Chapel at Beoley in Worcestershire, in the very church of which Langston was then the vicar.

Much of Langston's story was contrived, and yet the fact remains that a spare skull does reside in the ossuary beneath the Sheldon Chapel at Beoley. What is more, the skull exhibits features which compare with the posthumous images of Shakespeare.

The 'scar or indentation' above the right eyebrow of the Darmstadt death mask is matched by a discoloured region with two parallel scratches on the skull, occupying the same area as Ben Jonson is seen indicating with his finger in the Henry Wallis painting of *A Sculptor's Workshop* and which in a sketch made of the Shakespeare funerary monument in 1636 bears a distinctive black mark.

The cheekbones of the skull are missing. Sharp burrs on the outer edge of the left eyebrow correspond with the bulging protrusion visible on the Droeshout engraving and the Chandos Portrait of Shakespeare, and the orbital wall of the left eye socket is fractured, in line with the thin grey slit on the inner eyelid of the death mask.

Rev. C.J. Langston was desperate to tell the world that he had located 'THE VERITABLE SKULL OF WILLIAM SHAKESPEARE' at Beoley, 12 miles from Stratford. This required him to weave an intricate, improbable tale to explain how it got there. However, the chances are that the skull was not stolen from Holy Trinity Church in December 1794. It had been at Beoley all along.

The key to the enigma is Horace Walpole, whose offer of 300 guineas had instigated the adventure. Walpole coined the term 'serendipity', which he defined as 'making discoveries, by accident and sagacity, of things [one is] not in quest of'. This quality of serendipity appealed to Rev. C.J. Langston, who implied that his discovery of Shakespeare's skull was serendipitous.

Horace Walpole's ancestry was Catholic. The first martyr produced by Robert Persons' English College at Valladolid had been Henry Walpole. Inspired by the example of Edmund Campion, Father Henry Walpole was executed in 1595 – the same year as Robert Southwell – and is now venerated as a saint. Three of his brothers became Jesuits, active in

Shakespeare's London, and his cousin, Edward Walpole, also took holy orders in Rome before returning to England. Edward Walpole died in 1637, his Norfolk estates descending eventually to Robert Walpole, the father of Horace.

For many years, Horace Walpole enjoyed a lively correspondence with his Twickenham neighbour, Lady Browne, before her death in 1790. He captured the intimacy of their relationship in a playful verse:

When I was young and debonair
The brownest nymph to me was fair.
But now I'm old and wiser grown,
The fairest nymph to me is Brown[e].

Lady Browne was born Frances Sheldon, the daughter of Edward Sheldon and Elizabeth Shelley, in Beoley. Two of her brothers were Jesuit priests and her sister became a Benedictine nun in France. Her mother's ancestors had also been notable recusants. Willam Shelley, a servant of the Eighth Earl of Northumberland, was ruined in the aftermath of the Throckmorton Plot, which came to light after the arrest of Shakespeare's kinsman, John Somerville. The same William Shelley had married Mary Wriothesley, whose nephew, the Earl of Southampton, was Shakespeare's patron.

Many years later, Walpole's friend Frances Sheldon married Sir George Browne, a direct descendant of the first Viscount Montagu, who was the Catholic grandfather of Shakespeare's patron.

Ralph Sheldon – Lady Browne's great-great-great-grandfather – had been one of the wealthiest recusants in England. Mass was openly sung on his Beoley estate. A black marble altar table, which had been presented to him by the pope, was installed in the private family chapel which Ralph Sheldon built on the side of Beoley church.

Ralph's wife, Anne Throckmorton, was related to Shakespeare via Will's mother, Mary Arden. The Throckmorton connection linked the Sheldons with the gunpowder plotter Robert Catesby, with Shakespeare's friend John Combe, and with Ralph Huband of Ipsley, near Beoley, from whom Shakespeare bought his share in the tithe-lands around Stratford in 1605. Huband also owned Hillborough Manor, reputedly the home of Will's 'sacred nun', Agnes Whateley.

Ralph Sheldon had been imprisoned for his faith in 1580. He was named in 1583 as one of the Midlands magnates who had sheltered Father Hugh Hall. Sheldon came under suspicion again in 1594 for plotting to finance a Catholic uprising in North Wales, the knowledge of which might have led to Will Shakespeare being accused of 'misprision' of treason.

In the words of Cardinal William Allen, Ralph Sheldon was 'as good a Catholic as any in England'. He died in 1613. His daughter, Elizabeth, had married John Russell, whose half-brother, Thomas Russell, was an overseer of Shakespeare's will in 1616.

Rev. C.J. Langston, vicar of Beoley, would claim to have found Shakespeare's skull in the urn which had held the viscera of Ralph Sheldon. By the most extraordinary of coincidences, the skull was discovered in the family vault of Horace Walpole's intimate friend and neighbour, Lady Browne, and her Sheldon relatives.

Serendipity, indeed!

AT THE time when Horace Walpole supposedly initiated the search for Shakespeare's skull, another poet had put Beoley on the map. *Poems on Several Occasions* by Mrs Darwall appeared in two volumes in 1794, with a prefatory poem by a family friend, Rev. Luke Booker, a Doctor of Divinity and future chaplain to the Prince Regent during the madness of King George III. Mrs Darwall had first published her *Occasional Poems* in 1764, before her marriage to Rev. John Darwall of Walsall, when she was still Mary Whateley.

Born in 1738, the youngest daughter of William Whateley, a tenant farmer of Beoley, Mary received no formal education. The poems she had written by the age of 21 were described as 'not unworthy of the best of our poets' and attracted the interest of noble patrons. Like her contemporary, Frances Sheldon (Lady Browne), Mary Whateley had a connection with Beoley church: she was a close friend of the vicar's daughter.

Mary's great-grandfather William was the first Whateley to appear in the Beoley records. Her grandfather, John Whateley, is named alongside one of the Sheldons on a bell, cast in 1708, in the church tower at Beoley. The Whateley association with Beoley, however, predates this. Ralph Sheldon and his brother had supported the underground priests, John and Robert Whateley, in Henley-in-Arden. These priests were also funded by their brother, George Whateley, the draper of Stratford-upon-Avon whose sister, Agnes, was based at Hillborough in the parish of Temple Grafton.

The manor of Temple Grafton had been granted in 1545 to William Sheldon, the father of Ralph Sheldon, in whose funerary urn the skull of Will Shakespeare was found.

THE HISTORIAN Michael Wood recounted the Warwickshire legend that Will's heart was buried under a mulberry tree among the ruins of Wroxall Abbey, where Isabella and 'Domina Jane' Shakespeare had served as nuns. But it was to another ruined abbey – that of Bordesley, once the home of the 'old monk', Roger Shakespeare – that Will's head was taken.

The ruins of Bordesley Abbey had been bought by the Sheldons, who established a tapesty-weaving industry there, a mile from their Beoley home. Horace Walpole bought three of the grander Sheldon tapestries in 1781.

The Rev. Charles Jones Langston chose to open his tale of *How Shakespeare's Skull was Stolen* in 1794 – the year in which Mary Whateley Darwall's *Poems on Several Occasions* were published with a preface by the Rev. Dr Luke Booker. According to Langston, detailed notes on Shakespeare's skull had been entrusted to a Dr Booker; these notes allegedly went missing at about the same time as John Shakespeare's 'Testament of the Soul' vanished from the study of Horace Walpole's friend, Edmond Malone.

The elusive Frank Chambers, whose family owned Gorcott Hall in the parish of Beoley, had been prompted to track down the skull during a dinner party hosted at Ragley Hall, near Alcester, by Horace Walpole's second cousin. Also present at that dinner was Dr Samuel Parr, whose pupil, John Bartlam, became vicar of Beoley, and a Captain John Fortescue – possibly a descendant of the John Fortescue who had owned the Blackfriars Gatehouse before Shakespeare bought the refuge at the time of Ralph Sheldon's death.

The circumstances hint at a local secret, shared by Lady Browne with her neighbour, Horace Walpole, who therefore knew that the skull of Shakespeare was not in Stratford. It had been smuggled to Beoley, where it was preserved in the crypt beneath the chapel built by Will's friend, Ralph Sheldon.

The '2 or 300 pounds per annum' which Shakespeare was said to have left to a 'sister' would have been an illegal payment for prayers to be spoken and Mass to be sung for his soul. Where better for these devotions to have been observed than in Beoley, under the protection of the ardently Catholic Sheldons? And who better to have carried Will's head to safety than his 'sister sanctified of holiest note', Agnes Whateley?

This would explain why Ben Jonson was so determined to prevent a zealot like Bishop Bennet from digging up Will's headless remains. It might even account for the final part of the inscription on Shakespeare's funerary monument: 'SIEH ALL, Y^T HE HATH WRITT, / LEAVES LIVING ART, BVT PAGE, TO SERVE HIS WITT.'

Though Will had indeed left 'living art', then serving as a page, the statement seems to comprise a Jonsonian anagram, the reading of which hinges on whether *puta* should be translated via Latin or Spanish. Both possibilities are rendered here in italics: 'S i.e. Hall, *think you*, attributeth / Agnes Whately, *the whore*, her vigil to serve his wit. T.'

20

Look How the Father's Face

'WHAT'S THIS thing that gets between us and Shakespeare?' wondered the actor Al Pacino. That 'thing' is a misunderstanding based on an illusion.

Will Shakespeare had the (mis)fortune to live midway between the Dissolution of the Monasteries and the English Civil War. It was a period of considerable upheaval. For those on the make, there were unprecedented opportunities. The multitude was told what to believe – and how to believe it – by a remote government and bribed and bullied into betraying friends and family members who stuck to the faith of their forefathers. Those who remained true to their consciences lived in perpetual fear of the dawn raid – and yet, surprisingly many did. The human spirit is remarkably resilient.

No writer before or since captured the human spirit, in all its misery and majesty, as successfully as Shakespeare. Coming at his works from the viewpoint of a latter-day Puritan, George Bernard Shaw castigated Shakespeare's output: 'As to faith, hope, courage, conviction, or any of the true heroic qualities, you find nothing but death made sensational, despair made stage-sublime, sex made romantic, and barrenness covered up by sentimentality and the mechanical lift of blank verse.'

Shaw's assessment was grossly unfair. Clearly, he did not trouble himself to ponder why Shakespeare portrayed so much death and despair on the stage, or to wonder why the 'true heroic qualities' were so often sundered in his plays. Such a lack of inquisitiveness is the curse of Shakespeare studies. It stems from a reluctance, or a refusal, to engage with Will Shakespeare as a living author and a human being.

This is what gets between us and Shakespeare. His works are treated rather like the books of the Bible, as if they arrived fully formed from some higher plane, relevant for all time but somehow unrelated to the age in which they were written. If any consideration is given to his lifetime, it is on the false assumption that Will was a conforming *petit bourgeois*, a man so unassuming that he could die without anyone noticing.

That image of Shakespeare enrages those who claim that Francis Bacon or the Earl of Oxford or one of dozens of other candidates was the 'real' author of the *Complete Works*. By exposing the manufactured, tourist-friendly image of Shakespeare for what it is – a political construct – we remove the need to invent alternative authorship theories. The man of Stratford was who he was. It is our loss if we persist in not recognising him.

In 1999, listeners to BBC Radio Four's *Today* programme voted Shakespeare the 'Person of the Millennium'. Not bad, for a man about whom we claim to know so little!

Perhaps, subliminally, the Radio Four listeners knew that there is more to his legacy than fine words, neat phrases and memorable scenes. He had the courage to speak out, which makes him braver than those who try not to hear what he was saying.

WE CAN blame Ben Jonson for the thing that gets between us and Shakespeare: he started the process of divorcing Will from his contemporary world. 'He was not of an age, but for all time,' wrote Jonson in his prefatory poem for the First Folio.

In the same poem, Jonson hinted at another legacy that Shakespeare left behind. 'Look how the father's face / Lives in his issue,' said Ben.

William Davenant was 10 years old when Shakespeare made his sudden exit from the world's stage. His mother had achieved a sort of fame as Will's 'Dark Lady', his 'fickle maid full pale', his Cleopatra. Jane died in 1622 and was buried on 5 April at St Martin's, Carfax. Her husband, then six months into his term as Mayor of Oxford, promptly wrote up his will – a timely act, for he died on 19 April, two weeks after his wife was laid to rest.

A poem of the time suggested that John Davenant could not bear to live without his vivacious wife: 'No, no, he loved her better, and would not / So easely lose what hee so hardly got.' The poem does not explain why John had found it so hard to get Jane. A clue might survive in the churchwardens' accounts for St Martin's Church where, next to an entry for 1614–15, someone noted that John Davenant was 'Shakespears Vncle'.

A dictionary of *Buckish Slang, University Wit, and Pickpocket Eloquence*, dating from 1785, reveals that a privy or toilet could be referred to as 'mine uncle's'. A man who left his wife soon after marriage was said to have gone to visit his uncle; pawned items were also 'at mine uncle's'. The use of the slang term suggests that the nature of Shakespeare's relationship with the Davenants was well known in Oxford. John Davenant – 'seldom or never seen to laugh' – was Shakespeare's 'uncle', the tavern-keeper who cared for Will's soiled goods.

William Davenant was treated differently from his siblings in his father's will of 1622. Three sons of John Davenant had been sent to the Merchant Taylors' School in London; not so William, who was privately tutored in Oxford. John Davenant desired that the 16-year-old William should be 'put to Prentice to some good merchant of London or other tradesman', and that this should happen very soon, 'For avoiding of Inconvenience in my house for mastership when I am gone'.

Young William duly made his way down to London in the summer of 1622. Rather than entering into an apprenticeship, as his late father had wished, he chose to trade on the wit and good looks which he had inherited from his mother. He quickly secured a position as a page in the Holborn household of the Duchess of Richmond.

The duchess had been born Frances Howard (she was a distant cousin of her infamous namesake). After an early marriage to a wealthy wine merchant, Frances next married Edward Seymour, First Earl of Hertford, who died in 1621. Her third marriage, which took place within two months of her second husband's death, was to Ludovic Stuart, Second Duke of Lennox and First Duke of Richmond. Ludovic was the son of King James' first beloved favourite, as well as being the king's kinsman and the brother of Esmé Stuart, Ben Jonson's patron.

Jonson soon became aware of William Davenant's presence in London. Ben would observe in his inscription for Shakespeare's funerary monument that 'SIEH ALL' had left 'LIVING ART, BVT PAGE' to serve his wit. The young Davenant was indeed serving as a page. No doubt Jonson experienced a jolt of recognition when he saw his arch-rival reborn: 'Look how the father's face / Lives in his issue'.

Following in his father's footsteps, Davenant married while still in his minority. His first wife was named Mary, and their first child was baptised William on 27 October 1624, when Davenant was only 18.

He had also started writing poetry. One of his earliest poems was published in 1637 – the year of Ben Jonson's death – though it was written much earlier. It is an Ode, 'In remembrance of Master *William Shakespeare*'.

Davenant imagined the River Avon as being in mourning: every flower hangs its head; each tree:

Looks like the Plume a Captive weares,
Whose rifled *Falls* are steept i'th' teares
    Which from his last rage flow.

The piteous River wept it selfe away
Long since (Alas!) to such a swift decay;
    That reach the Map; and looke
If you a River there can spie;
And for a River your mock'd Eie,
    Will finde a shallow Brooke.

The river had not run dry. Davenant merely identified Shakespeare with the Avon, declaiming that where a great river had once flowed there was now nothing but a 'shallow Brooke'.

Sir Fulke Greville, Recorder of Stratford, had been raised to the peerage in 1621 as the first Baron Brooke. And within a couple of years of his arrival in London, William Davenant had moved from the Duchess of Richmond's household to the neighbouring Brooke House, the Holborn residence of Fulke Greville, Lord Brooke.

GREVILLE'S FATHER, also called Fulke, had made his home at Beauchamp's Court in Alcester, 7 miles from Stratford. Along with Sir Thomas Lucy of Charlecote he became one of the leading supporters in the region of the puritanical Earl of Leicester. It was members of the Greville family who had murdered Richard Quiney – the father of Shakespeare's future son-in-law – in Stratford in 1602.

The younger Greville was ten years older than Shakespeare. He formed an intense attachment to Leicester's nephew, the poet Philip Sidney, and fell into a nine-month depression when Sidney died in 1586. Greville then developed a lifelong love for Sidney's sister, Mary, who, as Countess of Pembroke, was the mother of that 'incomparable pair', William Herbert, Third Earl of Pembroke, and his brother Philip, Earl of Montgomery, to whom the First Folio of Shakespeare's plays was dedicated in 1623.

Greville's early activities as a spy for Sir Francis Walsingham soured his relations with Lord Burghley and his son, Robert Cecil, who eventually forced Greville – then Treasurer of the Navy – from office. He returned to favour after Cecil's death in 1612 and, as Chancellor of the Exchequer, took part in the investigations into the death of Sir Thomas Overbury in the Tower of London. His Calvinist views led him to adopt a fervently anti-Catholic stance, and he maintained close ties with some of the more extreme Protestants, including John Speed, who exposed Shakespeare in 1611 as a Jesuit mouthpiece. Greville was also a good friend and patron to Ben Jonson's mentor, William Camden, and to Francis Bacon, who in April 1616 was preparing to prosecute the Earl and Countess of Somerset.

Like his friend, Sir Francis Bacon, Fulke Greville is one of the many individuals put forward as the 'real' Shakespeare – this on the basis of a remark made in 1670. In *The Statesmen and Favourites of England since the Reformation*, David Lloyd wrote that Greville desired 'to be known to posterity' as 'Shakespeare's and Ben Jonson's Master'. It is far from clear what this meant. Greville had his own circle of Protestant poets and spies, including Sir Edward Dyer, and while he was undoubtedly a friend, and probably a patron, to Ben Jonson, there is no evidence to suggest that he had any sort of relationship with Will Shakespeare. Indeed, Greville's hatred of Catholics and his siding with the Earl of Pembroke's clique in seeking the downfall of Robert Carr, Earl of Somerset, make it highly unlikely that Greville and Shakespeare were friends.

On the death of his father in 1606, Greville inherited the post of Recorder of Stratford. He was, to all intents and purposes, the town's registrar and coroner. The decision not to hold an inquest into Shakespeare's death was his.

Greville was the 'Master' of Shakespeare and Jonson insofar as he was allied both with the murderer and the faction which wanted Will 'stopped'. He controlled the crime scene and ruled out any form of inquiry.

BY 1625, WHEN William Davenant entered his service, Greville was spending most of his time in Warwickshire. He knew that Davenant was a fellow poet. Davenant later published a poem, 'To the Lord B[rooke]. in performance of a vow, that night to write to him'. It is a strangely ambivalent piece:

Yet such my treach'rous fate, that I this night
(Fierce with untutor'd heat) did vow to write:
But happy those, who undertake no more
Than what their stock of rage hath rul'd before!

There were, wrote Davenant, 'degrees, that to the Altar lead; / Where ev'ry rude, dull Sinner must not tread', but 'where the High Priest should only be'. He concluded by praying that Greville would excuse a 'strong Religion here, though not a Muse'.

On 1 September 1628, Greville paid a brief visit to his London home. He was heard arguing with an ageing servant, Ralph Haywood. The word 'will' was mentioned.

Haywood stabbed his 73-year-old master twice, then locked Greville inside the chamber and ran to his own room, where he stabbed himself through the heart.

Greville's wounds were treated with animal fat. He died of septicaemia on 30 September 1628.

It is often claimed that Haywood attacked Greville because he had been left out of his master's will. Greville had, in fact, made generous provision for all his servants in his will, which Haywood had witnessed. The argument which resulted in the stabbing and the servant's suicide must have concerned another 'Will' altogether.

More attention might have been paid to the death of Sir Fulke Greville had it not been for the fact that George Villiers, Duke of Buckingham, had been assassinated on 23 August. The old king's favourite had become unpopular – he was suspected of harbouring Catholic sympathies. His death was greeted with popular rejoicing.

Davenant, however, saw it differently. Buckingham's assassination was 'the Peoples wound', he wrote to Buckingham's widow; 'for though it touch'd his heart, / His Nation feeles the rancour, and the smart.' The opposing view was expressed in a poem – possibly by Ben Jonson – to John Felton, the soldier who had murdered Buckingham:

Enjoy thy bondage, make thy prison know
Thou hast a liberty thou canst not owe
To those base punishments; keep entire, since
Nothing but guilt shackles the conscience ...

This poem was written by someone who knew that a guilty conscience was the only penalty for a justifiable homicide.

Jonson was interrogated about the poem. He pointed the finger at one Zouche Townley, who was then in the process of leaving the country. Ben had heard Townley preach in Westminster and invited him to supper two nights later, when he presented the preacher with the 'dagger with the white haft' which Jonson 'ordinarily wore at his girdle'. Both men had delighted in the fatal stabbing of Buckingham. Perhaps Jonson confided in Townley and gave him the white-handled dagger with which he had wounded Will Shakespeare.

The two men remained friends long after Townley's return to England.

LIKE HIS drunken master, King James I, Ben Jonson took the unusual step of publishing his complete works in 1616. Twelve years on, in 1628, Jonson was 'strucken with palsy'. The paralytic stroke might have been brought on by shock at the death of Sir Fulke Greville; Ben must have suspected that young Davenant had exacted revenge for Greville's collusion in Shakespeare's murder by coaxing an older servant into stabbing his master.

Davenant's brief service with the 'shallow Brooke', Fulke Greville, is something of an anomaly. His circle of friends was of a very different caste: they included Endymion Porter, raised in Spain and married to a zealous Catholic; Thomas Carew, who referred to himself and Davenant as 'we of the adulterate mixture' – 'So, oft the Bastard nobler fortune meets, / Than the dull Issue of the lawfull sheets'; and William Habington, who was born at Hindlip Hall, near Worcester, on 4 November 1605 and was just a few weeks old when Father Henry Garnet was captured in his family home.

Also telling, Davenant chose to dedicate one of his first plays, written while Greville was still alive, to the Earl of Somerset.

Somerset's trial as an accessory to the alleged murder of Sir Thomas Overbury took place one month after Will Shakespeare was buried. Lady Frances, Countess of Somerset, had pleaded guilty at her trial on 24 May 1616, and maybe she had tried to poison Overbury (her evidence was inconsistent). King James had been notably agitated on the day of Somerset's trial. The former favourite defended himself staunchly, but the outcome was already decided. Carr was found guilty of having 'stirred up, moved, commanded, abetted, aided, hired, counselled and assisted' those who had already paid the ultimate price for Overbury's death. When he heard the news, the king broke into 'a good disposition'. Somerset had said nothing to incriminate His Majesty.

The earl and countess were sentenced to be hanged. But while enormous pressure was exerted by their enemies at Court, the king was resolved to be merciful. Lady Frances received her royal pardon on 13 July 1616. Her husband, still protesting his innocence, had to wait until 7 October 1624 for his – more than two years after the couple had been released from their imprisonment in the Tower of London.

The Somersets were, of course, ruined. The Howard faction had been irreparably damaged by the scandal whipped up and exploited by the circle of the Earl of Pembroke, the Archbishop of Canterbury and Sir Fulke Greville.

In the light of Somerset's disgrace, Davenant's decision to dedicate his *Tragedy of Albovine, King of the Lombards* to the earl was a provocative one. Though Davenant had another play, *The Cruel Brother*, performed by the King's Men at the Blackfriars in 1627, *Albovine* was not licensed for performance. Davenant told the Earl of Somerset that it was not intended for the 'public Eye'. The play's portrayal of a king's passionate love for a male favourite ('He hath of late hung thus – / Upon my neck; until his amorous weight / Became my burden: and then lay slabbering o'er / My lips, like some rheumatic babe'), and the scheming courtiers who plot to destroy the favourite, made it dangerously contentious. It also offers us a glimpse of the sort of drama Shakespeare might have written in Somerset's defence at the time of his trial, and the reason why Will had to be silenced.

Albovine was published in 1629, with a verse from Edward Hyde commending the dedication to the Earl of Somerset, whom the author had addressed as 'Your humblest Creature, D'avenant'.

The affectation of signing himself 'D'avenant' provoked amusement. 'D'avenant from Avon comes', jeered one wit, alluding to Davenant's parentage. Others were kinder, praising Davenant as the 'sweet swan of Isis' – the literary heir to the 'Sweet swan of Avon'.

That a hostile faction opposed and undermined Davenant's efforts is clear from his writings. One of the mainstays of the anti-Davenant lobby was the Master of the Revels, Sir Henry Herbert, a kinsman of the Earl of Pembroke. Davenant would thank his friend Endymion Porter for rescuing his work from this 'cruel faction': 'I that am told conspiracies are laid, / To have my Muse, her Arts, and life betray'd.' Davenant handed his enemies another gift in 1630, when he lost part of his nose to a dose of syphilis. As one wag put it, 'Thus *Will*, intending *D'Avenant* to grace / Has made a Notch in's name like that in's face.'

KING JAMES I died, senile and debilitated, on 25 March 1625. He was succeeded by his son, Charles, who, in May 1625, was married by proxy to Henrietta Maria, the Catholic daughter of Henri IV of France and Marie de Médicis.

Davenant became a devoted 'Servant of Her Majesty', Queen Henrietta Maria. He also supplanted the ailing Ben Jonson as the chief writer of masques for the Court: his first, *The Temple of Love*, appeared in 1635. Five years later, he composed the last masque to be performed before King Charles and his French queen, a poignant plea for peace entitled *Salmacida Spolia*. The masque was presented on Tuesday 21 January 1640 at the Banqueting House – the same building from which King Charles would emerge on Tuesday 30 January 1649, to be beheaded on the orders of Parliament.

In addition to taking over Jonson's duties of composing courtly masques, Davenant succeeded Jonson as the unofficial Poet Laureate. Ben Jonson died on 16 August 1637, his funeral attended by 'all or the greatest part of the nobility and gentry then in town' – which might not have been many, it being the height of summer. Jonson had held the post of Poet Laureate by dint of his royal pension, granted in February 1616, for services rendered and yet to be performed. In March 1638, that same pension of £100 was transferred to William Davenant.

At the time, Dr Brian Duppa, Dean of Christ Church, was putting together a collection of Ben's poems under the title, *Jonsonus Virbius*. Davenant did not contribute to the publication, but he did write Dr Duppa an 'acknowledgement for his collection, in Honour of *Ben. Iohnson's* memory': 'How shall I sleepe to night, that am to pay / By a bold vow, a mighty Debt ere day?'

'This Debt hereditary is,' wrote Davenant, 'and more / Than can be pay'd for such an Ancestor'. The poem does not mention Jonson's name at all, although it does indicate that Davenant's 'hereditary' debt was about to be paid off. He had replaced Jonson as Court poet and now Poet Laureate, and this in fulfilment of a 'bold vow' he had made to his illustrious 'Ancestor'.

Davenant's claim, reported by John Aubrey, who knew his family, that he wrote 'with the very spirit' of Shakespeare and was (or 'seemd') happy 'to be thought his Son', has often been ridiculed. There was, however, very little of John Davenant in William, and a great deal of Will Shakespeare.

As the Civil War loomed, Davenant became Lieutenant-General of the King's Ordnance. In May 1641 he was wanted on suspicion of plotting to 'seduce the army against the parliament'. He was caught trying to leave the country – his nose gave him away – and heckled as a 'Superstitious Groom, / And Popish dog, and Curre of *Rome*' (Davenant later converted to Catholicism). He served as the queen's agent in France and a gunrunner for the Royalists. 'No man,' it was said, 'hath been a greater enemy to the parliament.'

Being 'in great renown for his loyalty and poetry', Davenant was knighted by King Charles at Gloucester in September 1643, a few weeks after the queen had stayed at New Place as a guest of Shakespeare's daughter. Sir William Davenant was later appointed Treasurer of Virginia, and then Lieutenant-Governor of Maryland, but his ship was intercepted by the Parliamentary forces in May 1650 and he was imprisoned on the Isle of Wight. He had with him part of the manuscript of his 'Heroick Poem', *Gondibert*, which featured a set-piece worthy of his (god)father. Davenant described a stag hunt in familiarly Shakespearean terms: the hounds are unleashed against the stag, 'As if the world were by this Beast undone, / And they against him hir'd as Nature's Foe'. When the stag has no more strength left in him:

> the Monarch Murderer comes in,
> Destructive Man! whom Nature would not arme ...

For she defenceless made him that he might
    Less readily offend; but Art Armes all,
From single strife makes us in Numbers fight;
    And by such Art this Royall Stagg did fall.

The metaphysical poet Henry Vaughan, commending *Gondibert* in 1651, remarked that Davenant's poetic fire had broken through 'the *ashes* of thy aged *Sire*'.

On 9 July 1650, Parliament ordered that Davenant and five others be tried for 'all Treasons, Murthers, felonies, Crimes and offences'. Though he expected to be executed, Davenant was spared. He was removed to the Tower of London, not to be released until 7 October 1652.

OLIVER CROMWELL became Lord Protector of England in 1653. Plays were forbidden under his mirthless regime, but that did not stop Davenant reviving the theatrical arts right under Cromwell's nose. He introduced 'opera' to London in 1656, and in that same year the first woman to act on the public stage appeared in his *Siege of Rhodes*.

With the Restoration of the Monarchy in 1660, Davenant was awarded a royal patent to form and run a theatre company. The patron of this company was the Duke of York – the future James II, the last Catholic King of England, who would visit St Winefride's Well to pray for a son; the theatre he opened in Lincoln's Inn Fields was known as the Duke's Playhouse. It was there that Davenant produced a number of Shakespeare's plays, drawing on the memories of those who had known and worked with Shakespeare.

Hamlet was performed in 1661, with women in the cast. This was followed by *Twelfth Night*, *The Law Against Lovers* (a misjudged adaptation of *Measure for Measure*) and *Romeo and Juliet* in early 1662. A spectacular revival of *Henry VIII* was criticised by Samuel Pepys as 'so simple a thing ... there is nothing in the world good or well done'. In 1664, Davenant staged his adaptation of *The Two Noble Kinsmen*, which he called *The Rivals*, and in which one of the performers was Moll Davis, soon to become a mistress of King Charles II.

One of Davenant's more notorious all-singing, all-dancing productions was his 'alter'd' version of *Macbeth*, with its aerial ballet of witches. It was first presented on 5 November 1664 – the anniversary of the Gunpowder Plot – and was seen by the diarist Pepys nine times. In 1667, Davenant produced his 'Comedy' of *The Tempest, or The Enchanted Island*, a collaboration with the poet John Dryden.

Dryden admitted that Davenant had taught him to admire Shakespeare: 'I could never have receiv'd so much honour in being thought the Author of any Poem how excellent soever, as I shall from joining my Imperfections with the merit and name of *Shakespear* and Sir *William Davenant.*'

It is to Davenant that we owe various traditions relating to Shakespeare, such as the story that the Earl of Southampton gave Will a gift of £1,000, and that King James had 'with his own Hand' written an 'amicable Letter to Mr. Shakespeare'. Davenant owned, and perhaps commissioned, the Chandos Portrait of Shakespeare and the Davenant Bust, which was salvaged from the Duke's Playhouse, where it was paired with a bust of Ben Jonson.

Will Shakespeare – as Jonson hinted in the First Folio – did not merit the honour of a burial in Westminster Abbey. Ben Jonson, however, did. John Aubrey would note that Ben 'lies buried in the north aisle' under a 'pavement square of blue marble about 14 inches square', inscribed with the words: 'O RARE BEN JONSON'.

Sir William Davenant died aged 62, on 7 April 1668. Three weeks later, a command performance was held at his theatre on 23 April, the anniversary of his father's birth and death.

Davenant's body was transported in a fine walnut coffin from the Duke's Playhouse to Westminster Abbey on 9 April. Five or six of his children, 'all boys', followed the hearse in the first of many coaches. He was buried in the south aisle of the abbey, under a marble gravestone which bore an inscription 'writt in imitation of yᵉ on Ben: Johnson': '*o rare Sʳ Will: Davenant*'.

No father could have hoped for a more loyal, courageous and industrious son.

Selected Bibliography

Shakespeare: Life and Works

Ackroyd, Peter, *Shakespeare – The Biography* (London, 2005).

Alexander, Catherine M.S., *Shakespeare – The Life, The Works, The Treasures* (London, 2006).

Asquith, Clare, *Shadowplay – The Hidden Beliefs and Coded Politics of William Shakespeare* (New York, 2006).

Barber, C.L., *Shakespeare's Festive Comedy – A Study of Dramatic Form and its Relation to Social Custom* (Cleveland, Ohio, 1963).

Bate, Jonathan, *The Genius of Shakespeare* (London, 1998).
  Soul of the Age – The Life, Mind and World of William Shakespeare (London, 2008).

Bearman, Robert, *Shakespeare in the Stratford Records* (Stroud, 1994).

Brown, Ivor, *Shakespeare* (London, 1951).
  How Shakespeare Spent the Day (New York, 1964).

Bryson, Bill, *Shakespeare – The World as a Stage* (London, 2007).

Burton, S.H., *Shakespeare's Life and Stage* (Edinburgh, 1989).

Duncan-Jones, Katherine, *Shakespeare – An Ungentle Life* (London, 2010).

Evans, Malcolm, *Signifying Nothing – Truth's True Contents in Shakespeare's Text* (Brighton, 1986).

Fox, Levi, *In Honour of Shakespeare – The History and Collections of the Shakespeare Birthplace Trust*, Enlarged Edition (Norwich, 1972).

Greenblatt, Stephen, *Will in the World – How Shakespeare Became Shakespeare* (London, 2005).

Hammerschmidt-Hummel, Hildegard, *The True Face of William Shakespeare – The Poet's Death Mask and Likenesses from Three Periods of His Life*, translated by Alan Bance (London, 2006).

Hammond, Brean (editor), *Double Falsehood*, The Arden Shakespeare, Third Series (London, 2010).

Harris, Frank, *Shakespeare & His Tragic Life* (Ware, 2008).

Holden, Anthony, *William Shakespeare – His Life and Work* (London, 1999).

Honan, Park, *Shakespeare – A Life* (Oxford, 1999).

Hughes, Ted, *Shakespeare and the Goddess of Complete Being* (London, 1993).

Knights, L.C., *Some Shakespearean Themes* (London, 1960).

Lamborn, E.A.G. and G.B., Harrison *Shakespeare – The Man and his Stage* (London, 1923).

Lerner, Laurence (editor), *Shakespeare's Tragedies – An Anthology of Modern Criticism* (London, 1982).

Nicholl, Charles, *The Lodger – Shakespeare on Silver Street* (London, 2007).

O'Connor, Garry, *William Shakespeare – A Life* (London, 1991).

Paul, Henry N., *The Royal Play of* Macbeth *– When, Why, and How it Was Written by Shakespeare* (New York, 1950).

Phillips, Graham and Martin Keatman, *The Shakespeare Conspiracy* (London, 1994).

Schoenbaum, Samuel, *Shakespeare's Lives* (Oxford, 1991).

Shapiro, James, *1599 – A Year in the Life of William Shakespeare* (London, 2005).
Contested Will – Who Wrote Shakespeare? (London, 2010).

Southworth, John, *Shakespeare the Player – A Life in the Theatre* (Stroud, 2002).

Thomson, Peter, *Shakespeare's Professional Career* (Cambridge, 1992).

Trussler, Simon, *Will's Will – The Last Wishes of William Shakespeare* (Richmond, 2007).

Waterfield, John, *The Heart of His Mystery – Shakespeare and the Catholic Faith in England under Elizabeth and James* (Bloomington, 2009).

Weis, René, *Shakespeare Revealed – A Biography* (London, 2007).

Wells, Stanley and Gary Taylor (general editors), *The Oxford Shakespeare – The Complete Works*, Second Edition (Oxford, 2006).

Wilson, Ian, *Shakespeare: The Evidence – Unlocking the Mysteries of the Man and his Work* (London, 1994).

Wilson, Richard, *Secret Shakespeare – Studies in Theatre, Religion and Resistance* (Manchester, 2004).

Wood, Michael, *In Search of Shakespeare* (London, 2005).

Other People and Places

Acheson, Arthur, *Mistress Davenant – The Dark Lady of Shakespeare's Sonnets* (London, 1913).

Barish, Jonas A. (editor), *Ben Jonson – A Collection of Critical Essays* (New Jersey, 1963).

Bengsten, Fiona, *Sir William Waad – Lieutenant of the Tower & The Gunpowder Plot* (Oxford, 2005).

Bevan, Bryan, *King James VI of Scotland & I of England* (London, 1996).

Boyle, Conall, *In the Footsteps of the Gunpowder Plotters – A Journey Through History in Middle England* (Warley, 1994).

Bradbrook, M.C., *The School of Night – A Study in the Literary Relationships of Sir Walter Raleigh* (Cambridge, 2011).

Bruce, John (editor), *Correspondence of King James VI of Scotland with Sir Robert Cecil and Others in England* (Westminster, 1861).

Caraman, Philip, *A Study in Friendship – Saint Robert Southwell and Henry Garnet* (Saint Louis, Missouri, 1995).

Cecil, David, *The Cecils of Hatfield House – A Portrait of an English Ruling Family* (London, 1975).

Cook, Judith, *At the Sign of the Swan – An Introduction to Shakespeare's Contemporaries* (London, 1986).
Roaring Boys – Playwrights and Players in Elizabethan and Jacobean England (Stroud, 2004).

Davenant, William, *Madagascar; With Other Poems* (London, 1638).

Donaldson, Ian, *Ben Jonson – A Life* (Oxford, 2011).

Dutton, Richard, *Ben Jonson,* Volpone *and the Gunpowder Plot* (Cambridge, 2008).

Edmond, Mary, *Rare Sir William Davenant – Poet Laureate, Playwright, Civil War General, Restoration Theatre Manager* (Manchester, 1987).

Enos, Carol, *The Shakespeare Encyclopedia: Stratford/London/Lancashire Links* (available online at: www.sunflower.com/~cenos/docs/ CompleteShakespeareEncyclopedia.pdf).

Fraser, Antonia, *Mary Queen of Scots* (London, 1970).

Garnett, Henry, *Portrait of Guy Fawkes – An Experiment in Biography* (London, 1962).

Greer, Germaine, *Shakespeare's Wife* (London, 2007).

Harbage, Alfred, *Sir William Davenant – Poet Venturer 1606–1668* (Philadelphia, 1935).

Harp, Richard and Stanley Stewart (editors), *The Cambridge Companion to Ben Jonson* (Cambridge, 2000).

Houston, S.J., *James I* (Harlow, 1973).

Hughes, Charles (editor), *Willobie his Avisa* (London, 1904).

Hutchinson, Robert, *Elizabeth's Spy Master – Francis Walsingham and the Secret War that Saved England* (London, 2006).

Joseph, Harriet, *Shakespeare's Son-in-Law – John Hall, Man and Physician* (Connecticut, 1976).

Kenyon, J.P., *The Stuarts – A Study in English Kingship*, New Edition (London, 1970).

Knight, Francis A., *Sea-Board of Mendip* (London, 1902).

Mee, Arthur, *The King's England – Worcestershire* (London, 1947).
The King's England – Warwickshire, New Edition (London, 1966).

Messenger, Ann, *Woman and Poet in the Eighteenth Century – The Life of Mary Whateley Darwall (1738–1825)* (New York, 1999).

Newdigate, Bernard H., *Michael Drayton and his Circle* (Oxford, 1941).

Nicholl, Charles, *The Reckoning – The Murder of Christopher Marlowe* (London, 1993).

O'Farrell, Brian, *Shakespeare's Patron – William Herbert, Third Earl of Pembroke 1580–1630, Politics, Patronage and Power* (London, 2011).

Orrell, John, *The Quest for Shakespeare's Globe* (Cambridge, 1983).

Owen, G. Dyfnallt (editor), *Salisbury (Cecil) Manuscripts Volume XXIV: Addenda 1605–1668* (London, 1976).

Palmer, Roy, *The Folklore of Warwickshire* (Felinfach, 1994).
The Folklore of Worcestershire (Herefordshire, 2005).

Patterson, R.F. (editor), *Ben Jonson's Conversations with William Drummond of Hawthornden* (London, 1923).

Redworth, Glyn, *The She-Apostle – The Extraordinary Life and Death of Luisa de Carvajal* (Oxford, 2008).

Rees, Joan, *Fulke Greville, Lord Brooke, 1554–1628 – A Critical Biography* (London, 1971).

Riggs, David, *The World of Christopher Marlowe* (London, 2005).

Rowse, A.L., *Ralegh and the Throckmortons* (London, 1964).

Russell, John, *Shakespeare's Country*, Fourth Edition (London, 1949).

Steane, J.B. (editor), *Thomas Nashe – The Unfortunate Traveller and Other Works* (London, 1985).

Trevelyan, Raleigh, *Sir Walter Raleigh* (London, 2003).

Trow, M.J., *Who Killed Kit Marlowe? – A Contract to Murder in Elizabethan England* (Stroud, 2002).

Weir, Alison, *Children of England – The Heirs of King Henry VIII 1547–1558* (London, 1997).

Wells, Stanley, *Shakespeare & Co.* (London, 2007).

Historical Events and Trends

Ashley, Maurice, *England in the Seventeenth Century* (London, 1975).

Barry, Jonathan (editor), *The Tudor and Stuart Town – A Reader in English Urban History 1530–1688* (Harlow, 1990).

Brigden, Susan, *New Worlds, Lost Worlds – The Rule of the Tudors, 1485–1603* (London, 2000).

Clark, Arthur Melville, *Murder Under Trust – The Topical Macbeth and other Jacobean Matters* (Edinburgh, 1981).

Doran, Susan, *The Tudor Chronicles – 1485–1603* (London, 2008).

Duffy, Eamon, *Fires of Faith – Catholic England Under Mary Tudor* (New Haven & London, 2010).

Edwards, Francis (editor), *The Gunpowder Plot – The Narrative of Oswald Tesimond alias Greenway* (London, 1973).

Englander, David, Diana Norman, Rosemary O'Day and W.R. Owens (editors), *Culture and Belief in Europe 1450–1600 – An Anthology of Sources* (Oxford, 1990).

Evans, G. Blakemore (editor), *Elizabethan-Jacobean Drama* (London, 1989).

Ford, Boris (editor), *The Age of Shakespeare* (London, 1982).

Fraser, Antonia, *The Gunpowder Plot – Terror & Faith in 1605* (London, 1997).

Grose, Capt. Francis, *A Classical Dictionary Of The Vulgar Tongue* (reprinted from 1811 edition, Chicago, 1971).

Hanson, Neil, *The Confident Hope of a Miracle – The True Story of the Spanish Armada* (London, 2004).

Harrison, G.B., *A Jacobean Journal – Being a Record of Those Things Most Talked of During the Years 1603–1606* (London, 1946).

Haynes, Alan, *The Gunpowder Plot* (Stroud, 1996).
Sex in Elizabethan England (Stroud, 2006).
The Elizabethan Secret Services (Stroud, 2009).

Hilton, Timothy, *The Pre-Raphaelites* (London, reprinted 1997).

Hogge, Alice, *God's Secret Agents – Queen Elizabeth's Forbidden Priests and the Hatching of the Gunpowder Plot* (London, 2006).

Ingleby, C.M., *Shakespeare's Bones – The Proposal to Disinter Them* (London, 1883).

Jones, Jeanne, *Family Life in Shakespeare's England – Stratford-upon-Avon 1570–1630* (Stroud, 1996).

Kingman, Tracy, *An Authenticated Contemporary Portrait of Shakespeare* (New York, 1932).

Leacroft, Richard and Helen, *Theatre and Playhouse* (London, 1985).

Lindley, David (editor), *Court Masques* (Oxford, 1995).

MacCulloch, Diarmaid, *Reformation – Europe's House Divided 1490–1700* (London, 2004).

Millward, Peter, *The English Reformation – From Tragic Reality to Dramatic Representation* (Oxford, 2007).

Milton, Giles, *Big Chief Elizabeth – How England's Adventurers Gambled and Won the New World* (London, 2001).

Nicholls, Mark, *Investigating Gunpowder Plot* (Manchester, 1991).

Norris, J. Parker, *The Death Mask of Shakespeare* (Philadelphia, 1884).

Parkinson, C. Northcote, *Gunpowder, Treason and Plot* (London, 1976).

Peach, Richard, *Is This Shakespeare's Skull?* (*The Village*, Issue 95: October 2009).

Pearson, Margaret M., *Bright Tapestry – Stories of the Great Houses of England* (London, 1957).

Plowden, Alison, *Elizabethan England – Life in an Age of Adventure* (London, 1983).

Porter, Stephen, *Shakespeare's London – Everyday Life in London 1580–1616* (Stroud, 2011).

Questier, Michael C., *Catholicism and Community in Early Modern England* (Cambridge, 2006).

Ridley, Jasper, *A Brief History of The Tudor Age* (London, 2002).

Rowse, A.L., *The Expansion of Elizabethan England* (London, 1973).

Smith, Lacey Baldwin, *The Elizabethan Epic* (London, 1966).

  Treason in Tudor England – Politics and Paranoia (London, 2006).

Somerset, Anne, *Unnatural Murder – Poison at the Court of James I* (London, 1998).

Stochholm, Johanne M., *Garrick's Folly – The Stratford Jubilee of 1769* (London, 1964).

Stone, Lawrence, *The Family, Sex and Marriage in England 1500–1800* (London, 1985).

Tawney, R.H., *Religion and the Rise of Capitalism* (London, 1926).

Thomas, Keith, *Religion and the Decline of Magic* (London, 1973).

Tillyard, E.M.W., *The Elizabethan World Picture* (London, 1972).

Travers, James, *Gunpowder – The Players behind the Plot* (Richmond, 2005).

Warwickshire Man, A, *How Shakespeare's Skull was Stolen and Found* (London, 1884).

Williamson, Hugh Ross, *The Gunpowder Plot* (London, 1951).

Wills, Garry, *Witches and Jesuits – Shakespeare's* Macbeth (New York, 1996).

Wilson, John Dover (editor), *Life in Shakespeare's England – A Book of Elizabethan Prose* (Cambridge, 1915).

Yates, Frances A., *Theatre of the World* (London, 1987).

Index